MAY GOOD,
PREVAIL!

Greg

WAS THAT THUNDER?

Imperfect book

Donated by Bryteag Publishing

- Not for Resale -

BT BRYTEAG
PUBLISHING

Was That Thunder?

More Than A Boston Marathon Bombing Story

Copyright © 2018 by Greg Kalkwarf

BT B R Y T E A G
P U B L I S H I N G

Author Photo: Kelly Photography / Kathleen Lavine

Editor: Catherine Jones Payne, QuillPenEditorial.com

Publishing and Design Services: MartinPublishingServices.com

ISBN: 978-1-7321312-0-0 (print), 978-1-7321312-1-7 (epub)

WAS THAT THUNDER?

MORE THAN
A BOSTON MARATHON
BOMBING STORY

GREG KALKWARF

 BRYTEAG
PUBLISHING

To Mom and Dad,
Kirsta, Bryce, and Teagan:
Much love always.

To the Boston Marathon bombing victims,
survivors and their families:
Your stories are far more important than mine.

CONTENTS

CHAPTER 1

THE BEGINNING

"I run so I can eat . . . more."

That's become one of my life mottos. I'm not a runner. I mean, I like to run, but I don't have a fancy GPS watch; I don't have a subscription to a running magazine; and I certainly don't precisely measure my water intake. But, I do have a sweet tooth, a bottomless stomach, and a mostly high metabolism. So, as an adult, running has become a way to overcome my insatiable appetite.

Growing up, baseball was my life. For Halloween, I dressed as a Kansas City Royal. On family vacations with my parents, my older brother Ron and I played catch at rest stops. We celebrated Friday nights with our dad hitting us fly balls until the sun sank below the horizon. I measured running in ninety-foot increments—the distance between bases on the baseball field.

As a freshman baseball player in college, however, I joined my fellow pitchers in one-mile group jogs for daily conditioning. Jogging along with my teammates, I always felt a strange urge to pull away from the pack. The mile loop created a gnawing feeling in my gut. Our group turned around at a park adjacent to a beautiful lake next to campus, but I wondered how much further I could go. Past the park? To the edge of town? *Gasp* . . . all the way around the lake?

When I realized in my late twenties that my metabolism was slowing, I decided to burn more calories by running around my Wichita neighborhood—and I liked it. The sweat streaming down my face. My lungs and legs burning as I pushed to longer distances. Exploring new areas on foot and discovering scenery invisible from a vehicle. Best of all, not feeling guilty having a second helping of appetizers, entrees, and desserts.

I liked running so much, in fact, that I signed up for the 2000 Wichita 10K River Run, part of the city's annual celebration of the Arkansas River that flows through downtown. I was pretty sure that I could run the 6.2 miles, but I had not trained as much as I thought I should have—so I did a six-mile run the day before my race. Looking back, I know how foolish it was to put in so many miles the day before a competition. Any real runner knows it's much smarter to save energy twenty-four hours before a run.

I lined up that next morning, unsure where to place myself in the starting corral. I felt in decent shape, so I started closer to the front than to the back of the pack. With my bib number pinned to my shirt, I blended in with the thousands of other runners, yet I felt like a cartoon character with a flashing arrow over my head, reading, "This guy has no idea what he's doing!"

My legs ached a bit from my excursion the day before—let's call it a rookie mistake—but as I eyed my fellow competitors, I figured I could run faster than any of the young kids or the sixty-year-old man. I didn't expect to win, but I thought I'd be among the earlier finishers.

Bang went the starter's pistol. Before I knew it, I'd crossed the first mile marker... in under seven minutes! That was way too fast for what I was prepared, but I hadn't learned that yet.

I jogged the first half of the run, feeling proud of my endurance. But before I reached the halfway point, I started seeing the race leaders running on the other side of the street, already headed back toward the finish line. I laughed to myself and at myself. "Those people are fast!"

After I reached the 10k halfway point, marked by a nondescript orange cone in the middle of McLean Boulevard, I turned and slowed to a walk. My inexperienced feet felt those nine miles in the last twenty-four hours, and they protested in tired, achy whines. They wanted to be out of shoes!

I kept trying to speed up my legs, and each time it seemed like someone much older or younger passed me. *Gulp.* It rapidly dawned on me that I wasn't quite the runner I'd thought. No way would I quit, but I could hear my La-Z-Boy recliner calling my name.

I managed to finish that 10K in 50:23—two seconds behind an eleven-year-old boy. I chugged a bottle of water handed to me after crossing the finish line and gnawed on a bagel that sat on the runners' refreshment table. I wanted to linger and savor the completion of my first timed run, but instead I limped and coughed back to my truck, drove home, and dropped my sore body and wheezing lungs in front of the TV for a nap.

After recovering from the pain in my lower extremities and the defeat of my ego, I decided to make a real commitment to running—I went to Target and bought a twenty-dollar digital watch with a timer so that I would have some idea of my running pace. Inspired to take another step forward, I drove the routes that I'd planned to run and measured not only overall distances but also specific markers like signs or telephone poles that would help me recognize splits and times. From my mailbox to the bridge measured one half mile; to the stoplight was one mile; to the interstate was two miles.

I was hooked.

At the time, I worked in the front office of Wichita's minor league baseball team. During our homestands, often ten or twelve games long, I worked twelve to fourteen hours a day, leaving little time for leisurely runs—though I bounded up and down many stairs at the stadium while entertaining our fans and performing in-game promotions. When the team hit the road, I pounded the pavement near my condominium or just a few miles north on the trails at Sedgwick County Park with its gorgeous tree-lined paths.

I still played baseball, too. On a few pleasant weekends while the team traveled the road, we front-office executives joined up with some colleagues and friends for casual hardball games on the stadium's field—a great perk for working in the industry.

This inspired us to enter some softball tournaments, which introduced me to the unexpected fact that I wasn't as young as I once was. For a weekend tournament, I volunteered to play third base, a position that requires one-hundred percent alertness during a game since the ball comes quickly down the baseline. I put my catlike reflexes to work, bending into a "ready" position for each pitch . . . for each of our games.

I woke up Monday morning with a back that refused to cooperate. I struggled to roll out of bed and hobble across the room. A week later, I sat in an orthopedic doctor's office hearing the news that I now had a herniated disc in my lower back, an injury that would remain with me in perpetuity.

———————

Between haphazard running and ball games, I kept my body active and gladly fed it accordingly. Yet, I still didn't know the length of a marathon, or whether Wichita even hosted a marathon. I maintained an average of ten to fifteen miles of running each week in three- to five-mile increments.

A 10K seemed like the ideal distance to me then. Any run longer than that seemed like it should require traveling in a vehicle. Why would anyone want to run so many miles when a car would get you there faster, with no shower necessary! Clearly, a no-brainer.

So, I kept up my short runs but didn't think bigger. And I continued to love it all—the euphoric feeling of crossing the finish line, the satisfaction of a sweaty, calorie-burning run, and the peacefulness of disengaging from the world.

Thus, I kept eating—more—and kept running.

CHAPTER 2

GETTING SERIOUS

I got serious—or perhaps really crazy—after moving to Denver in 2005.

I registered for my first marathon.

Five years earlier, a Kansas nurse moved into the condo next to mine in Wichita. The name of this cute neighbor was Kirsta, and after I hosted her at a few baseball games and a few non-sports dates, we grew our relationship to couple status. A year later, I realized that I wanted to watch baseball games with my best friend instead of working them. So, I retired from my baseball career and went to work as a marketing representative for an accounting firm. After starting with the company in Wichita, I had the opportunity to relocate to Colorado. Kirsta agreed to move with me, with the promise of a diamond ring and a wedding. Life was outstanding.

My wife is a baseball fan, too, so we were both excited to throw honorary first pitches at our wedding reception, which we held at a Colorado Springs Sky Sox minor league game.

In the months before the Denver Marathon in October 2006, I ran somewhat regularly, typically three or four times per week. This allowed our marriage to start off strong—just by keeping me out of the way of my new wife! I was clocking more miles than I had before that first 10K, but I still didn't follow any training regimen and wasn't technical in my approach. Well, I stretched a little bit before and after a run, if you want to call that a regimen.

My fuel during that first marathon was Tootsie Rolls. Real high-tech, right? The morning started out cold, and I ran the first thirteen miles in a long-sleeved cotton T-shirt. But as the morning wore on, the weather grew warmer and so did my internal body temperature. Kirsta agreed to meet me at the halfway point so I could switch into a short-sleeved cotton T-shirt. Ugh! Cotton clothing does not wick away sweat from the body like a performance shirt, but I was still hopelessly naïve.

As in my first timed 10K, I managed to finish, but I struggled through the last five miles to cross the finish line. My big toe started to ache so badly that I winced every time I landed on my right foot. And as time passed, the sun warmed the asphalt course until my body baked like a turkey in the oven, wrapped in a protective cotton sleeve keeping the juices—my sweat—next to my body. After twenty miles, I still wanted to run, but my body kept telling me, "You idiot, you have never done this before! What the heck are you doing?"

Although I sprinted across the finish line to impress the crowd of spectators, the last five miles really consisted of meandering, strolling, stumbling and only a little bit of running. The post-finish-line photos show me wincing, hands on head, and panting to catch my breath. I was happy to have completed my first marathon, but my 4:40 time—forty minutes short of the four-hour mark that signifies a good runner—left me wanting more.

Not often do you see photographers taking pictures after the finish line, but this one captured me in a great deal of pain at the end of the 2006 Denver Marathon, my first officially timed 26.2-mile run.

After recovering from my first marathon fiasco, I went super crazy. Kirsta and I had been doing a lot of mountain hiking, which inspired me to follow up on something I heard about when running behind three guys during the Denver Marathon: a marathon up and down Pikes Peak.

*Kirsta and I climbed our first 14er—a mountain that reaches higher than
14,000 feet elevation—on July 4, 2008. We were astonished to see a group
of people celebrating Independence Day with a cookout
at the top of Torreys Peak.*

Yes, the Pikes Peak that reaches more than 14,000 feet above
sea level.

When I decided to enter the Pikes Peak Marathon, I also
decided that it was an imposing-enough venture that people
might be willing to donate money to support my efforts. By
reaching out to my friends and business associates via email, I
managed to raise nearly $4,000 for Casey, a little boy who wanted
to take a trip to Disney World via the Make-A-Wish Foundation.
Fundraising provided a nice distraction from my training, and I
appreciated the people who donated on my behalf to help a kid.

At last, on a crisp, cool morning in August 2008, I found

myself in Manitou Springs, Colorado, standing at the base of Pikes Peak. Adrenaline surged through my veins as I gazed at the peak, standing shoulder-to-shoulder with eight hundred other climbers, prepared to begin "America's Ultimate Challenge."

With clouds above the summit ready to dump snow on Pikes Peak, I knew at the starting line that I would encounter inclement weather during the 2008 marathon.

Most of the Pikes Peak Marathon occurs on Barr Trail, named after the individual who carved a route among the tree and rocks that line the east face of the mountain. The primary difference between trail running and running on pavement is that you must watch for the random rocks and tree roots waiting to trip you when you aren't paying attention. On the positive side, the softer ground mitigates the pounding impact on your body.

Unlike a flat marathon, this route requires incredible physical exertion just to climb the mountain, not to mention saving energy for the thirteen miles back down. Although a flat marathon finish under four hours is considered a good time, a solid finish for the Pikes Peak Marathon is anything under seven hours. Sounds daunting, right? Maybe a bit terrifying?

But, I wasn't afraid of dying on Barr Trail, though climbers have had heart attacks on the mountain. My biggest concern was pooping. So, in the event I did have a bowel movement in the middle of nowhere and had to veer off course behind a tree, I brought along a small roll of toilet paper. Just in case.

At least this time I felt like I wasn't walking into the run completely unprepared. Pikes Peak definitely makes it into the top five toughest runs I've completed, but some of my earlier runs and my first marathon were more physically challenging because I was less experienced. My body felt ready for this marathon. My wife and I had bought property in the mountains, and I'd trained quite a bit on the roads and trails around our house at altitudes between 8,000 and 9,000 feet, which makes a good precursor for climbing to the top of Pikes Peak. Plus, earlier in the summer, I did a trial climb of the mountain, so I knew what to do expect along the trail.

Having fainted as a child while my family and I drove up Pikes Peak in the 1980s, I felt vindicated when I climbed the mountain for the first time in the summer of 2008.

The Pikes Peak Marathon occurs annually on the third Sunday of August. As if that's not enough, Manitou Springs also hosts the Pikes Peak Ascent, a half marathon going "only" up the mountain, on the day before the marathon. On Saturday, the weather turned ugly atop Pikes Peak, and those in the Ascent hit some tough times at the summit. In fact, race organizers turned nearly half of the participants around at the tree line because of bad weather—lightning, snow, ice, and sleet. Plus, many came unprepared, dressed only in running shorts and shirts, the typical attire for a typical marathon. I admit, even on days when I'd run in cold weather, I'd done so woefully underdressed—mostly because I'd never considered purchasing winter running gear.

"What the heck am I doing?" I cried out to Kirsta as I read about the weather conditions on the Pikes Peak Marathon website bulletin board.

"You're the one who signed up for it," she said, eyes not leaving the book in her hands.

Despite her lack of compassion, Kirsta helped me make the rational decision: I need more clothing. Shorts and a T-shirt were not going to take me to the summit. We left an extra hour early from our house and arrived in Colorado Springs to battle other unprepared climbers for the necessary equipment. Together we scavenged through racks of winter clothing—in August—to find running tights and a long-sleeved running shirt. In addition, I packed two sets of gloves, including my bulky ski gloves, three different winter hats, including a balaclava that covers my neck, and a pair of water-resistant wind pants from the closet at our house.

"Is this enough?" I asked Kirsta as I stared at the bags in the back of our vehicle.

"Beats me," she said with a smirk. "I'll be at the hotel."

We rolled into Manitou Springs, the start of the Pikes Peak Marathon, around four thirty in the afternoon. After I checked in at the registration tent, receiving bib #904, I started talking with people who had participated in the Ascent and confirmed the stories I had read about on the internet.

"Wow, it was freezing at the top!" said a Colorado native. "I'm glad I had my gloves."

A California runner added, "They made me turn around at tree line. I never thought I wouldn't be able to finish a half marathon in August because of a snowstorm!"

Their advice spurred my final preparations as I began to figure out how I would run up and down Pikes Peak in the middle of a winter storm.

With my bib in hand, I left the freezing runners behind to warm each other with their stories. Kirsta and I had a great dinner at Paravicini's Italian Bistro, allowing me to load up on carbs, and after a quick treat at Dairy Queen, we headed back to the hotel for an early night and earlier wake-up call.

Happily married for more than two years and dating for six more, Kirsta and I had already had many adventures together: exploring waterfalls and rainforests in Hawai'i, dodging pedestrians and taxi cabs in New York City, and moving from bucolic Kansas to the bustling Denver metropolitan area. Kirsta is a nurse by trade, and her quiet, steady demeanor is a perfect yin to the yang of my outgoing, Labrador-Retriever personality. Not only does she put up with my harebrained ideas, but she is also a terrific supporter when I decide to actually do some of them. We are both perfectionists at heart. So, just when I think I have a foolproof plan, she finds something I forgot and helps make it . . . perfect.

Like when the weather doesn't cooperate, and I need to buy winter clothing for a summer marathon up and down a mountain.

I woke at five thirty and was pleased to look out the window and see dry streets and sidewalks. I dressed in running tights, running shirt, long-sleeved shirt, and short-sleeved shirt, then pulled on a fleece pullover, gloves, and a cap to stay warm until start time. I packed the rest of my belongings—a few snacks and a water bottle—into a small backpack that lay snuggly against my back. Oh, and that small roll of toilet paper. Just in case.

We drove the short mile to downtown Manitou Springs and

walked a few blocks to the start line. After a picture with the start line banner and a kiss with my beautiful wife, I fell into place, ready for my timed, 26.2-mile trek to the top of the mountain and back. I took my spot in line next to a guy from Chicago who, in a previous year, had completed the Ascent in 4:07. I hoped to complete the climb portion of the Marathon in somewhere around four to four and a half hours, so I knew he would be a good companion with whom to start.

The runners stood in restless anticipation as the strains of "America the Beautiful" soared through the air. Katharine Lee Bates wrote this classic piece sitting atop Pikes Peak, and I smiled at the appropriate send-off.

The starting gun fired at 7:00 a.m., and we were on our way up from 6,300 feet. The first 1.6 miles on asphalt streets offered only a six-hundred-foot increase, and I jogged this with minimal effort. I smiled. "Yea, all of those hills during training paid off!"

My legs had plenty of energy, so I skipped the first aid station offering water and Gatorade. But, as the marathon route joined Barr Trail, I noticed everyone else walking, so I also decided to conserve some energy and slowed to a quick walk.

If you have ever driven in rush hour traffic in a metropolitan area, you know what it is like on the switchbacks at the base of Pikes Peak during the marathon. In this case, people, instead of cars, stack up one in front of the other; but on the trail, it's only one lane, with no place to pass. So, you run when the person in front of you does and slow down when they do.

One guy apparently placed himself too far back in the pack at the starting line and tried to pass. "Idiot," I mumbled to myself, practically hugging a mountainous wall on the right side of the trail as he stumbled through a bush to gain two seconds on his time.

Although the tight traffic continued for several miles, I glanced at my watch and realized that I'd completed the first three miles in forty-five minutes—definitely a good pace for me for this marathon. Somewhere around mile three, the trail opened, and we were finally able to run at our own rate. I made a few short stops to hydrate, and in just under two hours arrived at Barr Camp, the halfway point for the ascent, and I was on track to get to the peak in double that time. I stood at about 10,200 feet, astonished and pleased as I rewarded myself with a granola bar and about a three-minute rest.

Still, I knew that after a relatively easy first quarter of my journey, this is where the challenges really kicked in. Not least of which, my lungs would work much harder in the next six miles.

I continued with the same mentality that I did during my training—namely, run when I felt like it and then slow to a fast walk when I wanted. Basically, pushing myself but also recognizing that I needed to save something for the thirteen miles back down. Plus, I knew at some point I would likely encounter ugly weather because the same front that had dumped snow and ice on the peak for the Ascent was forecasted to redeliver for the Marathon.

So far, the day had been cool and overcast, with only a little moisture. We even saw our shadows for a while when the sun emerged briefly through a cloud. Nonetheless, my extremities grew increasingly chilly, and as the clouds darkened the skies, I put on a thin cap and gloves. At about the 8.5-mile mark is the stretch I'd been dreading. It is one long, straight incline. No switchbacks—just forward, forward, forward. Boring, boring, boring. Halfway through this stretch, I caught up with a woman who had a few years on me, as distinguished by a full head of gray hair.

"Hi," I gasped. "I'm Greg. How are you?

"Hello, Greg," she responded, barely missing a beat. "I'm Joyce and doing well. How about you?"

"My first Pikes Peak marathon," I gasped between huffs and puffs. A laugh morphed into a cough. "I . . . may . . . die."

"Oh, stop," Joyce replied. "You are doing great."

I smiled at the typical runner's response. I can't imagine a runner ever telling another runner what they really looked like. "You look like heck, and you probably are going to die," is what Joyce should have said.

However, I figured if she could keep up a steady pace, I should be able to, too. So, I marched behind her, plugging away and thinking about anything other than my legs, feet, and lungs. For good reason, my mind drifted to a dirt field outside of Wichita, Kansas, and I grabbed at my lower left back, pain throbbing near my left vertebrae, remnants of the herniated disc from playing softball many years prior. "Dang it! Why didn't I stretch better before that tournament?"

Knowing that the next aid station wasn't until just past the ten-mile mark, I put my head down and kept jogging, walking, marching—pick any verb that's the opposite of sprinting. I laughed to myself recalling my conversation during the Denver Marathon with the three guys who had previously completed the Pikes Peak Marathon. I asked if they had actually run the entire mountain trail, and they chuckled, "No, you just do whatever you can to keep moving."

I now knew what they meant.

My back pain intensified, but based on other climbing experiences, I knew it would hurt only as I traveled uphill, so if I could make it to the top, the problem would go away. Only about three more miles to put up with that pain. As I neared the tree line, I could hear lots of cheering, so I knew we were getting close to the next aid station at A-Frame, a cabin shelter, or the marathon leaders were passing on their way back down.

A-Frame is a small structure near the tree line on Pikes Peak that offers some protection from inclement weather.

Sure enough, eventual-winner Matt Carpenter, who finished first for the tenth time, sprinted by moments later. And in just a few minutes more, I arrived at A-Frame. I knew the temperature would drop quickly from here, so after a quick splash of fluids, I pulled on the balaclava, my ski gloves, and a wind/water resistant top. I welcomed the added warmth at a downright-cold 12,000 feet with three miles still to go before the summit.

Somewhere just past the tree line, the snow started falling. With no trees blocking my view, I saw nothing but gorgeousness for miles—beautiful, crisp white ground punctuated by only the occasional green shrubbery. Alas, the bobbing heads of other participants snapped me back to reality—I was in the middle of a snowstorm. In a marathon. On a 14,000-foot mountain.

I had seen some accumulation along the trail, but now we were getting serious. I couldn't see the Peak, nor could I see any of the trail behind me. I stopped around mile eleven to have a snack, and I discovered, to my disgust, that I'd forgotten to fill up my water bottle at A-Frame.

Plus, my cold fingers struggled to tear open an energy gel packet. A kind search and rescue volunteer offered to help. Unfortunately, the gel had pretty much frozen solid, so I couldn't squeeze it out. Instead, I found myself fighting to suck a flavored, energy ice cube through a tiny hole. I probably burned off any energy I gained from the vanilla-flavored gel just by trying to get it out of its packet! I then tried a granola bar, but remembering I was nearly out of water and wouldn't have enough to rinse the whole thing down, I only ate half, then shoved it away to continue the climb.

As I marched up to "The Cirque," the final aid station before the summit, my back ached, my fingers tingled with cold, and my throat felt parched. Looking around, I found myself above tree line trudging through four inches of snow with sounds of thunder echoing overhead.

Doubts echoed in my mind:

"I can't believe I am doing this."

"Why am I doing this?"

"A warm bed sounds wonderful."

Thankfully, words from my beautiful wife pierced through the clouds in my mind. "You can do it!" she'd written in a card she'd snuck into my running gear after I'd fallen asleep last night. My back straightened, and my resolve solidified. Kirsta's support and the fact that each step I took helped to raise money to send Casey to Disney World through the Make-A-Wish Foundation compelled me to push forward. "Just always move," I reminded myself, recalling advice I had read on the marathon message board.

Suddenly, I heard more yelling, which meant I had to be coming close to the Cirque aid station. Sure enough, one more turn around a rock and I could see volunteers doing the wave as runners passed.

Plus, they had water! And, reaching the final aid station meant just one more mile to the top. I could taste success. I was really going to do it! Excitement raced through my body, the shot of adrenaline providing a burst of warmth to counterbalance the freezing temperatures.

Then more thunder rolled in the distance. Despite reassurances from the search and rescue guys that we would not be turned around, I wanted to make sure that I did not climb this far and then fail to reach the summit. So, now hydrated, I picked up my pace slightly. Unfortunately, it didn't do much good. Because of the snow and ice covering the trail, and because those of us going up had to yield right of way to those coming down, we had to march single file up the last mile or so. This killed any chance of my making it to the Peak in four hours, but under the circumstances, I didn't care anymore. Time was not the issue; making it to the Peak was.

I realized then that I had a pretty good advantage now from growing up and living in winter climates. Runners from southern states were having trouble with their footing. Several people fell on their butts, and many others used their hands to navigate the ice-covered rocks.

"Here, let me steady you," I offered to the guy in front of me when he slipped. I braced his right arm as his left foot found purchase on the rock above. A minute later, as I waited my turn to climb the rock in front of me, I turned to the woman behind me and clasped her arm as she ascended another rock stair.

I enjoyed helping everyone, though, I realized the assistance slowed down my progress. Finally, at four hours and forty-one minutes, I reached the summit of Pikes Peak, 14,115 feet above sea level. *Ka-ching*!

An incredible feeling of relief swept over me, and my body tingled—maybe from the excitement of reaching the peak, but probably not. Despite all my clothing, I was cold, especially my toes, which couldn't escape the layer of snow clinging to the tips of my shoes. The temperature at the summit measured south of thirty degrees. Plus, ice covered the trail where all of the runners had tramped down the snow. Beautiful scenery, but not fun to run on.

I tried rewarding myself with a couple of pretzels at the small aid station near the banner marking the runners' turnaround point. My brain told my teeth to crunch them, but my frozen cheeks didn't want to cooperate. After downing some Gatorade and water, I realized I would rather get back down to the tree line so I could be warm again—and avoid any lightning.

We made our way slowly, again going single file and helping each other as necessary. But I soon realized that at the rate we moved, it would be a long haul. And, the sun had peeked out its head slightly, making the trail just a little slushy and providing decent footing.

I wanted to speed up to a jog, but three guys walked in front of me. Just as I realized I need to pass them, a young lady called out from behind me, "Do you guys mind if I slide by on your left?"

On her behalf, I asked them if the two of us could pass. The woman and I started to jog, watching for slick spots. With me in the lead, my new running friend and I deftly navigated the course and the runners still coming up Barr Trail. Within what seemed like just a few minutes, we had returned to A-Frame, just under 12,000 feet.

Just being back under tree line felt like rejoining civilization.

In fact, given the green trees and vegetation, I probably *was* breathing more easily from the additional oxygen in the air. I shed all the cold-weather clothes I had put on since I was now starting to sweat, and it would only get warmer as I headed down. I emptied my shoes of their accumulated pebbles and ate a few frozen M&Ms from the aid station.

With my mouth full of sugar, I learned the young lady hailed from Houston and was training to become an astronaut, hence her nickname "Buzz." I did not have my cell phone, but Buzz lent me hers, so I had a quick conversation with Kirsta to let her know that I was ahead of schedule.

"Hello?" Kirsta said.

"Can you hear me?" I asked.

"What?" my wife replied through static.

"It's Greg!" I yelled into the phone. "Can you hear me? I borrowed someone's phone. I made it to the top and am already headed back down. I should be at the finish line in about two or two and a half hours."

"Okay." Kirsta was studying for a nursing exam and engrossed in a book, so an update on my progress wasn't a huge priority, but she understood that she would need to leave the hotel earlier than expected to see me cross the finish line.

Handing the phone back to Buzz, I learned that she, like me, loved running downhill, so I knew I'd found a good descent partner. In a few words, we kicked butt. On this day, I had no trouble navigating the rocks and tree roots that haunt the trail. We slowed down only for the big drop-offs and the very rocky areas. In no time, we arrived back at Barr Camp—less than seven miles to go.

After quick refreshments at Barr, Buzz and I were back on our way, running at a great pace and only slowing down to walk a few of the up-hills that we encountered. My feet started to hurt, but we each pushed, knowing that we had an outside chance to finish at seven hours.

Time passed quickly, and we had a few others try to run with us, but none kept pace. By now, we were feeling good and skipping aid stations to pick up time. We made it through Rock Arch with no problems, but about three miles out, Buzz tripped. First her hands, then her knees took the impact, but thankfully her head remained off the trail.

"Crap!" I thought, fearing that she would be injured from the crash. My feet skidded to a stop. As much as I wanted to cross the finish line, I needed to help my new friend. While we had conquered the mountain as individuals, we came down the trail as a team.

I turned to offer a hand, but Buzz bounced up in no time, first going into a plank and then pushing herself to her knees and then her feet. I looked her up and down. "You okay?"

"My favorite ballcap," Buzz sighed. "It's broken. But I'm good!"

The future astronaut showed no signs of injury, so we took off at a quick pace again.

We crossed the back entry to the Incline and headed into the switchback portion of the trail called the *Ws*. Colorado Springs broke into view off the slopes. Traveling a straightaway, we came upon three walkers, and I called out, "Runners passing on your left!" But they were slow to move.

I hesitated and made a misstep. Like a cartoon character slipping on a banana peel, my shoes slid on loose rock, and I plummeted to the ground, ending up on my back. Buzz and one of the walkers asked if I was okay. I said, "Just need a hand up." So they pulled me up, and we were off again.

As we entered the final two miles of our mountain excursion, adrenaline filled my veins, and my heart beat in double time. I knew we would not make seven hours, but I calculated quickly and made 7:20 my new goal. And then Buzz wiped out again. I could tell this one hurt. She didn't even want to look at her hands to see if they were bleeding. But like a good trooper, she picked herself up, and we attacked the trail again.

We quickly made it to Ruxton Road, and I knew we would finish no problem. Buzz ran just a few steps behind, and I did not want to leave my wingman, but I knew we would have to run a seven-minute mile to finish in 7:20. So I called back, "Stick with me if you can," and as soon as we hit the pavement, I ran faster, past the COG rail station, past a little girl and a mom cheering with maracas, past other fans clapping and cheering.

After more than seven hours on my feet climbing up and down Pikes Peak, I push hard in the last 20 yards before the finish line in Manitou Springs.

I struggled mightily—feet burning, lungs chugging—until I heard someone yell, "Finish line is just around the corner!" and knew I couldn't stop now. I turned left, and there it was! I dashed across the line with "7:20:47" on the scoreboard overhead, which placed me at 325ᵗʰ of 631 male finishers.

My ascent time was 4:41:01, with a descent time of 2:39:46. I was amazed at my results until I learned that Matt Carpenter, the overall winner, had a finish time of 3:36:54, with splits of 2:11:54 up and 1:25:00 down. Not only was Matt finished before I had climbed the mountain, but he'd also probably showered, eaten lunch, and taken a nap! The rest of us competitors weren't ashamed, though. Matt's oxygen intake rate once measured as the highest among any runner ever, and he lives in Manitou Springs with daily access to train on Barr Trail.

I may not have Matt's oxygen intake rate, but I've always been the type of guy who doesn't leave anything left in the tank when crossing the finish line. So, of course, the medics always rush up thinking I need attention. For this challenging mountain adventure, it's standard operating procedure for attendants to eyeball each finisher, looking for any concerns. When two came up on either side, I said, "I'm okay, I just need to walk," and they let me go.

Buzz crossed the finish line about one minute behind me. We thanked each other and exchanged a smelly, sweaty hug after pushing each other for the last thirteen miles.

I felt woozy, but when I exited the finisher's tent to walk around, I realized my feet *really* burned. I stopped, and again someone asked if I was doing okay. I just stood there, leaning slightly forward, hands on hips, so someone shoved a chair behind me—and I sat down.

After catching my breath, I realized I really wanted to get my shoes off . . . and discovered a blister the size of a half-dollar on my left heel. No blister on my right heel, but the skin was soft and very close to becoming one. So, I borrowed another cell phone and left a message for Kirsta that I would be in the medical tent to get my blister treated. I tried putting on my shoes but really struggled until a volunteer told me, "Here, just hold on to your stuff," and he and another guy picked up my chair and carried me like royalty into the tent.

"Oh, what would Kirsta say if she saw this?" While embarrassed, part of me felt like a king, and I appreciated the gesture, as my feet were beyond sore. Thankfully, I am not aware of any photos that exist of this moment.

Three people, including a doctor, cleaned and bandaged the blister so I could put my shoe back on. I limped out of the tent again but still could not find Kirsta, so I crossed the street and started walking toward where I thought she might have parked. My feet had never blistered during runs before, so I recognized that I would have to investigate the problem, with my first thought being that it could be the result of downhill friction.

I made it as far as one-half block when I realized it would be fruitless to gimp around aimlessly. So, I borrowed another cell phone, left her another message, and sat on a bench in front of a pizza restaurant. Finally, Kirsta found me. She had been right across the street the whole time but somehow managed to miss me as I approached the finish line.

Kirsta made her way back to her vehicle, and the police let her stop near the finish line to pick me up. She rolled down the windows as soon as I got it in—I can't believe she thought I stunk! After I drank more fluids, we stopped at Chili's for an early dinner and enjoyed the ride home, but not before she made me change clothes and clean up with some baby wipes.

The electronic pedometer I wore during the marathon showed that I took more than 48,000 steps and burned more than 2,600 calories, or roughly the equivalent of five cheeseburgers—so I got a head start on catching up by eating one at Chili's, with fries!

CHAPTER 3

UP A MOUNTAIN, AGAIN

In early 2009, I received a phone call in my office from my friend Koree Khongphand Buckman, who had spent the weekend with her in-laws. While reminiscing with the family, her husband described the poor condition of donated toys that he and his siblings had received at Christmas when they were young. His older brother shared another memory, recalling that the kids received "slightly used" underwear, which allowed the family to spend money on other necessities. Can you imagine the indignity of wearing underwear that previously hugged the groin of a stranger?

Koree shuddered at the thought, and the next day she and two work colleagues developed the idea of a new not-for-profit organization called Underwearness to provide new underwear to children in need.

By the end of the phone conversation, Koree had me energized to help however I could. I believe passionately in helping those who can't help themselves, and children are among the most vulnerable members of society.

I committed to serving on the board of directors for the not-for-profit, and at our first meeting on February 14, I signed on as president of the board for Underwearness. We had little cash for the organization—Koree had paid for any filing fees, etc., out of her own pocket, and we board members made some minimal financial contributions. With the board's blessing, I registered for another Pikes Peak Marathon with the intent to raise money for Underwearness. In fact, for 2009, I signed up to be a D-D-Doubler . . . running the Ascent half marathon up the mountain on Saturday, and then doing the full marathon up and down the mountain on Sunday.

I coined my efforts "14er for $14,000" and built on my fundraising experience from the prior year. If my network had donated $4,000 to help send a child to Disney World, surely the combined board could raise triple that amount. I thought we would get one thousand people to donate $14 each to get to the $14,000 mark. Later, I realized naming a specific dollar amount had been a mistake, as people who might have donated more contributed the requested $14 in lieu of a larger contribution. I logged this info away for the future. Nonetheless, we board members spread the word about my Pikes Peak effort and generated more than $6,000 for the Underwearness coffers, a great financial start.

On the Friday before the 2009 Pikes Peak Ascent and Marathon weekend, the Colorado offices of the accounting firm for which I worked held an all-staff meeting involving one hundred people. As part of the get-together, I helped organized games to play before and after breaks. We distributed fifty small prizes for members of the winning teams and had plenty of leftovers, so I treated myself to tasty snacks like Krispy Kreme donuts, Rice Krispy Treats and Wendy's Frosty cups. Probably not the best things to eat before running in a half and full marathon, but as I always say, "I run so I can eat whatever I want!"

After the meetings concluded, I hurried home, finished packing my belongings, and Kirsta and I took the scenic backroads to Manitou Springs. Despite my day-long snacking, we were both starving.

"Straight to the restaurant?" I glanced at Kirsta.

The clock approached 7:00, so I was going to miss the evening's check-in for the Ascent. I also wondered whether my digestive system would be overwhelmed by eating so much food fewer than twelve hours before the run's start time. After all, stomachs are not designed to do both digestion and exercise at the same time.

"Ugh, this is gonna be interesting," I sighed to Kirsta, after we placed our order and handed the menus to our server.

During the months preceding, I had exchanged messages on the PPM website message board with a gentleman from Alabama who would be participating in the marathon for the first time. Jay and I eventually exchanged phone numbers and text messages as we shared our training accomplishments. So, as we waited for my lasagna and Kirsta's pizza, I sent a note to his phone.

Minutes later, the restaurant door opened, and a tall, trim guy strode through the restaurant's front door and to our table.

"Greg?" he asked.

"Jay!" I exclaimed, standing with a friendly hand extended. His wife Janie and my wife exchanged pleasantries while Jay and I shared strategies for the run.

"I have three goals, Jay," I said. "One, survive. Two, finish. Three, break seven hours."

"Sounds good to me," Jay responded with a smile. He and I were on the same track.

After their to-go order arrived, Jay and Janie left, but we knew we would likely see each other a few times during the weekend.

By the time Kirsta and I checked into the Comfort Inn and settled in, the clock neared ten thirty. After just seven hours of sleep, we woke at five thirty since I needed to check-in before the race at seven thirty.

"This is way too early to be awake," mumbled Kirsta, never one to be disturbed before the sun had broken the horizon.

As usual, and especially on a full stomach, I had a light breakfast: an oatmeal breakfast bar with a water and a G2 sports drink. Some people need their daily coffee; I need my G2. Unlike last year, however, Mother Nature provided outstanding weather this year, so I decided to run in just a pair of shorts and a single shirt, carrying only a handheld water bottle with two granola bars stuck in its carrying pocket.

Even at the early morning hour, the parking areas surrounding the start line were jammed.

"Bah," I muttered to Kirsta. "I hate to make you walk very far."

"Me, either," she added, with eyes only half-open. Kirsta was pregnant and due with our first baby in two months. She had already woken at a super early hour to drive me to the start line, so I thought I had asked enough from her without making her feet tired and her back ache from completing a 5k before the sun broke the horizon.

We found a somewhat illegal parking spot near the check-in tent; we weren't blocking a fire hydrant or anything—the sign just said, "No Parking Here to Corner," so it didn't seem like our rule breaking would lead to anyone's death.

Of course, something had to go wrong: I had forgotten my driver's license to verify my identification at check-in.

"Arrrgh," my knuckles massaged my forehead. With my best puppy dog eyes, I begged the volunteer behind the table. "Can I validate my existence in some other fashion?"

With a laugh, the helpful woman bent the rules and confirmed my registration by asking my birth date. The Pikes Peak Marathon scored serious points for customer service!

Kirsta and I now had thirty minutes to kill, so we snapped a few pictures near the starting line and visited with other participants. After some final stretching and a light jog down

Manitou Avenue, I had to desert my wife. Overemphasizing the situation, I dramatically played up my departure.

"If I don't return, take care of our child," I whimpered, patting our baby growing in Kirsta's belly and placing a soft kiss on my wife's cheek. "Be strong and raise him the right way."

I cradle our soon-to-be-born baby boy before saying farewell to Kirsta at the starting line of the 2009 Pikes Peak Marathon.

It was still dawn's early light, but I could sense her eye-roll as I found a place in line with the others preparing to ascend the mountain.

Compared to last year, this Ascent turned out to be fairly uneventful. A light jog put me at the end of Ruxton Avenue in twenty minutes, right on my usual pace. A highlight came soon after, as I spotted my coworker Katie volunteering at the aid station near the Incline, so I got to say hello and have her group refill my water bottle.

Like the prior year, traffic proved heavy through the "Ws," and I pretty much went at the same pace as the person in front of me, running when the group did. My goal was to be through Rock Arch in one hour, and sure enough, I hit it just under sixty minutes.

While my hope for the Ascent was four hours, I knew my number-one priority for the weekend was to break seven hours for the Marathon. So, I kept up a moderate pace, aiming for four hours, but not overly concerned if it missed it in my first year as a Doubler. I happily arrived at Barr Camp in two hours and decided to have a quick snack. I snarfed down a granola bar and some Gatorade and headed back to the trail.

The hike continued with no problems, and I was pleasantly surprised to arrive at the A-Frame aid station an hour later, around three hours total. Unfortunately, just after passing the tree line, I hit a wall. As I look back, I think it was a combination of everything—too much junk food, rushed travel, inadequate sleep—in the prior twenty-four hours that made me so worn out. I had to stop several times for thirty- to forty-five-second breaks, and as soon as I realized that four hours was out of the picture, I decided to take it easy in preparation for the marathon.

For the second year in a row, Mother Nature decided to have a little fun and throw some snow at us—in August! The wind and cooler temperatures made the last two miles a little uncomfortable, especially on my bald head. Hard snow pellets pounding a bald scalp is painful, kind of like those annoying paper cuts you sometimes get on your finger when you open an envelope. The type of annoying at which you laugh because something so small hurts so much.

The mini-storm lasted just a few minutes, thankfully, and I

soon arrived in range of the summit. I started picking up my pace a little bit. Unfortunately, I found myself stuck behind a slow-moving group of about five people, with no easy way to pass. As I checked my watch, I could tell that we would have trouble breaking 4:30 if we didn't pick up the pace. So, in as polite and energetic a voice as I could muster, I cried out, "Hey, guys, if we can pick up the pace a little bit, we can break four hours and thirty minutes!"

Another member of the group caught on and exclaimed, "Yeah, let's do it!"

It worked. While I was not able to pass them, they all sped up, and I crossed the finish line of my first Ascent in 4:26:13.

Since this was my first Ascent, I didn't know the protocol up top, and I was disappointed that no one directed me where to go. For the Ascent, you can drop off a bag of clothes at the starting line, and officials shuttle the bag to the top so you can dress warmly after you finish. The summit's chilly weather more than justified this precaution. After asking around, I finally found the bag pick-up area—now I just needed a place to put on a pair of pants and change into a long-sleeved shirt.

I thought I entered a side door of the summit house, where I plopped down in an empty chair near the entry point. After more than five hours on my feet, my heels needed a break. Someone offered me water and Gatorade, which I gratefully accepted. I took deep breaths and casually glanced around the room . . . and I realized I had invaded the first aid area. Oops!

Not wanting to draw attention to myself, I found my dry shirt and tried to pull it on so I could exit quickly. Uh, no—a muscle in my lower back spasmed, and I immediately dove facedown onto the floor so it would work itself out. Two people dashed to my side.

"Hey, sir. Are you okay?" I heard one of the concerned

attendants ask.

I was appreciative, though embarrassed. I didn't need help—previous back spasms always worked themselves out in just a minute—but I am sure it appeared like I was having a heart attack or other serious medical issue. I groaned, "Just a back spasm, but some ibuprofen would be great."

One of the attendants offered me some tablets, which I grabbed quickly and got out of there!

I had crammed ten dollars into my water bottle bag so I could eat at the summit if I were hungry. I wasn't, but I decided to buy some of the famous Summit House donuts as a surprise for Kirsta and a reward for me. I made it only a few steps into the Summit House. Holy moly, people jammed the place! After being nearly isolated for four and a half hours on Barr Trail, the noise and commotion overwhelmed me.

Instead of buying food, I pulled on my newly earned Ascent finisher's jacket and went back out into the cold to line up for the ride down. The air felt even colder while I stood around doing nothing, so I sat on the ground and pulled on my pants. After about ten minutes, I stood at the front of the van line and finally plunged into the warmth of the vehicle.

Thanks to a friend, Kirsta had found out about a huge clothing sale for babies occurring in Castle Rock, so she'd driven the fifty miles north as soon as I started running. I borrowed someone's cell phone on the ride down and learned that I would beat her back to Manitou Springs, so I decided to go to the food tent and enjoy some pizza and G2. As I sat on a curb, talking with another first-time finisher, Jay from Alabama came by. When his wife arrived soon after, they offered me a ride to the hotel, which I happily accepted.

Soon after, Kirsta arrived at the hotel, and I took a refreshing shower before we both went downstairs to soak in the hot tub—

just feet, for my pregnant wife. Let me tell you, the warm water on my tired muscles hit the spot! After some relaxation time, we headed to Paravicini's for our six o'clock reservations. Leveraging the knowledge I'd gained as a "veteran" runner, I combined the protein of chicken for muscle recovery with carbohydrates from fettuccine to provide energy for my run the next day. It'd been a long day for both of us, so we headed back to the hotel for an early night in.

I slept soundly and felt terrific when I woke up. The forecast called for a cold front to hit the area during the day, so I dressed in running tights and a long-sleeved shirt under my shorts and T-shirt. I again wore a small backpack on my back, but it carried far fewer items than last year: a G2 sports drink, a water bottle, a few granola bars, a hat, and light gloves—just in case. I confidently eschewed toilet paper.

At the starting line, we again ran into Jay and Janie and offered each other a hearty "Good luck!" I gave Kirsta a hug and kiss, then hopped in line for the singing of America the Beautiful and the starting gun. As we started, I knew I just needed to replicate the ascent time I had achieved yesterday and then run down in about 2:30 (I'd come down in 2:40 the last year) to break seven hours.

Competitors passed me quickly, so I checked my watch several times to make sure I was running at my pace. I reached Ruxton Avenue in about twenty minutes and again marched with traffic through the switchbacks at the start of Barr Trail. To pass the time, I chatted with the guy in front of me, a man named Frank who was a veteran Ascent participant but was running his first Marathon. Before long, we arrived at the side door of the Incline and picked up the pace. We hit Rock Arch at 1:02, just a couple of minutes slower than usual.

My philosophy became: maintain. I didn't want to go too fast, nor did I want to move too slowly or take many breaks. Without too much of a struggle, I reached Barr Camp in just less than two hours and detected no aches, no pains, and no issues with my body. I grabbed a granola bar out of my backpack, but this time ate as I walked to keep my pace—head down, just keep moving.

Many people like to run with earphones, listening to music to pass the time. For the Pikes Peak Marathon, that is not an option. Organizers want runners to be aware of the potentially dangerous surroundings at all times—you know, just bears and mountain lions—so earphones are banned. Without earphones, I just think. And in the stretch between Barr Camp and A-Frame, the part of the climb I found most challenging mentally, thinking is just what I did.

I thought about the support of people who had donated to Underwearness—and how a new not-for-profit, which started with zero dollars to its name, now had thousands of dollars in the bank to help provide a piece of comfort to children in need.

I thought about the words that my beautiful wife wrote in her "Good Luck" card and how blessed I was to have married a woman who supported my ridiculous endeavors.

I thought about my son arriving in just a couple of months. *I am going to be a father!* Heck, I could barely take care of myself, and soon I would be in charge of someone else's life?

If you have ever read On Walden Pond by Henry David Thoreau, you know the feeling I'm describing . . . of being so alone with your feelings. In this solitude, you delineate your priorities in life, but you also yearn for human interaction.

That's why the noise from the A-Frame aid station is so rewarding—you feel like you're back in civilization. I again reached it in three hours and felt energetic and inspired, ready to maintain a steady pace to the top, knowing that I was on track for my goal.

The Pikes Peak Marathon has a unique challenge. While climbing up, you must yield the right of way to downhill runners, especially the fast-moving leaders. Therefore, your time is slowed down somewhat because you must stop in some places. I took advantage of this handicap by using these small breaks as my only stops, unlike the many breaks I had taken the day before. I could also tell that my training had paid off . . . despite having now traveled nearly twenty-six miles in twenty-four hours, I had little fatigue in my legs.

Near the top, I ran across my Alabama buddy Jay, who had reached the summit in 4:03, coming downhill. His words: "It's kicking my butt, Greg." But Jay impressed me with his time, and I knew he'd be okay.

At 4:28:53, I hit the summit. Unlike 2008, the skies shone bright, and unlike 2008, I spent zero time at the top. I knew I could break seven hours, and I was holding nothing back.

In 2008, the first two miles were slow since we had ice and snow to traverse. This year, the only things slowing me down were other runners climbing uphill and a few rocks. As soon as I could, I ran fast and passed other downhillers regularly. I even stunned myself by how quickly I moved along the trail. In no time, I hit tree line and A-Frame, and I still felt solid.

Somewhere around the seventeen-mile mark, I spotted the back of a familiar runner: Frank, whom I had followed up through the Ws. He had beaten me to the summit by about thirteen minutes, and now I'd caught up to him. I'm not sure if I inspired him to pick up his pace, but we connected and started moving quickly together.

Unfortunately, disaster began setting in. I could feel a blister forming on my left heel. I'd adjusted my running style from last year, leaning forward more while going downhill, and now I could feel soreness in my right foot. I wanted to break seven hours so badly, but could I overcome the pain that was developing? I didn't want to come this far and not hit my target time. I checked my watch, did my math, and decided my goal remained in reach. I told Frank, and he responded, "Dude, I just want to finish, but seven hours would be great. Let's go for it."

So, we did.

I can't even come close to guessing how many people we passed. If you look at the marathon results, you can see people's "up" and "down" times. Of the twenty or so finishers on either side of my final marathon time, you will see only two or three others with down times as fast as mine. In fact, my downhill time was close to those who finished near the top 100. Not sure what I like about running downhill, but I do love it!

But as we approached Barr Camp, the pain escalated. Every step sent agony through the blisters on my left heel and right big toe. I coveted that seven-hour finish, though, so I pushed, but I could no longer keep the pain internal. I grunted stepping down from a rock. "Oomph!" I cried out when landing on my toe. "Ouch!"

Frank could hear me hurting, but instead of even considering leaving me behind, he became my leader and wingman. He set the pace, and I followed. If I needed to walk uphill, he walked uphill. I told him several times, "Go ahead. Don't let me slow you down," but he refused. I can't express how much I appreciated his encouragement.

By now, we checked our watches regularly, knowing seven hours was easily doable if we could persist. Frank kept his verbal outcries to a minimum, but he told me that his knees throbbed. Don't forget, this was his first Pikes Peak Marathon, and the downhill pounding can generate agony in the legs.

"Frank," I said, "I typically climb up to Rock Arch in sixty minutes."

"Me, too," he replied.

"So, if we can get there by six hours, and we can be down in sixty minutes, then we can break seven, right?"

"You bet," Frank said.

"I just want to get to Rock Arch," I repeated.

We pushed all the way to Rock Arch, passing it just as our watches passed six hours marathon time. Still on track to hit our finish goal! Blisters and sore knees could not slow us down.

We began to encounter hikers coming up the trail, who shouted out encouragement. We appreciated the comments, but I could only imagine how alarming each "ouch," "oooh," and other groan must have sounded to them as we lurched past. Then, without warning, Frank's foot caught a rock, and his six-foot frame tumbled to the rocky ground.

Since he'd served as my wingman, now was my time to take charge. "Good fall," I said. "Get up. You're fine. I don't see any blood. Let's go. We gotta beat seven hours."

He bounced back up, and with me breathing down his neck, he started moving again, glancing down at his hands and the rest of his body. Within a couple strides, blood started seeping out from an area near his right knee. I technically didn't lie—at the time, I didn't see any blood!

Laughing with Frank, I told him the blood would look impressive to the spectators near the finish line. Despite my attempts at humor, I hurt. After more than six hours of hiking, jogging, and running, my joints and muscles ached, and my brain wanted nothing more than to see the finish line. Even worse, I had to adjust how my foot landed on any given step, so I backed away a little from Frank so I could see his foot placement and thus eliminate any unpleasant surprises.

As we moved down the trail, I cheered at the sight of another familiar figure ahead on the trail: Jay from Alabama. Frank and

I slowed to pass him, and Jay gasped that he was struggling. I patted him on the back. "Dude, you've got ten years on me! And, you're from sea level! You are rocking this!"

Frank and I picked up the pace and, finally, reached the end of the switchbacks where Barr Trail ends and Ruxton Avenue marks the homestretch of the marathon.

"Frank," I said, "I gotta slow down. My feet can't handle this steep part. Go ahead of me. I'll be fine."

He agreed and ran ahead, leaving me by myself for the first time in miles and hours.

I was exhausted. I was hurting. I wanted to be done.

Wincing with each step, I took my final steps on gravel and dirt before I hit the blacktop near the Cog Railway. Here, spectators lined the route. So, to look my toughest, I needed to suck up the pain and jog the last mile. I tried to look triumphant for the crowd, and I ignored my physical distress by smiling and running as normally as possible. Okay—I encountered a spot with no one around where I walked for about thirty feet, but I really hurt!

I approached the finish line and could hear people saying, "Way to go, Greg!" I soaked it all in—waving to the crowd, smiling for the cameras, and otherwise enjoying the fact that I was going to break seven hours.

I again missed my wife, but that was because she'd found a spot in the shade instead of the planned location. Nonetheless, I expected she would look for me in the first aid tent. And indeed, she guessed—correctly—that after last year's experience, I would be there again.

I crossed the finish line at 6:50:06, hitting my goal to beat seven hours. Officially, my down time was 2:21:13, with which I was delighted, although I thought to myself, *Sheesh! If only I had not walked that thirty-foot stretch, I would have broken 6:50.*

Completing the 2009 Pikes Peak Marathon in under seven hours was an accomplishment of which I will always be proud! Thanks to Janie Hillis for capturing my finish.

The first aid tent is attached to the finish tent, so I just continued straight to a seat. Even more bothersome than my blisters, I was hot. The anticipated cold front hadn't arrived, so I was on fire. I stripped off the two shirts I was wearing, which allowed some heat to escape, and I felt even better when I got my shoes off.

Just as I settled in for my treatment, I saw Jay also entering the first aid area, so I waved him over to an open seat next to me. He had also broken seven hours, coming in at 6:54:19. Pretty darn impressive for a first-timer flatlander!

Frank Peloso (standing), Jay Hillis and I rehash our 2009 Pikes Peak
Marathon experience while receiving medical attention
inside the finish line tent.

Kirsta found me in my usual spot, and as she came to greet me, we overheard a woman who had just finished say, "That was harder than delivering a baby!"

I grinned, but my pregnant wife just rolled her eyes.

As Kirsta went to get her vehicle to pick me up, Jay and I gathered our things and said our goodbyes. He is a good man, and I am proud to have made his and his wife's acquaintance.

Sporting an Alabama shirt, my buddy Jay Hills says goodbye before we depart the Pikes Peak Marathon finish line. Both of us are wearing the official marathon finisher jacket.

This year, Kirsta and I stopped at my office building in Colorado Springs so I could shower and she could avoid my stench. Afterward, we couldn't come up with any better place to eat on the way home than the same Chili's where we had dined the prior year. I was astonished to find, though, that I couldn't even finish my cheeseburger! Feeling more exhausted than hungry, I was more than ready to get home.

One month after I rocked Pikes Peak, the Underwearness board hosted our inaugural event in downtown Denver. We had wanted something impressive and visually memorable for our Underwearness kickoff event. So, while brainstorming on a drive home from work, I had coined "Drop Your Drawers"—a terrific event that we held on September 24.

For our signature activity, the primary goal wasn't raising money. We wanted the publicity and a lot of participants and underwear. All board members invited friends, coworkers, business colleagues, and the general public to the upper-story, two-floor parking garage from which participants dropped packages of new children's underwear into baskets below. If the underwear landed in the appropriate containers, they won prizes donated by various businesses.

"Drop your drawers!" our emcee called out to passersby on Denver streets. "That's right. Bring new children's underwear and drop them from the top of the building for a chance to win prizes!"

Our participants discovered how much a lightweight package veers off course when traveling twenty feet through the air. "Oh, man, I just missed!" exclaimed my coworker Jami. "That was hard!"

My friend Katy attempts to win a prize during the "Drop Your Drawers" kickoff event we held for Underwearness in 2010.

The event succeeded in many ways—we garnered terrific media coverage, more than $1,000 in cash contributions, and nearly two thousand pairs of underwear to donate to Denver-area charities: Tennyson Center for Children and The Gathering Place. Supporters had so much fun that we heard reports of downtown stores selling their entire inventory of children's underwear! Combined with our fundraising efforts for my marathon run, Underwearness had officially launched.

As fall rolled around, my wife gave birth to our first child. Baby boy Bryce entered the world on October 12, 2009. Our world changed in so many ways: diapers, bottles, burp rags, and toys scattered around the house. Also on tap: less nighttime sleep because of regular feedings—though, as most parents would agree, more daytime naps were justified since the baby needed one, too.

Kirsta and I pose with our baby for our first family photo the morning after Bryce was born at Rose Hospital in Denver.

I continued to run as much as I could while maximizing time with my mini-me. I even brought him along on some of my running excursions. During one of those runs, I thought about how cool it would be to carry my son across the Pikes Peak finish line.

So, in 2010, I signed up for my second attempt as a Pikes Peak D-D-Doubler. Having raised $10,000 for charity the previous two years and having finished the marathon in under seven hours, I relaxed completely the weekend of August 21 and 22 with just one goal: carrying Bryce across the finish line.

Spotting my wife with a camera soon after starting the 2010 Pikes Peak Ascent, I jumped at the chance to say "hi" one last time before embarking up the mountain.

The weather was gorgeous that Saturday, my body felt great, and I had fun going up the mountain, mugging for the camera whenever I saw a photographer. My ascent time slowed considerably above the tree line when I came upon a struggling fellow participant from Arizona. I was in no hurry, so I made the decision to stay with him, not just to encourage him but because I was genuinely concerned for his well-being. I couldn't imagine leaving him alone and finding out later that he had died or suffered some serious medical issue.

We finally made it to the summit more than five hours after we started our climb, by far the slowest of any of my clocked times up the mountain. As we approached the finish line, I motioned to officials that my running partner needed assistance. As soon as he crossed under the finish banner, attendants moved to either side of the struggling climber and escorted him to the medical area. I followed them briefly until I was confident he would be okay. Mission accomplished.

The next day, I woke ready to run. With two years of Pikes Peak Marathon under my belt, I was mentally better prepared than ever for the challenge. Physically, my legs had rebounded from the Ascent, and since I had accomplished my goal of breaking seven hours, I didn't have any interest in pushing as hard as I had the prior year.

When we'd arrived in town on Friday, Kirsta and I had scouted a location on Ruxton Avenue about eighty yards before the finish line where she and Bryce would be waiting for me to come down the mountain. No missing each other this time!

As I approached that area at the end of my run, I began to scream out, "Who's your daddy?" This was the same thing I said each day as I opened the garage door at our house after a day at the office to be greeted by my smiling baby boy at the top of the stairs.

Bystanders looked at me like I had lost my mind on the mountain. Then, those same people moaned, "awww . . ." when they saw me stop along the road, take Bryce from Kirsta, and lightly jog across the finish line with our baby boy cradled in my arms. I struggled to hold back the tears after spending seven hours and thirty-four minutes alone climbing up and down a mountain and then celebrating the end of the marathon with my firstborn. Priceless. A memory I will forever cherish.

One of my favorite photos ever—carrying my baby boy across the finish line at the 2010 Pikes Peak Marathon. A few steps later, I handed him off to a medical attendant because he kept sliding out of my sweaty arms!

With four marathons now completed, including "America's Ultimate Challenge" three times, I thought it might be time to call it quits. I was in pretty good shape, and I thought I'd accomplished my running goals.

But Facebook had become popular, and in September some high school classmates, led by Stephanie Homan Groathouse, discussed online the idea of a mini reunion in Nebraska by participating in the 2011 Lincoln Marathon. I thought that it would be fun to catch up with old friends and see how fast I could run a flat marathon, compared to one up and down a mountain.

Plus, the idea of running across the fifty-yard line at Memorial Stadium, home of my beloved Cornhuskers football team, appealed to me. So, in May 2011, my family and I prepared for a trip to Nebraska.

On Wednesday, a day before we were to leave, I attended a business breakfast at the Denver Center for Performing Arts. The ballroom there has a suspended floor, but, oddly, the whole world seemed like it was shaking during the entire breakfast. I didn't feel up for walking back to the office, so I caught a ride with a coworker but still felt nauseated the whole way.

I spent another hour at the office before deciding I really was sick—and scheduled to run 26.2 miles in four days! Kirsta and I decided to wait an extra day before making the eight-hour drive to Lincoln, and, on Friday, I somehow managed to survive the journey. Yet, on Saturday, I vomited again and wondered how in the heck I would run a marathon.

Despite a good night's sleep at my brother Ron's house in Lincoln, I woke up Sunday feeling dizzy and wondering if I should attempt the run. But I was invested, financially and physically, so, at an early morning hour, Ron dropped me off near the starting line outside Memorial Stadium. Outdoors was chilly but sunny, and I slowly regained my energy and confidence. Instead of wondering if I would run, my mind started focusing on how fast I would run. I knew I was ready.

The first half of the marathon was packed—not just with runners, but with spectators. They were a little quiet, so at least a couple of times, feeling my strength and jovial attitude returned, I encouraged them to cheer by raising my arms and shouting, "Did the Huskers lose yesterday? Is this a funeral? Make some noise!"

I had a lot of fun those first thirteen miles, though I was slightly distracted to see an ambulance near the ten-mile mark. I figured someone was battling exhaustion or another minor medical issue, though I later learned a man had suffered a heart attack. Thankfully, his life was saved by those who witnessed his attack, including a pair of fellow runners who were doctors.

I had a terrific pace as I jogged down 10th Street approaching the halfway point of the Lincoln Marathon—notice the ambulance and medical workers in the background saving the life of a runner who had suffered a heart attack.

As we ran past Memorial Stadium, many runners veered off to cross the half marathon finish line. "Goodbye!" I cried. "Finish strong!"

Having hit the halfway point for my venture, I checked my

watch. I had completed 13.1 miles in 1:56:27—on track to break four hours! "That would be awesome!" I encouraged myself.

Unfortunately, the crowd enthusiasm disappeared. Heck, the *crowd* disappeared! Because so many participants—ten thousand—ran just the half marathon, fewer than two thousand remained for the full marathon. Which also meant the cheering section for the final 13.1 miles looked more like the opponents' section at Memorial Stadium during the fourth quarter in the 1990s after the Huskers pounded the visiting football team— sparse and quiet.

Running alongside heavy Lincoln traffic on a warm morning isn't exactly stimulating. It's a blur of engine noise, exhaust fumes, and heat radiating from the asphalt, separated from tons of molded metal by only a series of orange traffic cones. However, with my iPod keeping me entertained through the boredom, I carried a solid pace as the marathon headed south.

I neared the turnaround point outside of Holmes Lake Recreation Area, and my eyes opened wide to see that my family— Kirsta, Bryce, brother Ron, Mom, and Dad—had made it to 70th Street to greet me. I exchanged high fives and pleasantries, and then continued on, eager to hit the stadium with a strong finish.

But, when I turned north, the wind blew like a giant fan against me. I tried to push through it, but my hopes deflated as the group running with the 3:50 pacer passed me . . . then the 4:00 pacer . . . and the 4:10 pacer.

As I returned to the north side of the football stadium, my spirits picked up when I saw a familiar face. My high school classmate Stephanie, who had first floated the idea of a marathon reunion, had stayed after she finished the half marathon. She put a kick in my step as she ran with me for a minute to encourage me and tell me about the video camera ahead that would beam my face to those watching inside the stadium.

Sure enough, just around the corner, I spotted the camera and crossed my arms to flash the Husker football skull and crossbones like the players do on the field. I'm unaware of whether anyone saw me, but I sure laughed. Then, I stopped running for just a second to change my iPod to play the University of Nebraska's fight song and "Sirius" by The Alan Parsons Project—the song that plays when the football team storms the field for a game.

No one else could hear the music since I had in my earbuds, so people probably wondered why I had tears in my eyes and a crazy grin on my face, but for this native Nebraskan, entering the fabled stadium to those classic songs registered as a top-ten life moment.

As my feet hit the field turf, I quickly spotted my family in the spot I had recommended in the mostly empty east stands. At the end of my 26.2 my run, I posed at the finish line like the Heisman Trophy figure before spiking my water bottle. Goosebumps!

For a Nebraska native, posing as the Heisman Trophy as you finish a marathon at the 50-yard line of Memorial Stadium is about as Husker as you can get!

My finish time: 4:16. Close, but no cigar to breaking the four-hour standard for successful marathon runners. I set a personal record, especially impressive considering how sick I had been in the days leading up to the marathon. But I still had an objective on my bucket list that needed to be accomplished—running a sub-four-hour marathon.

CHAPTER 4

DEFINITELY INSANE

If I want to continue eating hamburgers, cookies, and ice cream, I will always need to do something to keep the excess weight off my frame. But training for marathons requires a lot of time, especially in the weeks that call for long runs. To maintain my health, I knew I needed to exercise, but after my fifth marathon, I also needed a break from marathon training.

Instead of just doing cardio workouts, I was game for adding muscle mass, but I dreaded the boredom of weightlifting. In fall 2011, I saw an infomercial for a video product called INSANITY. Intrigued, I began to investigate.

After comparing it to other products, especially P90X, I discovered that most programs require equipment to complete the workout, but INSANITY involves a series of exercises with only your body. Plus, if you document your completion of the 60-day program, you earn a free T-shirt. I'm a sucker for freebies.

My parents-in-law delivered INSANITY to me as a Christmas present in 2011. I started the "Fit Test" in the basement of their home, though low ceilings prevented some of the jumping—ha! I completed the first fifty-minute workout when I returned to our office building's workout facility the first week of 2012 . . . and promptly got sicker than a dog—not from the workout, but from a virus. That turned out to be a blessing in disguise, as my body was so sore from that workout I needed a full week to be ready to try again.

This time, fully recovered from all ailments, I began the program and pushed through all sixty days. Wow. Not only was it intense, it was insane! The program consists of a handful of thirty- to sixty-minute workouts that, if you follow the prescribed schedule, you complete six days per week with workouts titled "Pure Cardio," "Max Interval Plyo," and "Max Cardio Conditioning."

With sweat dripping from every possible pore, I often found myself finishing a workout with hands on head, struggling for my lungs to recover to normal breathing. Even in winter temperatures, I would poke my head outside to gather fresh air after pushing my body to limits not reached even when climbing a mountain. I had not been familiar with exercises like "Switch Kicks," Power Jacks," or "Power Knees" before INSANITY, but now I perspire just hearing the words.

On occasion while doing an INSANITY workout, I had a partner who lasted for a few minutes in his pajamas before deciding cartoons were a better option.

INSANITY also introduced me to new methods of stretching. The instructor emphasized the importance of keeping your body flexible, a reminder I definitely needed to hear. I discovered yoga poses like "Downward Dog" and "Table Top," and even learned the ballet technique called plié.

Ironically, a few weeks into INSANITY, I also started wearing Invisalign on my teeth. Dating back to my youth, I'd had a small gap between my upper two front teeth. But recently I'd noticed that some teeth on the bottom row had shifted and were slightly overlapping. In lieu of standard braces, my orthodontist agreed that I should use Invisalign to fix the problems.

Before Invisalign, the gap between my top front teeth was the perfect size for a toothpick—that's another story for another time.

Invisalign for me consisted of two hard molded plastic trays, one set each of the top and bottom rows of teeth. While you're not required to wear them twenty-four hours a day, and you have to take them out when eating, I wanted to wear them as often as possible to shorten the overall duration of treatment, guesstimated to be somewhere around two years.

So, between having plastic in my mouth and little air in my lungs, I dealt with multiple issues trying to breathe. Although I came close a few times, I never vomited during INSANITY. In fact, I became much better at breathing through my nose to avoid the braces-induced gagging.

Quick testimonial for INSANITY: even though I continued my not-perfectly-healthy eating habits, my before-and-after pictures showed a decrease in my belly size and my wife measured an increase in my bicep and tricep area. Impressive. Overall, INSANITY and Invisalign made me a better runner, and I became the fittest I'd ever been in my life.

CHAPTER 5

TRAGEDIES STRIKE

Shortly after I completed INSANITY in 2012, tragedy struck. On Monday, March 26, my wife, Kirsta, called me midafternoon to ask, "Wasn't that prescribed burn in the forest near our house supposed to be completed last week?"

From my north-side office, I had no view of the mountains, so I checked a website message board on which mountain residents discuss area issues. This confirmed that the fire had re-ignited and high winds were whipping it out of control.

I charged out of the office and made the forty-mile drive home as fast as I could. Radio news reports offered minimal information, but within ten miles of our house, I saw sheriff deputies blocking highway intersections that led to the fire area. When I crested the dirt road leading to our driveway, a massive plume of smoke greeted my arrival. The fire blazed just five miles east of our house.

Smoke billows from the Lower North Fork Fire a few miles east of our house, where I took this photo from our deck. The fire killed three residents, destroyed 22 homes and burned 4,140 acres.

"Holy crap!" I exclaimed, joining my wife on our deck to stare at the mess unfolding beneath us.

"Do we start loading our stuff?" Kirsta folded her arms.

"Give me fifteen minutes." I dashed back to my truck and drove one mile east to our neighbors' property, which offered a better angle. From here, the fire appeared much closer and bigger. Worst of all, I saw the dark smoke that indicates a burning structure, not just trees and vegetation. My heart sank as

I returned to our house.

"Structures are definitely burning." I sighed. "I think we are going to be okay, but let's pack a few things."

Indeed, our phones soon buzzed with a reverse-911 standby evacuation notice, and for the first time in our lives, my wife and I had to decide what items were most important. As Bryce sat in his high chair munching on dinner, Kirsta and I scrambled through the house, gathering wedding photos and dress, computers, birth certificates, and other irreplaceable items.

The evening news brought relief, to our house at least. Winds continued from the southwest, moving the fire away from us. Although we relaxed, we loaded cherished items into our vehicles—just in case.

Dusk brought milder temperatures and mitigated winds, as well as a fresh view of the inferno. Instead of viewing thick smoke clouds from our deck, we could now see red-hot flames consuming the dried terrain beneath us. Ironically, because of the wind direction, the distinct smoke smell didn't reach our house. It was very weird to see the fire without smelling it.

The next day, still on evacuation notice, I completed work responsibilities from a lawn chair on our deck, watching SEAT planes—Single Engine Air Tankers—drop slurry to prevent the fire from spreading. Kirsta and I watched in awe. For people who had never witnessed a forest fire before, the action was surreal.

Later in the day, I ventured out again, and I met a Denver television reporter at the media staging area at the fire station near our house. Later that evening, he and a photojournalist shot their evening report from our deck, with the flames visible over the reporter's shoulder. Bryce enjoyed crawling under the kitchen table as the local celebrities filed their news broadcast from their laptops above him. It provided a much-needed break from fire-related stress.

Dealing with a forest fire near our house was stressful, but Bryce enjoyed interacting with photojournalist Rico and reporter Will from 9News, the Denver NBC affiliate.

While we had sleepless nights and a precarious few days, we stayed safe. Many of our neighbors did not, including three individuals who died and hundreds who lost their homes or had property damage from the Lower North Fork Fire.

After five years of living in the mountains, this was our first experience with wildfire, and we emerged from the experience far more aware of the dangers of our home territory. We prepared a full evacuation list, which now always hangs from a magnet on our fridge, and we developed a better appreciation for lightning, fire mitigation, and the importance of moisture.

But later that week, it got worse for us.

Kirsta, a registered nurse in the Neonatal Intensive Care Unit, worked an every-weekend schedule at the hospital, so she drove to Denver as usual around 6:00 p.m. on Friday, March 30. After she left, I put Bryce in the bathtub and my phone on the charger. As he soaked in the water, we played with rubber ducks and other toys, laughing and enjoying some quality father-son time. Several minutes later, I heard my phone buzzing and grabbed it from the nightstand.

From several voice messages and a phone call to an in-law, I learned that Kirsta's dad had died less than an hour earlier in a tragic farming accident in southern Kansas. Emergency responders tried to help but had arrived too late.

Kirsta and I finally connected on the phone. Through tears, she quietly explained that she had turned her SUV around and was headed back to our house. I stood silently as Bryce giggled in the bathtub, splashing blissfully in the water like a typical two-year-old.

Days earlier, it seemed like a dream as we prepared to flee from a forest fire. Now, a nightmare had ensconced our family. Was this real? We had been on standby to evacuate from the fire. This was no drill.

As Kirsta pulled into the garage, I raced down the stairs and opened her car door. Speechless, I could only hold her as tears streamed down her face. In dismay, we threw clothes into luggage and left as soon as we could to drive through the night to her family.

Nothing would have changed the circumstances, but I felt horrible that I did not immediately answer the phone when Kirsta first called me. Knowing that she was alone with such news, even for just ten minutes, broke my heart, and I pledged to myself that my cell phone would be on my body or in close proximity at all times. While our lives would be forever changed, I did learn a lesson that would be critical later: my phone would be near me 24/7.

Making the tragedy even worse, Kirsta was two months pregnant with our second child. Since we were still in the first trimester, we hadn't told anyone yet. So, her dad never knew that he was going to have a (then) fourth grandchild. We had planned to visit our families at the end of April to share the news.

"How can you eat right now, Kirsta?" her sister questioned. Others looked on disapprovingly, not understanding that my wife *needed* to eat to keep our baby nourished. So, while friends and family visited to pay their condolences, my wife and I had to pull our immediate family members aside and share our happy news during a time of sadness and grief.

Kirsta's dad, David Wayne Lowe, was one of the best people one could ever know. In Kirsta's hometown, he was the guy to whom people turned whenever they needed something done. David was a longtime worker at the jet engine plant south of town, and he was a mechanical genius. In lieu of a blueprint, David would stare at a problem and magically resolve the issue in his head. His wife had the same vacuum cleaner for many years past its expiration date because David kept finding new ways to make it work.

Despite his gruff exterior, he genuinely cared for those around him. When I carefully approached him for Kirsta's hand in marriage, I had left baseball and did not have a full-time job lined up. His biggest concern? "Well," he responded to my request, "I'd like to see you get some health insurance." He'd always made sure that his daughter was taken care of.

The Lowe family helped move Kirsta and me to Colorado. We took a break from unpacking boxes and went for a drive in the foothills to the west of metro Denver, taking in the scenery so utterly different from the flatlands of Kansas. David drove, but he had trouble keeping the SUV on the road because he kept staring up in awe at the houses built high on the mountainsides. We laughed in fear as we reminded him to keep his eyes on the road!

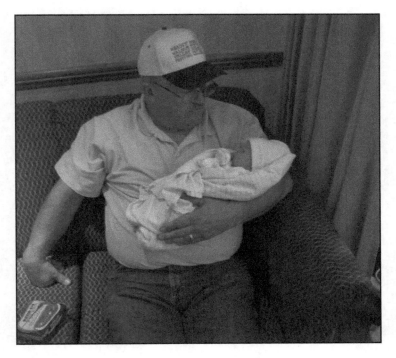

David Lowe cradles baby Bryce, his first grandson, in the hospital.

When Bryce was born, David eagerly welcomed his first grandson and third grandchild, with two prior granddaughters. Before Bryce's first birthday, David had already purchased a child's gun, eager to take his grandson hunting with him. We convinced David that it would be a few years before Bryce would be big enough to actually hold the gun, much less accompany him on a hunting excursion, though he remained optimistic about the opportunity.

David is dearly missed.

CHAPTER 6

A DISCOVERY

The next few months moved slowly. Life had changed, and my family was adapting to a new world. We now recognized the danger of fire in our mountain home, and Kirsta, in particular, mourned the loss of her dad, a person to whom she had often turned for guidance.

My energy level stayed pretty low until late July when I realized I needed to regain some fitness. I decided to tackle INSANITY again. It was as tough as the first go-round, and I enjoyed every minute of it—easy to say now. Completing the program requires tons of discipline, so I entertained myself by doing the workouts in unique locations, including hotel workout facilities while we traveled, the top of my office parking garage, even a park in my wife's hometown with a flock of geese as my audience.

After wrapping up the sixty-day workout, fall 2012 was approaching. I needed a new challenge.

Kirsta, pregnant with baby number two, was working one of her final night shifts before maternity leave when I decided to investigate the Boston Marathon. Bryce, soon to be three years old, entertained himself on the floor on a Friday night. Tired from the work week, I was just vegging on the couch, playing around on the laptop and hitting some websites before bedtime.

For kicks and giggles, I thought I would see what sort of qualifying time I would need to qualify for the Boston Marathon.

I knew the race typically occurred in the spring, and I had even posed on the finish line—ignorantly crossing the wrong way—when we visited Boston in 2010. But other than that, I didn't know much about the run.

When Kirsta and I visited Boston in 2010 to celebrate our fourth wedding anniversary, I asked her to capture a picture of me crossing the marathon finish line—I didn't know that I was running the wrong way! The word "FINISH" faces the overhead camera bridge on the east side of finish line so photographers can capture the words as runners complete their 26.2-mile venture.

Reality hit me, and I laughed out loud when the Boston Marathon qualifying times popped up on the Boston Athletic Association website. For my age bracket, a male would need to run at least a 3:15 marathon to qualify. My fastest flat marathon at that point had been Lincoln at 4:16.

"Bryce," I exclaimed, "I would have to shave nearly a full hour off my personal record. A full hour!"

With great delight, he laughed with me. Or maybe at one of the stuffed frogs with which he played on the floor.

Disappointed, I stared at the website, thinking how cool it would be to run the Boston Marathon. I learned that it was a point-to-point run versus a circular route, in which the start and finish line are near each other, and, from additional Google searches, I learned about all sorts of cool things that happened along the route.

"Bryce, the marathon goes right past an all-girls school," I commented to my disinterested son. "People call it the Wellesley College Scream Tunnel. Can you imagine thousands of women screaming at you?"

Bryce continued playing with his frog friends.

"Wow." I kept reading from the internet. "After the Red Sox game ends, the Fenway Park crowd empties into an area along the marathon path. More people screaming at me while I'm running—how cool!"

Goosebumps layered my skin just reading about it. Bryce yawned and snuggled a fuzzy frog to his face.

Ignoring my son's lack of interest, I perused the BAA website and discovered a tab that said, "Charity Program." *Interesting*, I thought. As I scrolled through the participating organizations, the Dana Farber Institute caught my eye; I recalled seeing their name and logo when we visited Boston in 2010. The organization performs outstanding work with children and cancer, so the idea of raising money appealed to me. After generating more than $10,000 for Make-A-Wish and Underwearness, I could handle the challenge.

Bedtime was nearing, so I started closing my internet browsers. As the Charity Program page appeared on the screen, a new logo popped into my Boston Marathon dream—Alzheimer's Association.

CHAPTER 7

LET'S ENDALZ

My grandfather Louis died of Alzheimer's when I was a teenager. I was young, naïve, and had no idea what that meant at that time. Let's face it, many people can't say or spell Alzheimer's, and until my family was affected by it, I didn't know the disease existed. But, a specific memory from that time is burned into my brain.

Grandpa and Grandma, my mom's parents, lived on a farm in southeast Nebraska. They owned about eighty acres, so my cousins and I always had fun running around the land, playing in the barn, exploring the pastures, sledding down the hills, and trying to get semi-trailers to honk their air horns as they roared past on the highway adjacent to the property.

One Saturday, I lay on their floor, watching a baseball game on one of the four channels they received on the TV at their house.

"Dean?" I heard my grandpa calling my uncle by his middle name. Allan Dean was the youngest child in the family and lived upstairs at his parents' house, helping on the farm. I heard Grandpa call his name a few more times, starting to get agitated. I sat up and realized that Grandpa was standing behind me, looking right at me. "Get out there and milk those cows!" he exclaimed, motioning for me to move outside to the barn.

I was perplexed. I was not Allan Dean, and there was certainly no expectation that I needed to milk the cows—that wasn't one of my chores, nor something I had ever done. I can't remember exactly what happened, but I think my mom or another relative intervened, as Grandpa was obviously confused over my identity. At age seven or eight, I was puzzled, but I went back to watching baseball and shrugged off my first experience with Alzheimer's. Sadly, it was not my last.

After Kirsta and I moved to Colorado in 2005, I had a phone conversation with my dad that brought the unfortunate reality that my mom had Alzheimer's. Dad said that Mom had been in the bathtub, and he had heard her call his name.

"Jerome," Mom said when Dad arrived in the bathroom, "What am I supposed to do with this?"

In her hand, Mom held a bar of soap, and, Dad said, she had no idea what to do with it. From five hundred miles away, I knew that this horrible disease had gotten her.

Brain diseases can be hard to diagnose. I mean, we can all be forgetful and many of us have joked about losing our memory because we're getting older. But that's not Alzheimer's.

Making a bad decision once in a while, like accidentally driving the wrong way down a one-way street, is not Alzheimer's. Sitting behind the wheel of a vehicle and having no idea where you're supposed to go or how to drive the car may be Alzheimer's.

Missing a monthly payment on a utility bill is not Alzheimer's. Completely disregarding your bills and having no ability to manage your finances is likely Alzheimer's.

Forgetting someone's name after you have not seen them in a long time is not Alzheimer's. Not having the ability to recognize and distinguish your grandson from one of your own children is likely Alzheimer's.

Going to the store and forgetting to buy a bar of soap is not

Alzheimer's. Sitting in a bathtub and not knowing what to do with the soap is likely Alzheimer's.

Although Mom soon began treatment, her decline continued.

When my family visited our Colorado home several years later, I lay on the couch with baby Bryce, trying to get him to take his daily nap. I was awakened by my mom asking, "Who are you?" Like her dad, she could no longer distinguish her own children.

My mom holds baby Bryce soon after he entered the world. Because of Alzheimer's, Bryce and Teagan won't get to know the woman who for many years provided wonderful care as a babysitter to so many children.

Bottom-line, Alzheimer's is a pretty crappy disease. Not that there are any good diseases, but it's especially painful to watch a family member slip away mentally while they are physically mostly healthy. It seems like we, as a culture, have not spent as much time and money on neurological diseases as we have on other issues. And since I'm not a doctor, I can't help find a cure— but I am pretty good at fundraising, so I thought it was time for me to step up.

CHAPTER 8

MY APPLICATION

I wasn't sure what my odds were of being accepted by the Alzheimer's Association to run the Boston Marathon, but I knew I had a compelling story—my mom was battling Alzheimer's, and her dad had already died from the disease.

Technically, the Alzheimer's Association's spots for the Boston Marathon were assigned by the Massachusetts / New Hampshire chapter, which had a panel to review detailed applications. Since I lived in Colorado, I was unfamiliar with the chapter, and I certainly had no relationship with anyone involved.

Still, I downloaded the application and began filling out the usual information: name, address, phone, and email address. Then I struck terrific questions about the applicant's connection to Alzheimer's and their strategy for raising money.

I had a few weeks before the application deadline, so I thoughtfully considered my answers.

> **What will your fundraising goal be for the Boston Marathon? (Minimum donation of $4,000 for a non-qualified runner and $1,750 for a qualified runner is required.)**
>
> Having raised around $4,000 and $6,000 in two

previous marathon fundraisers, the minimum donation amount did not intimidate me. I was afraid of setting too low of a goal and getting discarded by the review panel for not wanting to raise enough money. Conversely, I did not want to go too high and get disqualified for reaching for the stars.

I was confident the individuals who had supported my prior fundraising efforts would donate to such a personal cause, so I figured the combined amount—$10,000—was achievable. Brainstorming for a unique amount, I realized that the reason why I was running would be the perfect number for my goal. Thus, I wrote:

"In honor of my mother, who has been diagnosed with early-onset Alzheimer's, my goal would be $12,074.30—which coincides with her birthdate of 12/07/43. This amount is also roughly the equivalent of what I raised when completing two prior marathons."

What strategies will you use to meet your fundraising goal?

I laughed out loud. *Does strategy involve asking everyone whom I know to donate money to support me?*

When I'm passionate about a cause, I am not hesitant to ask for help. So, simply asking people was my strategy. However, I wanted to be more specific in my approach, so I highlighted what I had done in the past to illustrate what I would do in the future:

"When I raised money while completing two prior marathons, I was able to raise approximately $12,000 with basically no hard costs. My strategies include asking family, friends, and business associates through email, Facebook, LinkedIn, and in-person requests. As well, I designed a wallet-sized card with the pertinent information that I was able to hand to the many contacts that I would see while attending business functions. I anticipate using all of these strategies again, as well any new ideas that the Alzheimer's Association wants to share."

Please describe why you would like to run for the Alzheimer's Association.

This one was a no-brainer. Tears brimmed in my eyes as I typed.

"Most of the other organizations with which I have been involved have been for mostly selfless reasons—doing good for somebody else. But Alzheimer's is personal: my grandfather died from it, my mother is battling, and it is in my genes. Now, with one child and a second on the way, I want to do my best to help make sure we are on track to identify a cure so future generations don't have to deal with the issues my family is facing. It is time for me to be selfish."

Have you ever run a marathon? If so list date, your finish time and name of the marathon.

This question was an eye-opener. I guessed that since the Association was asking this, they would receive applications from people who were not avid runners, marathon participants or finishers. Or, the Association wanted to weed out people who were not serious about running 26.2 miles. So, I hoped that I would have a leg up in this category.

"I have completed five marathons total. Two were road runs: 10/15/06, Denver Marathon—4:41:03, and 5/1/11, Lincoln Marathon—4:16:10. Three were marathons up and down Pikes Peak (yes, the mountain), so the times are skewed (for this marathon, 7:00:00 is roughly the equivalent of 4:00:00): 8/17/08—7:20:47, 8/17/09—6:50:06, and 8/22/10—7:34:54."

What is your personal running time goal for the marathon?

Oh, man, I loved typing my response to this answer. I was still mad at myself for not breaking 4:00 during the Lincoln Marathon.

"3:59:00 - it's time to break 4 hours!"

In summary, I listed several items and tactics that I hoped would make me standout from other applicants. First, I thought it was important to make my fundraising goal a very specific, unique amount and to make it have some relevancy to my situation—thus, the goal of $12,074.30 in honor of my mom. I liked the 30 cents at the end to make it a number that stood out.

Second, I wanted the selection committee to know that fundraising was not a new experience for me. I had no idea what kind of applications they would receive, so I hoped that my background of raising money, completing prior marathons, and personal connection to the cause would give me the edge I needed.

I was nervous, but I thought I had a pretty good shot.

CHAPTER 9

GOOD NEWS X2

'd listed my direct office number on my application, and in late October 2012, the phone rang on my desk. Caller ID showed a number from area code 617—Boston. *Gulp.* Knowing this could be a very good—or very bad—call, I nervously answered the phone, "Good afternoon, this is Greg."

On the other end was Angela Floro, a development officer with the Massachusetts/New Hampshire Chapter of the Alzheimer's Association. Angela asked a very important, direct question.

"Greg, is the information on your application correct?" she asked. "Do you plan just to ask people to donate money for your fundraising?"

"Yes," I said hesitantly. I wasn't entirely sure what Angela meant or why she was asking.

Angela explained that other individuals often raised money by hosting special events, like a bar or restaurant donating a portion of that night's proceeds to the charity in return for the individual bringing people to eat and drink. That sounded like a good idea, so I said I was open to that and any other suggestions.

Angela appreciated my answer and said that everyone who was accepted would hear from the Association. I hung up, feeling optimistic.

About one week later, on October 30, I received a second phone call from Angela. I couldn't resist expressing my excitement on Facebook:

> *Just got an important call—of 140 applicants, I was one of 10 individuals selected to raise funds for the Alzheimer's Association by running the 2013 Boston Marathon!!!*

The next day, November 1, I received the official email:

> *Congratulations!*
>
> *You are receiving this email because out of the 140 applications we received for our 10 charity spots, you have either been selected on the team, wait list, or have secured your own bib into the Boston Marathon 2013 Run for the Memory team!*
>
> *We want to let you know upfront we truly appreciate the time and effort you will put forth over the next five months to train, raise funds and awareness for the Alzheimer's MA/NH chapter.*
>
> *Angela Floro, Development Officer, Special Events Alzheimer's Association, Massachusetts/New Hampshire Chapter*

Tears brimmed in my eyes as read the email. I couldn't believe it—I was going to run the Boston Marathon!

With baby number two on her way, I spent as much one-on-one time with Bryce as I could before his sister arrived. We attended Saturday story time at the library and spent time at a nearby schoolyard, taking batting practice and running around on the playground. We even included a quick trip to the dentist for Bryce, which he actually enjoyed. I think he may have a future on the other side of the chair!

Bryce is styling in his shades while swinging on a tire at an elementary school playground near our house.

On November 9, the three of us drove to a south Denver hotel, where we met my parents and Kirsta's mom and sister. We chose the hotel specifically so that all of us would be close to Rose Hospital a few miles north. We settled to bed early that night because, super early the next morning, we had a three-vehicle caravan headed to the hospital.

In the darkness of the early morning hour, I pulled our vehicle into the parking lot of the Emergency Room, where we had been directed to enter before regular hospital hours. As I walked through the sliding doors, the hospital looked different from when we had been there for Bryce's birth. I saw two gentlemen sitting in the lobby and asked, "Um, is this Rose Hospital?"

Oops. It was the Veterans Administration Hospital. My bad.

Of course, Kirsta laughed wholeheartedly as I returned to our SUV. She'd been wondering the entire time why I had pulled into the VA lot. "Shuddup," I muttered and then drove east a few blocks to the Rose ER parking lot.

Now at the correct location, we checked in and were escorted promptly to Labor and Delivery, where, at precisely 7:23 a.m. on November 10, 2012, Teagan Jayne Kalkwarf entered this world, and she had me wrapped around her pinky from the moment she came out screaming—definitely foreboding!

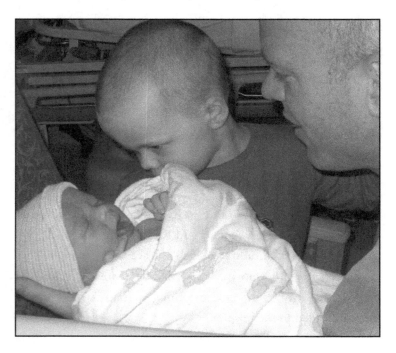

Kirsta's mom Brenda captured this terrific photo of Bryce eyeballing his baby sister soon after Teagan was born. Although they have their moments, they are usually pretty good siblings.

For both of our children, Kirsta and I each developed a top-ten list of possible first names. Each time, we did not have an immediate match. For the first child, I succumbed to Bryce and now love the name and the boy. For the second baby, Kirsta had written Teagan on her list. It was not her first choice, but I liked it. As the doctor held our loud, boisterous girl for the first time, Kirsta commented, "Yeah, Teagan seems appropriate for this screaming child. Kind of sounds like a heathen!"

We also wanted to do something symbolic for Kirsta's dad, so we developed Teagan's middle name to honor both of our fathers — "J" from my dad's name Jerome and "ayne" from David's middle name Wayne. A small tribute to two great men.

Everything went smoothly on this Caesarean section, so we were dismissed from the hospital after a three-night stay, compared to four nights for Bryce. Bryce had been twice nuchal— umbilical cord wrapped twice around his neck—and Kirsta had some recovery complications after his birth, resulting in the extra night. We were elated to bring a healthy baby girl back to our mountain home!

November passed quickly: trips to the pediatrician for Teagan's well-checks, Thanksgiving, and visits from more family members. I snuck in some training runs some mornings before work, but I admit I focused on cuddling my baby girl. I knew in a few weeks, the challenges in my life would increase: winter driving conditions, training for a marathon, and lots and lots of fundraising.

CHAPTER 10

FUNDRAISING STRATEGY

When I'm passionate about a cause, I don't have trouble asking people for support. I have found that, typically, if I believe in a cause, others are willing to contribute to my fundraising efforts.

I have raised funds for many terrific not-for-profit organizations. Since I had completed fundraising for Make-a-Wish and Underwearness while running the Pikes Peak Marathon, I was confident that a grassroots approach would be successful.

During my conversation with Angela of the Alzheimer's Association, I mentioned that I was open to trying some event, like a car wash, selling candy for a percentage of the sales, or a restaurant night with the eatery donating a portion of the evening's revenue to the cause. But I was also confident that just asking for contributions, which had worked in the past, was my most reliable move.

As I mapped out my strategy, I relied on my previous efforts to determine five main methods. I thought many of the people in my business network would help, so I would try LinkedIn posts and direct messages. Without being redundant, I wanted to send emails directly to my personal and work contacts. Then, I hoped that my connections on Facebook would respond to posts—that's what friends are for, right?

I also printed front/back pocket-sized cards with information about my quest, which I could keep in a pocket to give to people I saw at lunches, meetings, or events. Lastly, I decided to write letters to a handful of high net worth individuals whom I had met, hoping I could secure a few large donations that would eat up a sizeable portion of my goal.

 END ALZ **Goal: $12,074.30**
Our vision is
a world without Alzheimer's.

Greg Kalkwarf ~ 2013 Boston Marathon

Show your support by contributing one of these ways:
1. www.alz.kintera.org/Boston2013/gregkalkwarf
2. Cash donation (give to Greg with your address)
3. Mail a check (payable to Alzheimer's Association):
Greg Kalkwarf
1700 Lincoln St. Ste. 1400, Denver, CO 80203

www.alz.kintera.org/Boston2013/gregkalkwarf

I have raised money for many charities, but this time it is personal. My grandfather died from Alzheimer's, my mom is battling it, and it will likely affect me. That's why I am fortunate to have been selected by the Alzheimer's Association to raise money for the organization by running the 2013 Boston Marathon on April 15, 2013. In honor of my mom's battle, **my fundraising goal is her birthday**: 12/07/43, or $12,074.30. I welcome any support you can provide to help me reach that goal. Proceeds will help improve the lives of those affected by Alzheimer's by providing enhanced care and support for all affected and through the advancement of research.

These are the front and back of the pocket-sized cards I used to educate people about my fundraising efforts. The mailing address and website link are no longer valid, but if you want to make a donation to the Alzheimer's Association, I would be happy to connect you!

Jeffery McAnallen became my first donor at 2:06 p.m. on Thursday, December 6, 2012. I know because I received an email every time that someone contributed via my personalized website at kintera.org.

Jeff is an attorney and worked in the same building I did in downtown Denver. We often found each other in the workout center at the same time—me running, Jeff biking. As a guinea pig attempt, I'd given him one of the pocket-sized cards that very Thursday morning. Needless to say, I was pumped to see Jeff follow through on his word and put me on the fundraising scoreboard. Many thanks, Jeff!

I became like one of Pavlov's dogs—every time my phone vibrated with a new email, I checked to see if it was a donation. Phone vibrated? Discreetly slide my phone out of my pocket during the meeting. Phone vibrated? Grudgingly open one eye while lying in bed half asleep. Phone vibrated? Oh, no—that was a phantom vibrate. I swear I felt something.

Serious about hitting my goal, I knew getting there would be a marathon in itself: step by step, dollar by dollar.

Next came a Facebook post. I was a little leery of this method, as I've always thought people respond better to a direct request compared to a timeline post. In hindsight, I think it helped when I personalized my posts for specific dollar amounts, but I started out on December 8 with a generic post that became my standard language throughout the fundraising campaign:

> *I have raised money for many charities, but this time it is personal. My grandfather died from Alzheimer's, my mom is battling it, and it will likely affect me. That's why I am fortunate to have been selected by the Alzheimer's Association to raise money for the organization by running the 2013 Boston Marathon on April 15, 2013.*
>
> *In honor of my mom's battle, my fundraising goal is her birthday, 12/07/43, or $12,074.30. I welcome any support you can provide to help me reach that goal. Proceeds will help improve the lives of those affected by Alzheimer's by providing enhanced care and support for all affected and through the advancement of research. Thank you for your consideration!*

Then, I decided to tap into my business connections on LinkedIn. Most of them will tell you that I am a pretty generous person, always eager to help others achieve their goals, so I anticipated that my network would respond to my request for help.

I labored efficiently the morning of December 10 to complete my work obligations, and then worked just as hard during the afternoon to send out a fundraising request to my more than one thousand LinkedIn connections. I used the same request message that I had on Facebook, with the subject line, "Boston Marathon—a little help?"

The response proved unbelievable. The dollar amounts—big, medium, and small—quickly added up, as did the comments. People inspired me by sharing how someone they knew had been affected by Alzheimer's, like this message from Deems Hargleroad:

> *Hey, Greg. Sent a check your way. I have to be honest that your charity of choice helped push me over the edge. My aunt passed away from Alzheimer's five years ago after battling the disease for 15 years. IMHO it is the crappiest of all them because it steals your personality first before your body. I know I speak for both of us that if this disease can be wiped out in our lifetime, we would both be very happy. Congrats on getting in and best of luck!*

Comments like this made it easy to keep pushing forward, both in my fundraising and training. By December 20, I had raised $3,000, nearly one-quarter of my goal. I was thrilled with the support.

To supplement my one-on-one efforts, I compiled a small list of media outlets that I thought may be willing to promote my efforts, though it was by chance I developed some relationships that paid lots of benefits. On December 13, while reading *The Denver Post*, I noticed a submitted article in the "Your Hub" section written by Sara Spaulding, then Vice President of Marketing and Communications for the Colorado chapter of the

Alzheimer's Association.

I emailed Sara early that morning, asking if the Colorado chapter would be willing to support my efforts, even though the funds I raised would be for the Massachusetts/New Hampshire chapter. Her response brought me joy and relief: "We would be happy to promote you here in Colorado."

Sara helped connect me with others at the Alzheimer's Association in Colorado, all of whom became huge allies and advocates for my cause. Additionally, she knew the woman who led communications for the Association in Boston, so I quickly felt like part of the family, working together to help maximize publicity in a variety of outlets.

One of those outlets was *The Crete News*, the weekly newspaper in my Nebraska hometown. Thanks to my cousin, Julie Reetz, I connected with the newspaper editor, Jenn Lampila. With the holidays approaching, I knew that my family and I would be in Crete for Christmas, so Jenn asked to interview me while I was in town. On Christmas Eve, I stopped by her office and provided quotes for an article, headlined "Reason to Run," that ran in a January edition of the paper.

This picture of me ran in The Crete News with a story about my running the Boston Marathon for the Alzheimer's Association.

The picture of me on the front page was one I had given to Jenn that showed me at the finish line of the 2010 Pikes Peak Ascent "throwing the bones"—the crossed-arms symbol for the Husker football team. It just seemed fitting for a Nebraska newspaper!

I got another surprise when we returned to our Colorado home after traveling for the holidays. I've always enjoyed reading the daily newspaper, in this case, *The Denver Post*. When we travel, I ask the carrier to deliver the missed issues upon our return.

As I flipped through those papers, I saw a picture of myself! In December, I had seen another athlete profiled in the Post as a "Trail Blazer" so I'd submitted my information. They ran it in their January 1 edition—a great way to start the new year!

Trail Blazer: Conifer's Greg Kalkwarf is a marathoner to support the Alzheimer's Association

By The Denver Post

POSTED: 01/01/2013 12:01:00 AM MST   ADD A COMMENT

Who: Greg Kalkwarf of Conifer

The cause: Alzheimer's Association

The feat: The Boston Marathon

The story: After conquering "America's Toughest Challenge," the Pikes Peak Marathon, Kalkwarf decided to try the Boston Marathon on April 15. His team, Run for the Memory, will raise money for the Alzheimer's Association.

Kalkwarf's grandfather died from the disease and his mom is battling early-onset Alzheimer's. "And it will likely affect me," Kalkwarf says. His goal is to raise $12,074.30, in honor of his mother's birthday (Dec. 7, 1943).

Image courtesy of The Denver Post

I don't know if the publicity generated any new donations, but it didn't matter. Merely creating a buzz about the Alzheimer's Association and its efforts was an equally important part of the media campaign.

On January 7, 2013, I crossed the $4,500 mark—an insignificant number from an outside perspective, but huge for me personally. As a charity runner, I needed to provide a credit card number to the Alzheimer's Association when I registered. Because they have specific hard costs related to their efforts in coordinating the marathon team, they require team members to guarantee a specific amount that they will fundraise—and if not, team members' credit cards will be charged the difference!

Paying for our Boston airfare and hotel would be a sizeable expense itself, so it was a relief to know that after hitting the quota amount, we would not have to pay any additional amount out of pocket. Whew! "Good to know that we will be able to pay the mortgage this month" was Kirsta's reaction.

Although I enjoyed the buzz of my phone from each online donation, I also enjoyed receiving checks and cash because they seemed so personal. In particular, I loved when people sent a personal card or note with their donation.

One that stood out came from Brian Van Haaften. Brian worked in Wichita when I worked for the Wranglers baseball team. His company was the sponsor of our mascot Wilbur T. Wrangler's Birthday Bash, and Brian and his family became my friends. Even after they moved to Tulsa, I paid a weekend visit for a golf outing and spent the night at their house. They lived in Minnesota in 2013, and I received a mailed donation on January 6 that included a sticky-note, handwritten message from Brian:

> *Greg,*
>
> *Thanks for reaching out! I hope this note finds you and your family well overall. Keep training hard. I know you can have a PR for this race.*
>
> *Blessings,*
> *Brian Van Haaften*

A simple message from Brian Van Haaften gave me tons of confidence. This sticky note hung at my office desk for months as a reminder to keep pushing.

I stuck that note on my office wall, and it motivated me every day for the next four months. Amazing how just a few words, in this case, "*I know you can have a PR*," can make such an impact.

By mid-February, my fundraising approached the $7,000 mark, more than halfway to my goal, and donations continued to roll in. With more than one thousand LinkedIn connections, I decided it would be worthwhile to send another request to those individuals. Being careful not to send to those who had already contributed, I posted a second request to these connections on Friday, February 15, with verbiage almost identical to my initial message. My request sparked another flurry of contributions and another round of people sharing their connections to

Alzheimer's—mothers, grandfathers, etc., who had battled and died from the horrible disease.

One supporter who shared her personal story was Donna Jared, who worked as part of the development team for Mercy Housing, a national affordable housing organization based in Denver. I had served on their Colorado advisory council and thought very highly of the organization and Donna, whom I had met at one of their fundraising events. In an email exchange, and later in person, Donna explained that her family had such a prevalence of Alzheimer's that they had been asked to participate in a research study at Columbia University and had been featured in the HBO documentary series "The Alzheimer's Project," hosted by Maria Shriver. Wow!

Hearing these stories from people around the country made me more driven than ever to hit my goal. Alzheimer's is a global disease and learning how people were affected made my fundraising not just about me, or my mom, but about a culture. Ending Alzheimer's is a team pursuit with lots of players making contributions.

I treasured each check that came in the mail and every time my phone buzzed with an alert of a new contribution. In particular, the donations of unique amounts really made me smile since they mimicked what I had done with my fundraising goal of $12,043.70.

My orthodontist is Dr. Anil Idiculla. When I decided to proceed with Invisalign, I had met with three orthodontists and received price quotes from each. I had selected Dr. I because he had such a positive environment in his office—a reclining, vibrating chair in his waiting area, a kids' video game play area, and a west-window view of the mountains that looked like something out of a picture. His office reflected his personality, and when I mentioned my marathon fundraising efforts, he was immediately onboard. When his donation came, I got tears in my eyes: $127.43. He took out the zeros and nailed my mom's birthday. Very touching.

Julie Reetz did something similar, except she honored her father-in-law Lavern Reetz, my mom's brother. I have always liked Julie since the day cousin Terry, her future husband, brought her to a family event way back in the 1980s. She is a high-energy person, radiates positivity, and was very supportive during the years that Lavern battled Parkinson's until his death in 2010. Lavern was born January 2, 1931. Thus, Julie wrote a check from her and Terry for $102.31. Super cool, and so appreciated.

As I posted updates on my fundraising status on Facebook and LinkedIn, I often pointed out that I was a specific dollar amount from hitting a milestone. It seemed like if I said that I needed $50 to reach $7,000, someone immediately stepped up and made a contribution so that I surpassed that amount. For example, Tara Rojas, a fellow 2010 *Denver Business Journal* Forty Under 40 honoree, contributed $50.14 because I was that amount short of a goal. Thanks, Tara—I still owe you a Braum's ice cream.

With great pride, I sent this email on April 11 to those who had donated on my behalf:

We did it—thank you!

With support from more than 200 individuals, I am proud to say that I will be traveling tomorrow to Boston with more than $13,400 in donations for the Alzheimer's Association—surpassing my goal of $12,074.30 in honor of my mom's birthdate (12/07/43).

I hope to send another email next week with results and photos. In the meantime, thank you for your

*support of me, my family, and the Alzheimer's
Association. Someday, we will live in a world
without Alzheimer's.*

Very Sincerely,
Greg

In return, I received a note from a Colorado Springs friend,
who succinctly summarized the thoughts of most of my
supporters:

Greg,

This truly touches my heart.

Thanks for supporting the fight of Alzheimer's.

Good Luck and Have Fun!!

CHAPTER 11

MENTAL PREPARATION

Not breaking 4:00 during the 2011 Lincoln Marathon stayed in my brain for many months. Finishing below that magic number seems to define those who are terrific marathoners.

To break four hours, I knew I needed to prepare better both physically and mentally for the Boston Marathon.

I spent another evening on the couch with my computer on my lap—this time, looking for books written about the Boston Marathon. I found a few and grabbed them from the library in the days ahead. Some focused on the fascinating history of the Boston Marathon, and I devoured the stories of legends and symbols connected to the marathon.

I could hardly contain my excitement as I read. Nothing against any other marathon, but I was going to run *the* Boston Marathon. Now, some people say that everyone should have to qualify for the marathon. I get it. Someday, if I can keep running a consistent pace as I age, I would love to get a time that would allow me to run Boston as a qualifier. But I appreciated the comments I saw on a Runner's World message board that said charity runners are just as deserving of their bib numbers as anyone else.

However, what I truly needed to prepare for the Boston Marathon was a book that described the route mile by mile so I could run myself mentally through each part of the course. The

BOSTON MARATHON LEGENDS AND SYMBOLS

THE BOSTON MARATHON has been run on Patriots' Day since 1897 to celebrate the holiday.

PATRIOTS' DAY is a Massachusetts holiday celebrated the third Monday in April in honor of the first battles of the American Revolutionary War.

ATHLETES VILLAGE is the location in Hopkinton at which thousands of runners rest "patiently" outside a high school and a middle school waiting to walk the 0.07 miles to the marathon starting line.

HEARTBREAK HILL is the last of four hills on the marathon course in Newton, Massachusetts, and on which in 1936 Ellison "Tarzen" Brown broke away from Johnny Kelly to win the marathon, thus, "breaking" Kelly's heart.

KENMORE SQUARE is west of the Back Bay area of Boston, just north of Fenway Park, home of the Boston Red Sox. Major League Baseball allows the Red Sox to play at home each Patriots' Day with an 11:00 a.m. start, which means as the game typically ends, fans spill into Kenmore Square to cheer on marathon participants.

BOYLSTON STREET is the thoroughfare on which the last 0.2 miles of the marathon are run, with the finish line on the street immediately north of the Boston Public Library. Participants then pass Copley Square, a beautiful public square on Boylston Street just east of the library and the marathon finish line.

only book that I could find was one written by a bandit, a person who runs the race route without a bib number. It pained me to buy the book because it seemed like I was endorsing the idea of running as a bandit; nonetheless, I paid the price and absorbed each description of the author's experience. With no better mile-by-mile description, it seemed the best way to learn the course and plan a strategy.

For the Lincoln Marathon in 2011, my mile splits averaged 9:47. For comparison, running mile splits of approximately 9:10 is equal to a four-hour marathon. To break the 3:59:59 mark, I would need to cut at least sixteen minutes from that time, or about forty seconds from each mile. Simply put, I needed to run nine-minute miles. I could do that. I mean, I had run that pace. I just needed to sustain it for twenty-six miles and then coast for that final 0.2. Years ago, that would've been laughably impossible. Now, that seemed very feasible.

I thought about buying a fancy GPS watch, but thanks to a coworker, I discovered a phone app called Strava, which shows your pace while you're running. I didn't want my phone in my hand as I ran, though, so I just started the Strava app at the beginning of my training runs, stowed it in a case on my waist, and then reviewed my mileage splits afterward. My gait is close to nine-minute miles naturally, so I worked on sustaining that pace for longer distances, pushing myself to go harder and dig deeper.

I also had a few things going for me that served as psychological boosts. First, I was running at 5,280 feet or higher in Colorado, and science shows that I'd have more oxygen at sea level in Boston. Plus, I completed a lot of up and down training in the mountains near our house, so the idea of "Heartbreak Hill" (about an eighty-foot incline over a half-mile span) wasn't very intimidating.

Also not intimidating was the marathon route: even with the four hills in Newtown and a few other bumps in the road, the marathon is primarily run downhill—and I love running downhill, as evidenced by my times in the Pikes Peak Marathon. And, those who had run the Boston Marathon said the crowd support would be tremendous during the entire 26.2-mile route— no let down in the cheering like had happened in Lincoln—so I knew I could count on energy surrounding me in the later, challenging miles of the marathon.

Just knowing that I had a shot at breaking four hours was quite the motivation. The carrot dangled in front of me, and I was chasing it.

While at work one day, I read in the newsletter from a health care organization about a woman in Steamboat Springs who had run the Boston Marathon after having a cervical neck fusion performed. Using LinkedIn, I discovered that a friend knew Jennifer Schubert-Akin, the woman featured in the article, and we got in touch.

Among the advice that Jennifer provided in an email exchange, I took this comment most to heart:

Heartbreak Hill—no, it is not as nasty as portrayed. It is actually a series of four hills, each one a bit longer with a bit more incline than the last. What makes it so challenging is that these hills are between miles 16 and 21, when most runners are starting to hurt. If you add hills to the latter portions of your long runs, it will help you at Boston.

Jennifer is a veteran Boston Marathon competitor, with more than twenty now under her belt, so I welcomed her input. Knowing that Jennifer trained in the Colorado mountains and learning that she also had completed the Pikes Peak Marathon, I built confidence that I could conquer Boston hills without a heartbreak.

On February 5, the process became real. Not that it wasn't before, but it's like the difference between seeing the ultrasound of your baby and holding your child in your arms for the first time. The Alzheimer's Association emailed the 2013 Boston Marathon 117th Annual Invitational Entry Form. Filling it out was just a formality, but completing my registration was absolutely priceless. It even took away the pain of paying the $300 nonrefundable entry fee.

Then, on February 16, more goosebumps—an email from the Boston Athletic Association officially notifying me that my entry had been accepted. My child was in my arms, and I smelled the baby powder!

Dear Greg Kalkwarf,

This is to notify you that your entry into the 117th Boston Marathon on Monday, April 15, 2013 has been accepted, provided that the information you submitted is accurate.

A Confirmation of Acceptance card will soon be mailed to you via US Postal Service mail.

We look forward to seeing you in April! Best of luck in your training!

Sincerely,
Boston Athletic Association

My teammates provided additional motivation and inspiration, even though I trained one thousand miles away and had never met them. One was Ms. Dale Ann Granger-Eckert, the glue of the Boston Marathon Alzheimer's Association team. Dale Ann took photos of everything and everyone, and she made the personality of team members come alive, including that of her husband, Dale Bob Eckert. Yep, that's right—they're both named Dale. Ironically, Dale Bob's sister, battling Alzheimer's, also lived in the mountains outside of Denver, so we had a connection before we ever met.

*Dale Ann Eckert is an amazing friend and teammate. She is typically the
person behind the camera, but I snapped this pre-marathon photo
of her on the Alzheimer's Association bus.*

It was cordial, informative, and inspiring emails like this from
Dale Ann on March 10 that would make me feel at home in
Boston:

> *Hi Greg,*
>
> *Great pictures on Facebook. Nice to see the family
> and the "neighborhood."*
>
> *Most of our Friday snow is gone, and we are
> hanging on to 40's for temps. It was great to run in
> the sun yesterday.*

Our point-to-point long run as you may have heard was canned due to snow. Instead, we made the most of Heartbreak and the hills in Newton for improvised long runs. We kind of scattered but regrouped with Rich at the top of Heartbreak at the end.

I must say your driveway will certainly take some of the sting out of the hills when you get there. Any marathon, but particularly Boston, as you know, is all about pacing, not letting the adrenaline burn you up in the first three miles or the Wellesley scream tunnel pick up your pace gives you something in the legs when you finally get to the hills. I will be creeping along at the back of the pack hoping to stay near the 5-hour mark.

Five weeks and counting.

See you then,
Dale Ann

The next day, March 11, teammate Ted Lombardi sent an email to the team that got everyone excited: BAA had posted bib numbers! I don't know what it is about bib numbers that gets us runners so excited—maybe because it is our ticket to the show, so to speak. I stared in awe at my Boston Marathon ID: 21264.

Then, on March 12, for the third day in a row, another teammate's email, this one from Chrissy Horan, brought more good inside information. The insight complemented what Jennifer Schubert-Akin had indicated.

The hills start more around 16. Through 13 is a lot of downhill . . . don't go for your half marathon PR because you'll bust in the second half. 13-16 are pretty flat with a big downhill at the end of 15. There are actually 4 hills in Newton, depending on who you talk to, some say 3, some 4. Might as well not try to fool yourself, I think and acknowledge the first one :) after heartbreak hill, it's mostly downhill to the end.

Hope that helps!

Chrissy's advice did help. My mind was marathon sharp. I'd read everything that I'd found and had memorized everything I could. Outside of the weather, I thought I was prepared for anything.

CHAPTER 12

TRAINING

Possibly the worst part of the Boston Marathon is the timing. Because it occurs in early April, training for the marathon takes place in the winter months, which means that many people preparing for Boston get to do runs in terrifically cold, and sometimes downright nasty, weather.

I coped as best as I could: dressing appropriately when running outside and moving indoors to a treadmill when the weather proved unbearable.

Thanks to my Pikes Peak experience, I now had winter running attire—long-sleeved technical shirts, running tights, etc. I'd also learned the concept of layering clothes and typically had no problem staying warm . . . except for my extremities. To cope with cold fingers and toes, I purchased an abundant supply of hand and foot warmers—the kind you insert into your gloves and shoes, like if you are going to sit outside for a football game or hunting expedition.

These worked great, and at the end of runs, the warmers still had lots of heat in them. On any given run in downtown Denver, I would cross under a bridge and see a homeless person huddled next to a cold, cement wall. The first time the idea of giving the warmers away occurred to me, I was a bit nervous.

"Hey, excuse me," I said to the unkempt, middle-aged man. "I have been wearing these hand warmers during my run. I don't need them anymore. Would you like to have them?"

He peered up at me from the midst of his blankets and responded, "Oh, yes, that would be great! Thank you!"

"You're welcome," I countered, saying a prayer of protection for him—and sometimes her—as I jogged away.

These small gestures warmed my heart and hopefully warmed the individual for a few hours.

At the time, my company's office was located in a building just east of the hub of downtown Denver activity. Immediately across the street, the building management group provided a small-sized workout facility for tenants: a few treadmills, stationary bicycles and ellipticals, some weight machines and free weights, a single television consistently tuned to CNN, and men's and women's shower facilities with warm water and clean towels. It was nothing fancy, but I loved it.

I captured this picture of myself and the equipment
in the building's workout facility.

Because it was in a central location, I had several options

to keep my training runs fresh and enjoy some of Denver's landmarks. To the east, I could run a six-mile route around Denver Zoo. To the north, I had a nice five-mile route that went up the only substantial hill in downtown Denver to the Highlands area. To the west, a six-mile route around Mile High Stadium, home of the Broncos. And to the south, I could run two miles to connect to a trail along beautiful Cherry Creek, which opened up many possibilities.

The southern route became a lot of fun as I challenged myself to go farther. First, to the Cherry Creek Shopping area. Then, to the Colorado Avenue bridge. Just past the bridge sat a hotel with a water fountain near its entrance, so I could refill my water bottle about midway through my run. It may not seem like a big deal, but it beat having to carry a second water bottle during my long runs.

While the Highlands route offered some elevation, I knew that I needed to spend more time on hill work, both down and up, to reflect the Boston Marathon route as much as possible. In fact, I wanted to overtrain so that the hills outside of Boston would offer little or no challenge.

Several years prior, a coworker told me that he ran laps in the building's parking garage located directly across the street, above the workout facility. "What?!" I exclaimed. "That doesn't sound safe!"

But after trying it, I discovered the controlled, often empty environment worked downright perfectly for me—I could run uphill and downhill, over and over again. The garage is thirteen stories tall, and a lap up and down is about one mile. I'd start at six in the morning and complete a few miles before traffic increased and parking spots filled on the lower levels. My rule was to start no new laps after seven o'clock. Continuing after that time would require running inches away from vehicles moving at twenty miles per hour—not safe.

To prevent any surprises for a driver or for me, I also ran against traffic. Then, if I spotted headlights, I either stopped or moved to an area where no cars were parked to make sure I didn't get in the way of a moving vehicle. In fact, though we never spoke, it seemed like I knew some of the people because I would often see the same cars and could predict where they were going to park!

To add diversity to my workouts, I also did stairs. First, I started off climbing the thirteen stories in the parking garage Then, it hit me. I could climb the office building stairs—fifty-four floors!

My company office was on the fourteenth floor, so I would typically go down the stairs to the first floor, and then start the trek up to top before coming back down to fourteen—about twenty minutes roundtrip. I tried to vary the climbs for different days and different flights: one step at a time, two steps at a time, backward, crossover left, crossover right, or climb ten floors, stop at a landing and do ten push-ups.

Climbing the office building stairs offered a nice change of pace from running on a flat surface.

I'm not sure if this helped improve my running, per se, but I loved the dexterity challenge, and it seemed to improve my overall fitness.

Living at a high elevation, I had plenty of hills around our home on which to train. But, Kirsta worked every weekend until our daughter was born in November, which left me in charge of Bryce. With no sidewalks and snow often on the ground, it was too much of a hassle to attempt outdoor runs with a stroller. But, when I could, I had a couple of different routines that I completed near our house.

"Driveway Drills" was the creative name I labeled the path between our garage door and our mailbox. For a city dweller, that might be five steps. For us, it was a bit more of a journey.

"Here we go," I thought to myself the first time I headed down, starting my stopwatch as I began a slow jog down our seventy-five-yard-long asphalt driveway. From there, I picked up the pace as I turned left to head 0.2 miles down a dirt lane.

"Hey, guys!" I called out to a neighbor's white and brown horses in their pens about halfway down the lane. As the dirt leveled off to the paved cul-de-sac that housed a wooden frame of mailboxes, I grabbed our newspaper, made the turn, and headed back up the same route, repeating the trip a handful of times.

The up part of Driveway Drills was a lung-burner, and I knew I was in great shape when I could jog the entire route without stopping. The down portion turned out to be great preparation for the immediate downhill at the start of the Boston Marathon.

"Back and Forths" was a simple way to describe the approximately 1.5-mile route between the property of two neighbors who lived at the top of separate mountains. I never worried about my time while completing Back and Forths—with views of mountain peaks and green forests, the goal was a relaxing workout. Plus, with altitudes ranging up to 8,500 feet, this was another breathtaker . . . in more ways than one if you include the sights.

Gorgeous views like this made it real easy
to run on the roads near our home.

Most of my workouts took place before 8:00 a.m. and were completed on an empty stomach, so I knew I would need to find ways to gain energy for my long runs, and especially for the marathon, which would not start until nearly lunchtime in Boston. I made it through four marathons mostly with Tootsie Rolls and granola bars, but I needed to adapt to more conventional running energy sources.

Via observations at runs and the Runner's World website forum, I learned about Gu packets. Gu Energy products were created for daily training and competition. They're condensed into small packets that are easy to carry and consume on the run, which is the perfect combo for fueling long-distance runs. While I had used them a few times during the Pikes Peak Marathon, I knew I would need to use them smarter, more regularly, and more efficiently than I had in the past.

I stopped by an outdoors store to pick up the product and could not believe the plethora of flavors: chocolate, mint chocolate, peanut butter, vanilla bean and more. Had I known there was such a selection, I'd have started using them a long time ago! I mixed them up on my first long run along the Cherry Creek Trail and quickly decided that—even though I am choclaholic— vanilla bean worked best for me. I think more people would complete marathons if they knew they could have tasty snacks along the way!

It seems like such a small thing, using a supplement on runs, but I was confident that having this additional energy would benefit me during the marathon. And, if I wanted to break four hours, I would need something more appropriate than Tootsie Rolls!

I felt confident about my preparation. I just needed to keep running, and, barring any unforeseen circumstances, I'd be ready to roll on April 15.

CHAPTER 13

RUSH HOUR COLLISION

With one month before the 2013 Boston Marathon, I set out on a beautiful Thursday, March 14 morning for a twelve-mile run in downtown Denver. The planned route for the day was to go south to the Cherry Creek Trail, which I had run before, so I wasn't expecting any adventure—just a beautiful morning to be outside.

Making the turn at the halfway point, I ripped open a gooey gel and sucked down the contents. My energy level kicked up, and I blazed—for me—down the asphalt trail. I glanced at my phone to see mile ten and eleven splits of 8:24 and 8:26. "Dang, I rocked those miles!"

Smiling, I jogged lightly up the switchback ramp from the trail to the Lincoln/Speer Boulevard intersection. It was just before eight and traffic was heavy, but nothing unusual. Northbound vehicles proceeded with a green light, and some slowly turned west from Lincoln onto Speer. Seeing the "walk" light on for pedestrians, I waited patiently at the corner for a car to slow enough that I could cross.

As often happens, though, people in cars forget that pedestrians in crosswalks have the right of way. More cars passed, and I decided it was my turn. As I tried proceeding into the intersection, a woman driving a PT Cruiser did not want to stop for me. I hesitated and motioned toward the crosswalk. Her vehicle slowed and finally stopped, and I started jogging across the street.

I quickly looked at the pedestrian light. It was now blinking, but when running, I can dash across the street in two seconds. If I hustled, I would be fine. I glanced up to see the auto traffic light turn yellow and—*Bam*!

My world stopped as a vehicle hit me hard. I heard the crunch of something breaking, and I rolled down the street from the impact, doing my best stunt-double imitation. Conscious but stunned, I came to a rest on my hands and knees in the middle of the Speer Boulevard asphalt. Traffic stopped. Thankfully, my breathing continued. My right side ached, a sharp pain emitting from my rib cage.

A tall gentleman in a cowboy hat stepped out of a big Ford truck, sauntered over to me, and asked if I was okay. "I don't know," I huffed, as my left hand cradled my right ribs.

From my knees, I swiveled my head for a quick 180-degree assessment: A minivan taxicab sat on my immediate left. I glanced at the intersection and discovered a double turn lane. The taxicab driver hadn't seen me from the second lane, and, though he stopped upon impact, the vehicle had likely been traveling 25-30 mph when it hit me.

Although I thought the crunch was my iPhone, it turned out to be part of the minivan's left headlight, broken pieces of which scattered on the street. The impact spot on my right side hurt like hell, but I could move and didn't sense any other significant bodily harm. I was lucky I hadn't hit my head; I was lucky to be alive.

At least one person had called 911 and asked if I needed an ambulance. As people helped me up, I realized that I was mostly okay. Several individuals who witnessed the collision wrote down their names and phone numbers, as well as information from the taxi cab driver. They also captured the license plate number of the PT Cruiser that had originally hesitated to yield right of way to me in the crosswalk. While she didn't hit me, I still think she was part of the reason for the collision.

The woman who had 911 dispatch on the phone asked again if I wanted medical attention, and I politely told her that I was okay and that I ran marathons and was going to finish my run. I am either really tough or really stupid.

So, the scene was over. The witnesses returned to their vehicles, traffic resumed and the taxi cab driver turned onto the quiet portion of 7th Street so we could communicate further. Walking toward the taxi, I did a full self-assessment. I saw two small holes on the right hand of my $1 gardening gloves and, when I pulled them off, discovered a bruised and slightly bleeding right pinky. I looked down further and saw a small hole in the right knee of my running tights, and then a small tear in my left shoe.

My lower right ribs stung like a large nail had been hammered into them. I approached the cab with labored breathing. The cab driver apologized repeatedly in broken English. After assessing the overall situation, I decided we could settle it one-on-one, no need to involve cops or attorneys.

I told the cabbie that my pants had cost me about $20 and my nearly new shoes had been $80. If he had the cash on him, just give me $100 and—unless I discovered something else or if my situation worsened—we would just let bygones be bygones.

Visible relief washed over him. "Oh, thank you very much!"

I saw no reason to pursue additional action. God lets things happen for a reason, and I am confident that the cab driver and everyone who witnessed the collision will be better drivers—and I a better pedestrian.

The cab driver offered me a ride, but I said "No thanks" since I wanted to finish my run. On the mile back to the workout facility, I held my left hand over my right ribs, almost the reverse of what I would do standing for the National Anthem. I hit pretty much every red light along Lincoln Street—that happens when you slowly run a fourteen-minute split.

Back at my office's workout facility, I decided I should probably call my wife.

"What?" she greeted me as she answered the phone.

"Just checking in," I said casually via speakerphone. "What's going on?

"Well, my hands are full of poop. Bryce filled the potty with poop, and now Teagan exploded in her diaper."

"Well," I countered, "I think I can beat that. I just got hit by a car."

At first, Kirsta was in disbelief, but after she heard the story, she agreed that I was having a worse morning—and she insisted that I visit the doctor. A few hours later, I painfully walked the mile east to the office of my primary care physician. After a few rounds with the stethoscope, the doctor saw no need for X-rays and confirmed that my ribs were not broken. "Take it easy for a few weeks," he said, as he wrote a prescription for pain medicine.

I did take it easy for a few days—which pained me as much as the taxi cab had. Although I was fortunate not to have been seriously injured or killed, I was disappointed that I couldn't complete my planned long run the day after being hit. Instead, I sat on a stationary bicycle in the office workout facility.

"Hey, Greg!" said my friend Jeff McAnallen as he entered the workout facility. "What a gorgeous morning!"

After weeks of cold weather, a warm front had moved through Colorado overnight and provided for a beautiful Friday morning that took the temperature to fifty degrees by eight o'clock.

"It is," I replied, "but I'm not enjoying it."

"Why, what's up?" Jeff questioned.

I explained that I had been planning to wake up super early and complete my final long training run before tapering for the marathon. I had been planning to complete a twelve-mile route around Denver's City Park, through downtown, and into the Highlands neighborhood, which would have given me some late-run uphill experience to simulate Boston's famed Heartbreak Hill. I had been planning to run the route twice for twenty miles.

"So, instead, here I am on this stupid bicycle. I've gone twenty minutes, and I'm done."

"Wowwwww," was all Jeff could say.

But, early the next week, I climbed back on the stationary bicycle to keep up my heart rate and then, within a week, I started on the treadmill stepping softly and slowly, but putting in some miles.

I replayed the accident in my mind as I inched forward on the treadmill and played the "What If?" game. What if the taxi driver hadn't slammed on his brakes and had instead driven over me? What if I had been paralyzed? What if I had lost my legs? What if I had died? My wife is tough and would be strong without me, but the thought of Bryce and Teagan losing their dad hit me hard. They had already lost a grandpa, and their grandma's battle with Alzheimer's robbed them of much connection. With watery eyes, I shook off the emotions, turned off the treadmill, and headed to the shower.

CHAPTER 14

FINAL LONG RUN

I resumed a slow-paced jog outside later the next week and knew that I had to battle through the pain to complete at least one more solid long run. It was closer to the marathon than recommended, but I could tell my legs needed to do it. They'd only received a couple of small scrapes on the knees and were ready to turn loose for some intense exercise.

Also, a significant date approached on the calendar—the one-year anniversary of the death of my father-in-law. This anniversary coincided with Easter, so we'd decided to spend the weekend in Kansas with Kirsta's family.

Instead of my originally scheduled final short run in Kansas, I developed a plan to run twenty-four miles. Her parents' ten-acre property sits just north of Strother Field, so I used Google maps to determine a six-mile loop along Highway 77 between the two locations. Running four loops along a four-lane thoroughfare with traffic at seventy-five mph wasn't ideal, but it would work. Plus, if my rib cage proved too sore at any time, I could call Kirsta to pick me up without her having to drive too far out of the way.

I figured if I bought a gallon of water, I could leave it at the intersection near my in-laws for a pit-stop once every loop. To replicate the marathon, I brought the same number of gels that I would use in Boston in fifteen days.

*Running solo along a Kansas highway required me to provide my own
refreshments—a jug of water at the base of a sign post—
and entertainment—laughing about running in the
vicinity of a waste disposal site.*

That Saturday morning, March 30, just sixteen days after being
hit by a taxi cab, my legs were ready to go, especially after an
eight-hour hour ride. As I woke up, I had an idea—I sat $154
short of my fundraising goal and really wanted to hit my amount
before the day ended. So, before I hit the pavement, I posted on
Facebook:

> *Facebook friends, I am just $154 short of my goal,
> sitting at $11,920.30 of $12,074.30. I am going
> for a three-hour run. Would you be willing to push
> me past the $12,000 mark while I am out? Thanks
> to the MANY who have donated already! I feel
> your support with each step I take! (or maybe that
> is my sore ribs ...)*

I placed my water jug near the base of a signpost, started my watch and Strava tracking app, and ran south on the shoulder of the broad four-lane highway. The weather was gorgeous with clear, sunny skies, mild temperatures, and a gentle wind. As I set my cruising speed, I decided to check Facebook for some motivation. My coworker Audrey had stepped up with a donation. Not only did her kindness put a spring in my step, but it also brought me peace of mind to know that I'd entered the home stretch of fundraising.

In a relaxed mood and enjoying the beautiful running conditions, I determined to have a fun twenty-four miles. In my head, the run became something like a Jerry Lewis telethon: I entertained myself—and perhaps others—by waving to cars as they passed and by interacting with "my audience" on Facebook with updates, dedications, and continued pleas to donate to the Alzheimer's Association in support of my efforts.

My ribs held up solidly for the run, but I was tiring toward the end of my final loop. I thought I'd accomplished enough physically in my third and final training run of twenty-or-more miles, and the run inspired me to make a final plea for fundraising help. I promised to run an extra mile into town to the city Easter egg hunt if someone would make one final contribution. The Facebook silence was deafening. I ended my run along the highway and began a slow walk back to the house, where I saw Kirsta loading up the kids for the Easter egg hunt.

As I trudged down the gravel road, I checked my email one more time . . . and discovered that a Nebraska cousin, Lori, had contributed. I was elated and exhausted at the same time. I yelled to Kirsta, "I will meet you in town!" and turned back to the highway to add a couple more miles. The temperature had warmed, and my body sagged, but I continued running for Lori just as I'd promised.

Kirsta holds Teagan while giving Bryce strategic advice before the Winfield, Kansas, Easter Egg hunt.—photo by Brenda Lowe.

I was tired and smelled worse than the costumed Easter Bunny we saw at the egg hunt, but I finished—twenty-six miles, or pretty close to it. I also knew that I had to be close to my fundraising goal, but with my phone battery ready to give out, I waited until I returned to the house to check details on the computer. I'd received multiple donations, but were they enough to push me over the top?

I logged on to my fundraising page and checked out the numbers. I had surpassed my goal! A huge weight fell off my shoulders. Then, I looked at the details. With her single donation of nearly $200 at the start of my run, Audrey had pushed me across the $12,074.30 mark.

CHAPTER 15

FINAL PREPARATIONS

I've been blessed to meet so many wonderful people in this world. I received donations from administrative assistants to CEOs, from people in my office to people around the country, people I knew in elementary school to people I'd met just days before. The more people contributed, the more I knew that I wanted complete the Boston Marathon not only for myself, but on behalf of each of my donors.

As the marathon date approached, I decided that I wanted each donor to be with me at the finish line, so I visualized a personalized shirt to wear during the marathon. I hated not to wear the purple singlet provided by the Alzheimer's Association, but I needed a white shirt with more space. So, I spent fifty dollars for a custom-designed shirt, and Kirsta added with markers the words "Boylston or Bust" on the front. On the back, she wrote "In Honor of Mom Donna" and "In Memory of GPA Louis." Then I wrote the names of my more than two hundred donors, and the names carried all the way over the shoulders!

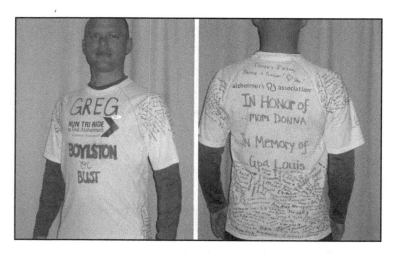

I loved wearing my custom-designed shirt that included the names of those who donated to the Alzheimer's Association on my behalf—can't believe I made them all fit!

At any timed running competition, I've always thought it is nice to have people I know at the finish line to greet me, and maybe even have someone along the course cheering.

For my first marathon, Kirsta greeted me in Denver near the halfway mark and again at the finish line. For my Pikes Peak Marathons, Kirsta and I connected near the finish line each time. In Lincoln, my family greeted me on the course and at the end of my run.

So, as I prepared for the Boston Marathon, I knew I wanted Kirsta and the kids somewhere near the finish line. I also knew that Boylston Street would be packed. Most online information that I found indicated that the crowds for the last half mile would be at least five to six people deep—not very conducive for getting a "front-row" spot unless you were willing to camp out for hours.

I also realized that Kirsta would be carrying a five-month-old girl in one arm while trying to corral a three-year-old boy with the other. Plus, the idea of them in the middle of a massive crowd in an unknown city terrified me.

"Oh my gosh, this finish-line area looks nuts," I called out to Kirsta from the living room couch. "How early do you want to get there to hold your spot?"

"Not at all," she dryly responded.

"This stinks," I moaned, looking at comments on a marathon website message board. "I want you guys there, but it's going to be beyond crowded."

"Whatever," my wife responded, staying focused on dinner preparations in the kitchen.

I knew that while Kirsta was supportive and would stand among the masses if I asked her, it would be an absolutely miserable situation.

As I kept investigating, I discovered that while the north side of the finish line stood open to the general public, the south side was set up as restricted-admission bleachers for VIPs. Thus, I just needed to figure out how to become a VIP . . . or, more importantly, how to make my wife and children VIPs for the Boston Marathon.

I checked a couple of websites and found that some people sold their VIP tickets—going rate of approximately one hundred dollars per ticket. That's a decent amount of money, but not out of line with what I would pay for a ticket to a major baseball or football game. Plus, if my family was willing to fly across the country to support my 26.2-mile run, I wanted them at the finish line, and I wanted them to be as comfortable as possible.

That's when a small miracle happened.

As a member of the Alzheimer's Association team, I was on an email distribution list with my other teammates—usually to talk about upcoming meetings or practice runs, but sometimes the emails produced small talk about aches, pains, or other fun things that happen when you're training for a marathon.

One of my teammates was Erica, whose grandfather had died from Alzheimer's. In a March 15 email, Erica indicated that because of her connections to a sponsor of the Boston Marathon, she had two VIP finish-line tickets and would award them to the person who pledged the largest donation to her fundraising efforts.

This was it—exactly what I needed. I emailed Erica about our interest and asked if she could find out if our baby girl would need a ticket. At five months old, Teagan would not be able to sit by herself, so Kirsta would just hold her, which would usually mean the baby didn't need a ticket.

It took a few days for Erica to hear back from her contact, but she confirmed that we would need only two tickets. She also said that the passes were not valid until after 2:00 p.m., but as I did the math in my head, I knew that would not be a problem. I was scheduled to start at 10:40 a.m., so unless I ran a 3:20 marathon time—absurd, since I aimed just to break 4:00—Kirsta would have plenty of time to enter the VIP area and settle into a spot in the bleachers.

Erica and I exchanged a few additional emails. Convinced this would be the best option for my family, I provided her a larger dollar amount than the other offers, and on March 22, she let me know the passes were ours. I cheerfully donated to the Alzheimer's Association in Erica's support, marking the contribution from "Your Friends in Colorado."

On April 5, I received one of the best items ever—two VIP passes for the Boston Marathon, which meant that my family would not have to scramble in the finish-line crowd along the north side of Boylston Street. Instead, Kirsta, Bryce, and Teagan would be elevated in the somewhat-comfortable VIP bleachers on the south side of the street to see me finish the Boston Marathon!

These passes from my teammate Erica put my family in the VIP bleachers on the south side of Boylston Street.

In an April 7 email to Erica, I typed, "I can recall only three other times that I felt this 'tingly'—the weeks before my wedding and the births of our children!!"

More good news popped up in early April—the Alzheimer's Association announced that they had also secured some finish-line VIP passes, and they would be awarding two each to the top three marathon fundraisers. At the time, I sat in third place, but I'd already hit my fundraising goal and needed to spend the next three weeks preparing for the trip. Plus, I'd already secured the passes from Erica, so my immediate family was set.

While that piece of the puzzle was now in place, we still had other details to figure out, and worry about.

Teagan, at only five months old, hadn't flown before. Now, this shouldn't be a big deal, but Kirsta and I are the type of parents who don't want to have "that kid" on an airplane. We were confident that Bryce, who had already flown several times, including a trip to Boston, would handle the four hours of confined time no problem. But, Teagan—well, she's Teagan. She came out of her mother's womb screaming and hadn't really stopped since, so we were scared that she would not be at her finest on an airplane.

We had picked a flight time (9:25 a.m. MDT) that we thought would be conducive to the kids' schedule. They'd wake up slightly earlier than usual, eat a packed lunch on the airplane, and then, hopefully, nap a few hours before our scheduled landing in Boston at 3:15 p.m. EDT.

Things went about as perfectly as they could. We found a terrific parking spot at the Denver airport with a short walk to the terminal; we secured three adjacent seats on our Southwest Airlines flight; and the kids were all smiles as the plane departed— Bryce enjoying his view out the window.

Since Teagan did not need her own seat, we flew comfortably to Boston in three adjacent seats on her first flight.

Teagan behaved very well and even received a few compliments on her pleasant demeanor. Toward the end of the flight, my legs felt tight, so I stood up and walked up and down the aisle, carrying Teagan and showing off my precious baby girl. The flight attendants were very friendly, and as I approached the front of the plane, one of the female attendants asked if she could hold our soft, cuddly baby. "Of course!" I responded.

And all hell broke loose.

I don't know what set off Teagan, but she started crying. And screaming. And wailing. And the cabin door flew open, and the wings fell off the plane! Okay, maybe not that last part, but Teagan's lungs disrupted the serenity that covered the first three hours of the flight. The flight attendant apologized profusely, but the dam had broken loose and even Kirsta, NICU nurse and best mom ever, couldn't repair the damage.

Mercifully, the plane's wheels finally touched down in Massachusetts. Passengers complimented both kids on their behavior as they exited the plane, so I'm sure it was not as bad as it appeared to Kirsta and me, but we were relieved to breathe the fresh air of Logan International Airport.

We had minimal travel plans once we arrived in Boston and no plans to rent a car. We'd considered using their subway system but decided it would be easiest to catch a cab.

Of course, young children require special seats when riding in a car. It's the law. And Kirsta and I typically follow the law. For this trip, we'd left the kids' usual car seats at home and had brought two smaller, more basic car seats for travel.

It was a wet, cool day in Boston, and as we approached the airport's taxi stand, I feared the worst—how were we possibly going to fit two car seats, two kids, two adults, and multiple luggage pieces into a cab? As we approached, the attendant recognized our plight and handled us professionally—he waved us over from the front of the line and moved other cab-seeking passengers into position to catch the waiting cars, and then brought forward the sole minivan that had been in line—an absolute godsend. I couldn't help but smile at the recollection of the minivan taxicab that crashed into me just three weeks before on the streets of Denver. Perhaps the good karma of my accident had come back around.

As I waited inside with Bryce and Teagan, our cab driver loaded our bags and waited patiently as Kirsta installed the car seats to mom-satisfaction. The cabbie navigated the drizzle and Boston traffic, and we arrived for our second stay on Beacon Hill.

Unfortunately, the hotel did not have our room ready. And, our terrific travel day screeched to a halt. I sighed in frustration, and Kirsta scanned the surroundings for a private spot, knowing that Teagan would soon demand to nurse. Bryce remained his easygoing self, talking with his frog stuffies.

When we had stayed at this hotel during our 2010 Boston visit, the hotel had carried the Holiday Inn flag. Since we are part of their Priority Club, we'd received a free night's stay and other benefits. Although the hotel was about 1.5 miles from the Boston Marathon finish line, we liked its location and did not hesitate to book it for our 2013 Boston Marathon stay. But, after I made the reservation, the hotel switched flags and now operated as a Wyndham.

So, while we would not necessarily receive the same perks as in 2010, the price did compare to other hotels, and we knew the area and the property. Plus, we made a special request for a room similar to that which we had during our first visit: a corner, oversized junior suite that allowed plenty of space for the kids to move around, as well as a super-sized walk-in closet in which we could put Teagan down for a nap.

Knowing that the hotel management staff had gone out of

their way to get us a specialized room, we waited patiently in their lounge area for nearly an hour before they bestowed our room keys upon us. Despite the wait, the front office manager and his team delivered fantastic service to make us comfortable.

As Kirsta and the kids finally settled into our room, I called Regina's Pizzeria in the North End to place an order.

"You're going to run over there?" Kirsta unpacked luggage and organized clothes in her usual get-ahead-stay-ahead manner.

"I need to get loose," I explained. "The rain will feel good, and we can microwave the pizza when I get back."

On the jog to Regina's Pizzeria, I snapped a picture of Faneuli Hall, the site of many Revolutionary-era meetings and protests in Boston. The building is named after Peter Faneuli, a Boston merchant who funded construction of the facility.

Actually, the moisture felt awesome! The rainy night had me

questioning whether I was in Seattle instead of Boston. So much rain, in fact, that I thought about a cab ride back to the hotel, but my lungs loved the fresh air too much, so I eschewed any vehicle and quickly hoofed it back to our room, no problems with the pizza.

I run so I can eat—more—but hydration is important to me, too. Sure, water is accessible at any hotel, but after a while, I want something with flavor. And for a marathon, I would be drinking a lot to stay hydrated.

Adjacent to the hotel sits a shopping center with a Whole Foods and a CVS Pharmacy—part of the reason why we wanted to stay at the Wyndham again. In the week before our trip, I had called the CVS to make sure they would have grape G2—my beverage of choice for hydrating and refueling. As promised, they did indeed have grape G2, and I bought several large 32-ounce containers to store in our mini fridge.

Some people say don't sweat the small stuff, but I needed those small pieces put away first. Now, I could finally focus on enjoying the big picture. I felt like a small child on Christmas Eve!

CHAPTER 16

SATURDAY, APRIL 13

I admit I woke up Saturday a bit anxious. We had a long day ahead of us, and I had a lot to get done. Would my bib number be ready? Would I find my teammates at the expo? Would the kids behave at the evening reception?

First up, the Alzheimer's Association team had agreed to meet at the Hynes Convention Center at eight forty-five to pick up our marathon bib packets en masse. I had some rattled nerves because I didn't know where the convention center was, and I had not met any of my teammates. Having only seen pictures and heard their voices on phone calls, I wasn't sure if I would even find them!

The forecast called for chilly weather, so I pulled on a pair of jogging pants and a long-sleeved pullover and headed out the hotel's doors. The ground remained wet from the prior evening, and my lungs enjoyed the moist, crisp air. I used Boston Common as my North Star, making my way to the park and then west down Newbury Street to the convention center.

The clock read just 8:30 a.m., so the marathon expo wasn't open yet, and only a few people lingered in the lobby. Near a staircase, I saw a single man who seemed to be lingering, perhaps waiting for others. "Are you with the Alzheimer's Association team?" I asked. The man answered affirmatively. I had met my first teammate, Ed Taglieri, and his warm greeting put me at ease.

Within a few minutes, more teammates arrived, and I

introduced myself to Chrissy, Ted, Bill, Jeremy, Dale Ann and Dale Bob, Nicolle, and Erica, who had given us the VIP tickets, as well as the others who were part of the Alzheimer's Association team. At nine, the expo officially opened, and we gathered for a team photo on the staircase where Ed and I had met. Then we hurried upstairs to pick up our bibs.

Before we picked up our marathon running bibs, Alzheimer's Association team members gathered outside the expo for a group photo. Although each of us has our own stories and backgrounds, our connections to Alzheimer's brought us together.

For most runs, I grab my bib and make a quick dash through the expo, usually making it in and out in under five minutes. This, however, was *the* Boston Marathon. As we picked up our bibs, each teammate posed for a picture or two, or ten, and then we re-gathered for another group photo, posing with our newly acquired identification number. I had been assigned 21264 to wear during the 26.2-mile excursion.

Then we moved to the shirt pick-up area. I was pumped— the official Boston Marathon participant shirt to wear proudly for years to come! The 2013 edition included in registration fees sported bright yellow with blue lettering and the Boston Athletic Association logo. Next up came the Adidas merchandise area. Here I hesitated. One hundred dollars to buy the official 2013 Boston Marathon jacket, bright blue with yellow striping and logo.

"That's a lot of money," I confided to a fellow runner who was also eyeballing a jacket.

"YOLO," she smiled. I noticed she had on a Boston Marathon jacket from a previous year.

"Do you wear it quite a bit?" I asked. "Get your money's worth?"

"Oh, definitely," she replied, holding up this year's style. "But never before I finish."

"Don't want to jinx it?" I offered.

"You know it!" she said, folding the jacket over her arm and heading toward the checkout line.

I stared more at the jackets and asked a few other people their opinions about when it is okay to put on the special gear. Most agreed that neither the shirt nor the jacket were to be worn until you completed the marathon. I concurred and planned to keep mine in the bag until Monday afternoon.

I carried that bag around the expo, the largest I'd ever seen for a run, and loaded up on stickers and other freebies, including some King's Hawaiian sweet rolls that I knew Bryce would enjoy snacking on later. Finally, I realized that I had been there for more than an hour, and I needed to get back to my family.

I started walking a different route back toward the hotel.

This time, I traversed the blocked-off Boylston Street, now in full marathon preparation mode. I eyeballed the VIP stands in front of the library and paused for a few photos at the finish line, including one with the guys who had just laid down paint for the new finish line.

I happened upon a group of guys painting the Boston Marathon finish line. They were having a blast and I couldn't resist jumping in for a photo.

I praised the painters. "Guys, this is so cool! I can't believe it stays in such good shape during the entire marathon."

"Nah, man," one of them commented. "We paint a new line each year, but then we also lay a mat over the paint. We'll put that down tomorrow."

Either way, I could not wait to cross it for real!

The jog back the rest of the way became a challenge since I carried two heavy bags of swag I'd picked up at the expo. The air remained cool, but I was sweating heavily by the time I made it back to the hotel. Although Kirsta and the kids had eaten a big breakfast, they were ready to get out of the hotel and eat more food.

With marathon day approaching, I wanted something reasonably healthy and safe for my digestive system—a runner's worst fear is having stomach issues on race day. As we walked toward the Common, we spotted a Subway along Tremont Street, and I devoured a chicken sub—about as reliable and safe a food as I can find.

The cooler temps prevented us from enjoying the day as much as we would have liked, but we wandered around the Boston Common area and found the *Make Way for Ducklings* statues. Bryce hesitated at first, but after I posed on the big statue, careful not to break it, he had fun sitting on the little ducks for some pictures.

Bryce was hesitant at first, but eventually agreed to sit on the
Make Way for Ducklings statue so Mom and Dad could
take pictures in Boston's Public Garden.

Despite the chilly air, the swan boats were operating, so we bought tickets and boarded, bundled up for a ride on the water. Teagan's eyes were barely visible between her blanket and head wrap, but Bryce thoroughly enjoyed cruising on the pond. Again, I thought how fortunate I was to have my entire family together for this journey. We were creating awesome memories.

Temperatures were chilly, but we braved the cool air for a Swan Boat ride on the lake in the Boston Public Garden.

As we disembarked and walked through the park, we spotted the carousel. Although Bryce was nearly three and half years old, he had yet to ride a carousel—and after one ride, he was addicted! This time, we limited Bryce to two rides, but we knew we'd found a new favorite source of entertainment for him. Baby Teagan stayed bundled in the stroller, and we headed back to the hotel for an afternoon nap because we had a big night ahead of us.

Bryce had not experienced a carousel ride until he climbed on this horse in Boston Common—he loved it!

Around four thirty, team coach Rich Schilder came to our hotel in his BMW. Much like the cab driver who picked us up at the airport, Rich waited patiently as Kirsta installed the child seats in the back of his car. After securing the children, Kirsta somehow managed to squeeze between them in the back seat, and I sat shotgun as Rich drove us to Papa Razzi, an Italian restaurant in Wellesley at which the Alzheimer's Association was hosting a celebration dinner for its Boston Marathon runners.

Bryce and Teagan were the only children in attendance, and we were much relieved that they behaved well all evening. And what an evening—a group photo of the runners, a terrific buffet loaded with energy-rich carbohydrates, and an awards ceremony, which included an emotional video of photos submitted by each of the team's members, and quotations about why they ran—all set to poignant music. While those in the room came from many backgrounds, we were all united in our mission to end Alzheimer's.

The Association recognized several individuals for their

contributions to the fundraising efforts. I raised more than $14,500, including several hundred dollars contributed after the marathon, which was good for third place in the group.

I proudly carried Teagan with me to the front of the room when the emcee called my name as a top fundraiser. "This," I proclaimed, displaying my baby girl for all to see, "is why I'm running." I recognized that it might be too late to save my mom from Alzheimer's, but we needed to stop the disease from affecting the next generation.

Most importantly of all, we clapped thunderously when the emcee announced our combined money raised: $200,000 to help assist those battling Alzheimer's and those who are trying to find a cure.

CHAPTER 17

SUNDAY, APRIL 14

If I'm going to a city with a Major League Baseball franchise, the first thing I do is check the team's schedule—if they are in town, I'm likely going to a game. The Red Sox are always granted a home game on Patriot's Day, and I was elated to discover they played home the entire weekend before the marathon.

My friend Christine and I spent one season working together for the minor league baseball team in Wichita. When not busy with baseball, we chatted about NASCAR and country music or hit a local park for rollerblading. Although Chris moved on to work for a Major League Baseball team, she and I remained friends. She helped secure tickets for Kirsta and me when we visited Boston in 2010, and she came through in a big way again in 2013, getting us four awesome seats for the Sunday's Red Sox game.

As my family and I walked across the parking lot behind the hotel to Whole Foods for breakfast, I knew it would be chilly at Fenway Stadium that afternoon. I thought about wearing the Pikes Peak Marathon pullover that I had worn most of Saturday. I picked it up, sniffed, and recognized it stunk.

"Kirsta, do you mind if I wear my sweaty Pikes Peak jacket all day?"

"Ya' think?" she called from the bathroom while applying her makeup.

So, in order not to scare anyone off, I decided to break my promise and don the blue Boston Marathon jacket. Stepping out of the elevator, I sported some swagger in my walk with the special jacket on my back. I'd joined the club of Boston Marathon participants . . . and hopefully not jinxed myself by wearing the jacket early.

First pitch of the Red Sox game versus the Tampa Bay Rays was set for 1:35 p.m. I was super excited to take Teagan to her first Major League Baseball game. Of course, she wouldn't remember it from five months old, but how many kids can say they attended their first baseball game at such a historic stadium in the first year of their lives?

But, before the game, we had some business to complete.

First, I wanted Kirsta to see the VIP bleachers so that we could coordinate as close as possible the spot where she and the children would be sitting at the finish line. I knew there would be a crowd during the marathon, and I wasn't sure how easy it would be to spot them sitting in the bleachers. So, we walked at a leisurely pace through Boston Common over to Boylston Street, making our way through the throngs of people hanging out near the finish line or also walking through the Back Bay to the baseball stadium.

From the street, we identified an area in the bleachers that looked like it would be easy for Kirsta to access while managing two kids. They would go through the entrance, walk up a set of stairs, and then take the bleachers as high as they could go, hopefully providing good sight lines to see me coming down the street without other people blocking their view. I turned toward the finish line and looked to my right, mentally noting the location as if coming to the end of my 26.2-mile path.

The Boston Athletic Association creates a VIP section with bleachers on the south side of Boylston Street in front of the public library. In both 2013 and 2014, Kirsta, Bryce and Teagan sat near the top of the bleachers in front of the word "Boston." In the background of this photo is the media bridge that is assembled a few yards past the finish line. Beyond the media bridge, also on the south side of Boylston, sits the medical tent.

Because I'd finished as third-place fundraiser for the Alzheimer's Association, I'd earned two extra VIP finish-line bleacher tickets. Now, we had a mile walk to Fenway Stadium and two VIP passes to distribute.

"Are you allowed to sell them?" Kirsta asked me.

"I guess." I stared at the passes. While I had won them as part of my fundraising efforts, we had also made a $180 contribution to the Alzheimer's Association to receive the original two from Erica. "It's not like we're going to make money from them. I'd be happy to get even a little bit for them."

That, of course, is if we could even find someone who wanted them—since the passes were only valid after two o'clock, the user would likely need to be someone who wanted to watch a runner in the third wave, which would start at ten forty. Plus, what was the likelihood we'd be able to find someone who needed *two* passes? I mean, if someone wanted to watch their spouse cross the finish line, they would only need one pass. Or, someone could watch with one guest, but that just seemed like an odd arrangement.

So, as we started walking east, I nonchalantly held up the two passes like someone trying to sell tickets to a sporting event. It seemed a little awkward since we were a mile away from a game. Would anyone even know or care about the passes?

Incredibly, within just a few blocks, we had a taker—a husband and wife from Birmingham, Alabama. The woman was running the marathon, and the man, Jeff, had yet to figure out where he would stand to watch her. I reassured them that the passes were real and explained the timing. Amazingly, she was a wave-three runner.

Since we'd donated close to $200 for the original two passes, I hoped we could get a reasonable amount from one pass. Then, anything we received for the second pass would be icing on the cake. I suggested $60, and Jeff accepted, handing me three $20 bills.

As excited as I was to earn cash for one of the passes, I was more pumped to know that Jeff would be in the grandstands to see his wife cross the finish line. Once the grandstands were assembled and in place along Boylston, it was easy to see how convenient it would be to sit there versus the madness to ensue on the north side of the street.

The family and I continued our trek toward the stadium with a few other inquiries, but no serious takers. Plus, Kirsta lugged

Teagan, and I carried Bryce for a little while, so I had trouble holding a ticket in the air while balancing a three-year-old boy in the other arm. Finally, as we neared the stadium, a woman approached with sincere interest. She and her husband were also going to the baseball game and asked for more time to consider, so I gave her our seat location, and she said she'd find us.

We cleared the entrance and found our seats on the first base side behind the Red Sox dugout in the fourth row behind the walkway. Thanks again, Chris! As we settled into Section 120 Row DD, lunch hour arrived.

"What do you want to eat?" I asked Kirsta as she rummaged through the diaper bag.

"This," she said, holding up two containers.

In another twist of fate, representatives of a hummus company had been along Boylston handing out free samples, so Kirsta and Bryce enjoyed a healthy meal while I headed to the concession stand and grabbed a chicken sandwich, picking up some carbs and protein in preparation for the marathon.

The afternoon was chilly, and even though Teagan was swaddled in layers of clothing, Kirsta took her to stay warm inside the large merchandise shop at the corner of Van Ness Street and Yawkey Way, still part of the "stadium" on game days. Not long after, someone filled the empty seat: the woman who wanted to buy the VIP grandstand pass. We settled on $40, and she left very happy to have the accommodations.

Food done, VIP passes gone, and the girls warm in the merchandise shop, Bryce and I focused our attention on the game. As I scrutinized the scoreboard, I noticed a lot of zeroes in Tampa Bay's row. Clay Buchholz was throwing a no-hitter for the Red Sox! I am a huge baseball fan and have attended hundreds, maybe thousands, of games in my lifetime, but I have never seen a no-hitter, at least not on the professional level.

To avoid a jinx, no one talked about the magic taking place on the field, but the tension was palpable. I couldn't say anything to the fans around me, and Bryce was too young to understand what was happening, but I had to tell someone. I took out my phone and sent a text to my brother Ron.

"Check out the Red Sox game," I typed. "It's Teagan's first game. Ever. This is amazing."

A few minutes later, Ron responded. "Cool!"

He had gotten my subtle message. Wouldn't it be something if Teagan's first game ever was a no-hitter?

Buccholz mowed down the Rays through six innings. Kirsta and Teagan returned during the seventh inning to sing "Take Me Out to the Ball Game." Both teams posted more zeroes, and then all 35,000 fans stood to dance and sing to "Sweet Caroline."

I took this family photo just after the seventh inning stretch during Teagan's first baseball game—our goal for each baseball game we attend is to last through middle of the seventh inning so we can sing Take Me Out to the Ballgame.

In the top of the eighth, just six outs from history, the Rays burst the bubble. Left fielder Kelly Johnson led off the inning with a solid single to right field to break up the no-hitter. Although he was erased by a double-play by the next batter, Johnson had spoiled what could've been a historic occasion for Teagan's first game.

After sitting for the length of a ballgame, my legs were ready to move. With a Red Sox win and Patriot's Day coming, Boston citizens were in a good mood. Bar crowds overflowed onto sidewalks, music jammed from inside cars, and laughter echoed through the streets.

We moseyed out to Boylston Street to begin the journey back to our hotel, stopping at several shops along the way so Kirsta could buy herself a souvenir T-shirt.

With the marathon start time now less than eighteen hours away, I had to make sure only safe items went into my stomach— so, we again stopped at the Subway near Boston Common. Since we'd eaten at this location just the day before, I felt comfortable choosing it for my pre-marathon dinner. Nothing fancy, just a grilled chicken breast with some cheese and lettuce, which I carried back to the hotel to enjoy with some G2.

To avoid some hills, we walked a blocked out of the way and did some sightseeing along the way. Bryce ran along the red painted bricks that marked the Freedom Trail. He didn't appreciate the occasion, but when we visited in 2010, he was not yet walking, so I loved taking pictures and videos of him along this historical marker.

Bryce walks along the Freedom Trail, a 2.5-mile route that meanders past historically significant sites in Boston. He wore the same monkey backpack to the marathon finish line so Kirsta could keep him corralled by its straps.

We made a stop at the Whole Foods buffet for Kirsta and Bryce to pick up some dinner. Then we laid our spread out on the table in our spacious room and devoured it while watching the traffic come in and out of the parking lot beneath our hotel window.

As I kicked back before the big day, I thought about how much had happened in the last year. We'd sat on our house deck watching a raging forest fire as firefighters battled the flames. We'd suffered through the tragic accident that took Kirsta's dad. I'd been selected by the Alzheimer's Association to run the Boston Marathon and had friends from near and far help me raise more than $14,000 in my mom's honor. I'd completed hundreds of training runs, pounding the pavement and trails. And, I'd narrowly averted death by taxicab.

Before making my last preparations, I made a final communication with the world, posting on Facebook:

So, I will be running THE Boston Marathon on Monday at 10:40 a.m. Eastern time. I will have my phone with me, so all text, Facebook posts, and emails are appreciated. I probably won't respond, but I will likely pull out my phone for some inspiration when needed! God Bless Us Everyone!!

I slid from the Facebook app to the weather.com app. The forecast called for nearly ideal running conditions on Monday, and since the Alzheimer's Association team members were going to get to stay on our bus while waiting at the start of the marathon, I wasn't too concerned about what to wear before we ran. Plus, we would be able to check a bag near the starting line, and race organizers would have it waiting for us at the finish line. Lastly, I'd purchased some throw-away clothes on discount at Walmart, so I'd be able to discard these as I approached the starting line, and marathon volunteers would collect them to give to charity.

I reviewed my run-preparation list and laid out "Flat Greg" on the floor of our hotel room, getting Kirsta's help to insert the safety pins through my bib number into my shirt. I swear, I poke myself silly whenever I try to do it; plus, she always seems to make it look just right and connects the bib perfectly so that it neither flaps nor stays too tight.

It struck me again how special it was to have Kirsta and my family there. Sure, I could have traveled to Boston by myself and called Kirsta and the kids from the finish line, but it wouldn't be the same. Absence may make the heart grow fonder, but experiences are a heckuva lot more fun when the people you love are there with you.

CHAPTER 18

WAKING UP

During our stay in Boston, Bryce and I shared a pullout couch bed so that Kirsta could have the big bed with Teagan, who, at five months old, was breastfeeding frequently.

The queen and princess slept like royalty on their king bed, and thankfully Bryce didn't stir, which should have meant a good night's sleep for me too. Nope. I stared at the ceiling, and by 3:00 a.m. my stomach did not feel good.

"Dang it, what did I do?" I typically have good control over my digestive system and know what sorts of foods cause issues, so I wasn't blaming the Subway chicken sandwich I had the night before.

My mind zipped through everything that could be causing stress: different time zone, changed sleep habits, anticipation, etc. I pushed these emotions aside and processed the marathon route in my mind. In lieu of sleep or rest, I pulled out my phone's calculator app and for the hundredth time computed the times necessary to break my 4:00 goal, sixteen minutes faster than my previous personal record.

Each time I did the math, I comforted myself that not breaking 4:00 would not be the end of the world. I had trained well and knew I could still set a PR, but figured that a finish of 4:04 to 4:06 was more likely. Odd times, I know, but those numbers kept popping into in my head as I calculated my run and finish time.

My alarm buzzed at four o'clock, and after a couple of snoozes, I rolled out of bed at four twenty, groggy, but excited. I was going to run the Boston Marathon!

As I pulled on my clothes, energy coursed through my body. I was ready to fulfill my commitment to the 250 donors to the Alzheimer's Association in support of my marathon run. I worried only about two things: if the weather would continue to cooperate, and if I could break four hours. I figured the stomach problems would settle down with a couple of Tums, which I always take before any run of more than sixteen miles.

As my final preparation before leaving our hotel, I finished packing a backpack with items I would use before, during, and after the race, including snacks, my iPod, a phone charging cord, and warm clothing. I also packed a second, smaller bag with items I would take to the starting area in Hopkinton, and then check at a school bus before beginning the marathon. Volunteers would drive the bags to the finish line for participants to pick up afterward.

My family and I planned to reconnect after the race at the Westin hotel one block from the finish line for a post-race Alzheimer's Association reception—the same site where I was to meet my teammates and ride a bus to Hopkinton, the start of the Boston Marathon.

*Kirsta surprised me by dressing both kids in customized
designed shirts for my Boston Marathon run. The color purple
represents awareness about Alzheimer's.*

As they slept, I kissed Kirsta and the kids goodbye and headed
out the door. I typically skip the elevator and use the stairs, but we
were on the seventh floor, and I didn't want to risk tripping down
the steps in my excited state. "Wouldn't that be something?" I
laughed. "Break an ankle the morning of the Boston Marathon!"

I tried to stay calm this far in advance of the race, but I
bounced from the elevator and out of our hotel onto the quiet
streets of Boston.

CHAPTER 19

PRE-MARATHON

The air was crisp with just a few clouds in the sky—all the makings of a beautiful day. I slow-jogged through Boston Commons to Boylston Street, absorbing the moment. To make it real, I whispered to myself, "This is the morning of the Boston Marathon. I am walking the streets of Boston. I am going to run the Boston Marathon!"

As I neared the finish-line area, one half block from the Westin hotel, I made a stop at the huge white tent that I had seen earlier. I thought it might contain VIP features that Kirsta could enjoy with the passes we'd obtained, but when I poked in my head, I was stunned to see that it was committed one hundred percent to medical purposes, lined on both sides with cots and other related equipment. I laughed as I took a picture, joking with the attendants that I would see them later.

Cots line either side of the medical tent near the finish line. It was pure serendipity that I took the picture early in the morning as I walked to the Westin to meet my teammates before the marathon.

I made my way to our team's meeting room in the Westin, where my teammates assembled. In the hour or so that we were there, I used the restroom again, and my stomach seemed a bit better, though something was still happening in there. Time moved quickly, and by six o'clock we headed back downstairs to board the bus to Hopkinton.

Members of the Alzheimer's Association Boston Marathon team make our way down the hallways of the Westin Copley Place en route to a coach bus that would take us to Hopkinton and the starting line.

We chatted and joked for a few minutes before the mood grew quiet. Our coach bus carried just part of our team, so the fourteen of us stretched out comfortably. I dozed off and on during the forty-minute ride, checking out the suburb terrain for my first visit outside of downtown Boston.

When the bus pulled off the interstate at seven o'clock to approach Hopkinton Middle/High School, I moved forward a couple of rows to the front seat so I could enjoy a full view and take more pictures out the front of the bus. "Wow, it's like a sea of busses!"

The Boston Athletic Association arranges for school busses to transport runners from downtown Boston to Athletes Village near the starting line in Hopkinton. Most busses drop off runners and return to Boston to pick up more participants. The Alzheimer's Association provided a charter bus that remained parked in Hopkinton, so we runners relaxed in comfort.

Unlike the majority of runners, who had to vacate their school bus and proceed to Athletes Village, my teammates and I got to hang out on our bus as long as we wanted since it would remain parked until after our start time. However, I was jittery, so I exited and walked through the staging area, where I viewed throngs of people scattered on the large grassy areas designed for football and baseball. Some stretched, some read, some huddled to stay warm, and some were already in line at the swath of porta-potties lining the outskirts.

While I planned to take my phone with me during the marathon, I wanted to focus on running during the actual race.

So, at the Village, I snapped many photos, knowing that I would leave the disposable camera in my checked bag and could use my phone camera to take pictures and video at the finish line.

2013 marathon runners kill time in Athletes Village in Hopkinton, home of the Boston Marathon starting line. Porta-potties line the background of the photo, while many runners hold bags that they will leave pre-race at busses, then pick up after crossing the finish line.

Loud music pierced the still air and created a party atmosphere, but while the sun shone brightly, the air was chilly, and I was ready to get back to our bus. But as my stomach continued to rumble, I spotted a row of porta-potties near the back of the Village with short lines. I thought I might be able to clear my bowels once more. While I knew I could use the bathroom on the bus, I did not want to be "that guy" who made the bus stink.

I gag easily, and as soon as I opened the porta-potty door, I started retching. The smell emitting from the bowl was beyond disgusting. With eyes watering, I did my thing. Holding my breath as best I could, I cleared my bowels and am lucky that I did not clear my stomach.

The fresh air seemed like heaven, and while still making some noises, my stomach felt tremendously better. I headed back to the bus to remain comfortable—and use the hand sanitizer that I had packed in my checked bag.

The elite runners start the marathon no later than ten o'clock. I was in wave three, home of most of the charity runners, and scheduled to start at 10:40 a.m. Eastern Time. That translates to 8:40 a.m. Mountain Time, which is about two hours later than when I typically started my morning runs and the other marathons I had run. This would be a challenge. I'm a man of routine, and I wasn't sure how my body would respond to a change in that routine.

So, I chilled as best as I could for a couple of hours. I snacked, drank, debated what to wear, and jogged a few short laps around the parking lots. I also enjoyed chatting with my teammates, taking pictures, etc.

As showtime approached, I decided the weather would allow me to run with only a shirt and a pair of shorts, but kept on my throwaway gloves and cap. To loosen up one final time, I jogged a lap down the sidewalk in front of the elementary school. Every muscle, tendon, and bone in my body was in prime condition; the only ache was that rib that had been punched three weeks earlier by the taxi cab. But, I'd survived the twenty-four-mile run in Kansas, so I wasn't concerned the rib pain would interfere too much. Besides, the Boston excitement overwhelmed the dull ache I still felt.

We checked our bags at the appropriate school bus and began the 0.7-mile walk to the starting corrals. I decided to make another stop to urinate—guilty of drinking too much thanks to the late start. Unfortunately, when I decided to hit these porta-potties, I got separated from my teammates.

I'd been placed in Corral Four of the third wave. I am not sure how this was determined—possibly by the anticipated finish times that we'd provided—but being placed closer to the front of the wave versus the back, which was Corral Nine, meant that I would have fewer people jostling me. It's not like I was going to be one of the fastest of the 27,000 people scheduled to run the marathon. But I was also confident I wouldn't be the slowest, so the closer I could be to the front, the more likely that I'd be able to run my pace—and the better my shot at breaking four hours.

This corral assignment—and the few minutes earlier that I started—also turned out to be crucial for the developments that occurred later in the day.

So, separated from my teammates, I stepped solo to the front of Corral Four surrounded by hundreds of others ready for 26.2.

CHAPTER 20

THE BOSTON MARATHON

I waited. And waited. And waited.

After six months of preparation, the final minutes hung in the air like a last-minute shot in a tied basketball game. I just wanted to run!

Other runners packed the street. We bounced on our tippy-toes, trying to harness the energy cascading through our bodies. Standing shoulder to shoulder in the corral, we swayed foot to foot waiting for the gates to open.

I was tired from lack of sleep, but adrenaline would soon push that away. My only problems: my bladder was full again and my intestines still had not completely settled down. Suddenly, a mint candy, the red and white striped kind, fell at my feet. I looked down to see a woman picking up three or four that had fallen. "Do you want one?" she asked. "I'm not sure why I brought so many."

The candy was like a gift from above—mints have always helped settle my belly, so I graciously accepted her offer and sucked away.

I don't recall anything special taking place before the start of wave three, just a countdown of the minutes and then the seconds. We were off! I knew the start was downhill, but it was steeper than I'd imagined. I tried my best to hold back, but I absolutely love running downhill, so I maneuvered to find a running lane that allowed me to go at my own pace.

The crowd roared as one voice in celebration of another wave entering the parade route, which immediately justified my decision to run without headphones. No music could compete with the motivation provided by those cheers.

Although my eyes focused on the course in front of me, my peripheral vision spotted feet moving all around me and hands alongside the street, waving in a blur as we passed. I am not sure where there were more people—on the race course, or along the race course. The only time other time I'd seen this many people in one spot was in Times Square in New York City.

Despite my finger getting in the photo, this picture I took during the 2013 Boston Marathon shows how crowded the route is with runners.

Thankfully, I'd received good intelligence from my teammates and discovered a wooded area on the left side of the road just a half mile into the run. Several other runners were also emptying their bladders, and I took advantage of this small, crowd-free area to water the ground. After that, I felt fantastic and ready to run.

Placing one foot in front of the other, I could not believe I was running *the* Boston Marathon. I absorbed every breath as I cruised the pavement and decided that I could, and should, have a little fun . . . and I committed a big faux pas.

To my right, I noticed a young boy trying to give a high five to runners, but no one slapped his hand. Thinking of my own children, I wanted to make his day. I glanced to my right and cut over to the side of the road. To my horror, my foot tangled with that of a woman who had been running in my blind spot. She hit the ground, and I stopped in dismay.

"I am so sorry!" I exclaimed. I offered my hand to assist her in regaining her feet. She gave me a not-so-friendly look, so I just said, "My apologies," turned, and ran away as someone else helped her up. I swear I checked around me before I made my cut, but her fall had been my fault, and I carried that guilt with me.

I regained my focus and made a conscious decision to make running my priority, not interacting with the crowd. I liked my pace, and I stayed focused on my goal of breaking four hours. The miles clicked by quickly, and I hit the 10k mark in 52:51.

I wish I could share more about the first half of the route, but honestly, nothing really stood out, other than a consistently noisy crowd. Several times, I yelled to the crowd, "Where am I?" to confirm my location on the marathon route, but mostly I ran harder than I ever had in my life.

Around mile thirteen, the crowd noise increased a few decibels. I'd reached the Wellesley "Scream Tunnel." For more than a quarter mile, students from the all-girls school lined the route, screaming and begging for kisses, hugs, and high fives. I felt like Elvis Presley, the Beatles, and every other rock and roll star who ever sold out an arena. I scanned the crowd for any girl that mentioned Nebraska or Colorado, and I would have at least said hello or given a high five, but the closest I saw was Iowa, so I passed, staying focused on my time goal.

Leaving the Scream Tunnel, I hit the halfway mark at 1:51:32, a very fast time for me. Calculating in my head, I stayed energized knowing that I was rocking a solid pace.

At the sixteen-mile mark, I found an inspiring sight—the Alzheimer's Association cheering section. At least fifty people joined together in the mission to EndAlz and, clad in purple in support of my teammates and me, were cheering, clapping, ringing bells, and yelling our names. I left feeling energized for the next four miles, likely to be the four toughest.

The loud bells and cheering from the Alzheimer's Association cheering station provided me an amazing boost of energy—this photo from the Association shows me running strong near mile 16.

Thanks to insight from veteran runners, I knew that the four hills started with an overpass, so I put my head down and just ran. Also thanks to pre-marathon tips, I knew that each hill had its own recovery. My training paid off, and I cruised through the next two hills until I reached the infamous Heartbreak Hill.

This was it. The moment I'd prepared for since I first found out I'd been accepted into the Boston Marathon. I could not and would not disappoint myself.

The Hill lasts only 0.4 miles and increases in altitude by just ninety feet—nothing compared to Colorado mountains. The Driveway Drills I'd completed outside our home were tougher. I knew I just needed to push through it. The crowd yelled my name, visible on the front of my shirt, and I kept my head down and put one foot in front of the other. Any slowdown here would not only be an insult to my training but could cost me precious seconds in my quest to conquer four hours. I could not slow down, and I definitely could not stop.

As I crested the hill, I spat on the ground triumphantly and whispered, "Take that, Heartbreak Hill!"

Based on advice from several people, I moved to the side of the road after I crested the hill and slowed to a walk to give my legs a break—and to do a quick body-check. Ribs hanging tough, though still sore; knees had no issues; toes solid; bottom of feet were hot and sore, likely the beginning of blisters; hamstrings and quads were achy, but manageable. Time to finish the marathon.

I knew the Citgo Petroleum sign from watching Red Sox games on television—the sign is visible over the left field wall of Fenway Park. To see it during the marathon knows that the end of your run is near!

I can't believe how many people I began to pass, or how many times I heard spectators spot my name on my shirt and yell, "Looking good, Greg!" I may have looked good, and I thought I was running solidly, but I was starting to feel the pain. I was tired. I desperately wanted to be done. Somewhere around mile twenty-three, a family offered me Pringles. I grabbed a handful, and that salt hit the spot!

At this point, my watch became my best friend. 3:59 was quickly approaching, and 26.2 seemed to be getting farther away. A headwind hit me when we turned straight east, and now it was batting me down, though the crowd was doing its best to pick me up. For the first three and half hours, I'd acknowledged everyone who yelled my name with a wave of some sort. But now, I just hoped they knew I'd heard them.

I've fainted only one time in my life—ironically, as a child near the top of Pikes Peak during a family vacation, but around the twenty-four-mile marker, I began to wonder if I might hit the ground again. My vision had gone foggy, my head was down, and my body hurt. I began to wonder if 4:00 was out of reach. "If I don't break four hours, I can still set a PR," I thought to myself. My gait began to slow.

Suddenly, another voice commanded: "Dang it, Greg, you didn't come this far *not* to break 4:00—Go!" I don't know if the voice was God, or perhaps Kirsta's dad looking down on me from heaven, or just my internal compass, but the voice sounded so passionate that I listened to it.

I looked down at my watch, and I knew if I pushed, I could still break 4:00. I just had to keep going.

Soon, I saw the famous Citgo sign and knew I had about one mile to go.

I had memorized much of the marathon route, so when I made the right-hand turn onto Hereford, I knew I simply had to run two blocks to Boylston Street before the finish line would come into my sightline. I pushed on as the crowd roared. I'd heard that it would feel like everyone cheered just for you, and honestly, it felt that way to me, too. The yelling and screaming hung over me like a noise arch. I'd never experienced anything like it.

The tall media bridge just past the finish line inched closer with every step. I checked my watch a final time and knew for sure—I was going to become more than an average runner. I was going to break four hours!

Moving forward, I saw the VIP bleachers on my right. In my

dazed condition, I was thankful that we'd pre-arranged a specific location. Slowing my pace, I blocked out the noise, the crowd, and the commotion around me and focused strictly on spotting my family.

"There they are!" My heart leaped as I waved, smiled, and flashed, "I love you!" in sign language to Kirsta, Bryce, and baby Teagan. My wife pointed and held up Teagan high so I could see her, and then the small hand of my mini-me son waved as a huge smile spread across his soft face. All the money we'd spent, all the hassles we'd encountered, all of the stomach problems at the start of the race, were worth that five-second exchange. I registered another top-ten life moment.

Grudgingly, I turned away, and took thirty more steps, totally forgetting to use my camera phone to record any pictures or videos. More than ready to be done, I cruised across the finish line, ready to celebrate.

I finished my 26.2 miles quest in 3:56:03, shaving more than twenty minutes off my previous marathon personal record. And, thus, for the first time in my undistinguished running career, I had broken the 4:00 barrier!

My wife had her hands full with a 5-month old and a 3-year old, so I excused her bad photo of me crossing the finish line–you can see the back of my white shirt underneath the cap bill of the gentleman on the right.

Being a cheeseball, I typically pose for the cameras at the finish line. For Boston, I had practiced flashing "I love you" with one hand while holding up four fingers of the hand that also held my water bottle because I *knew* I was going to break four hours.

I forgot to do any of this.

Instead, a few steps past the line, I needed help. Instead of my mugging for the camera, the photographers caught pictures of me holding up a finger, signifying I needed assistance. My legs were weak, and I felt dizzy. It took me a few seconds to find an attendant, but when I did, a pair of guys quickly got their arms around me. I thought I would just need to walk it off, but when they asked if I needed to go to the medical tent, I accepted their offer.

Even more inviting, they offered to push me to the tent in a wheelchair. After more than four hours on my feet, counting time in the corral, the idea of sitting down suddenly seemed appealing. I slid with relief into the wheelchair, my feet elated to be off the ground. The attendants rolled me into the large medical tent about thirty yards from the finish line—the same tent I'd photographed much earlier in the day.

I knew I'd recover soon enough, but I figured I'd be delayed a little bit from returning to the Westin to meet my family. So, as the attendants pushed me to the medical tent, I sent a text message to Kirsta: "I'm okay but in medic tent."

I didn't want her to worry about me since I knew she'd have her hands full with two young children—one tethered to her arm with a backpack hand strap and the other one in a Moby wrap. I didn't give much thought to what my family would be doing. I just figured I would see them at the reception. I closed my eyes and breathed.

CHAPTER 21

EXPLOSIONS

There were only a handful of runners in the tent, which stretched nearly an entire block long and about a whole street wide with cots lined up like pews in an old-fashioned church. As attendants rolled me through the entrance facing Boylston, laughter and smiles from fellow Boston Marathon finishers created a jovial atmosphere inside the tent.

My handlers took me to a cot on the west side of the tent near the entrance. I thanked them for their assistance, and as I maneuvered my body from the wheelchair to the cot, three or four extremely cordial women hovered about me, asking me questions: name, medical history, how my body felt. "Angels taking care of me," I smiled to myself.

I reiterated that I would be okay; I felt just light-headed and dehydrated. I sat on the cot, and my angels covered me in blankets and offered me a cup of warm salt water. My nose cringed, but I took a drink—and immediately spat out the fluid on the cement beneath me. It may have been healthy, but it tasted nasty.

My angels countered with a cup of cold water and a bag of potato chips, which I gratefully accepted and devoured. One angel wrote down my information on her clipboard, another took my blood pressure, and a third recorded my vitals. I lay on my back, eyes closed. I was tired and very relaxed.

Suddenly, a loud *boom* cracked the sky.

"Was that thunder?" I asked. The noise reminded me of the thunder at our mountain home when it seems like Mother Nature is lighting fireworks on the roof.

Seconds later, we heard a second explosion, not quite as loud as the first. My eyes were now wide open, and I saw looks of concern in the faces of the angel attendants above me.

While the women stayed with me, other medical personnel rushed out of the tent. Because the tent was enclosed, other than the doors on both the north and south sides, we could see nothing outside the structure.

Within a minute, an announcement came over the medical tent PA system. The voice said something to the effect of, "There has been an incident. We need everyone to please remain calm. We need to move the runners to the rear of the tent."

My attendants helped me to my feet, and I shuffled toward the back of the tent as my senses adjusted to the new emotions dangling in the air. Other runners calmly did the same; tired, we were happy to cooperate and take direction.

There had been tons of equipment at the finish line, so my instinct told me that a generator had blown up, or some other sort of electrical accident had occurred. Slightly dazed, a small handful of us runners congregated around some chairs and cots at the southwest corner of the tent. In front of us, medical personnel rushed around the tent laying down more cots and opening more blankets. In an organized and orderly manner, they reminded me of a scene from the classic TV show M*A*S*H when the voice announces, "Incoming wounded!"

Knowing that something big had happened, I turned on my phone's video recording as I half sat, half stood on a stool. In moments, new individuals were brought inside from Boylston Street, through the door I'd entered minutes earlier.

One of the first arrived in a wheelchair, with his legs ending at his knees. For a millisecond, I thought, "Oh, no, something happened to a wheelchair racer!"

Then, seeing the exposed bone of his right tibia, I realized he was a victim. I subtly recorded a man in jeans and a cowboy hat helping a medical attendant push the wheelchair past me—not stopping at the cots but rushing him straight through the tent to the south door, where an ambulance stood waiting.

In my heart, I knew that was the same wheelchair I'd ridden into the tent minutes earlier.

Right behind the first victim, attendants wheeled another man on a gurney into the tent. He also appeared to have a severe leg injury. I turned off my phone's video. After 25 seconds of recording, I didn't have the heart to be a journalist. "Holy crap."

More medical personnel hustled throughout the tent, setting up more cots, grabbing supplies from storage cabinets, and attending to additional victims coming into the tent—some in wheelchairs, some on stretchers. I saw blood on the equipment, blood on clothes, blood on skin.

As I absorbed what had happened, I began to feel fortunate that my legs were only shaky. I still had my legs.

I stared at the scene unfolding in front of me. "What the hell is going on?" I wondered to myself.

My phone buzzed. A text from Kirsta. I still had no idea what had happened outside, so I hadn't been concerned for my family's wellbeing. Her text told me they were in the hotel room, which I took to mean the reception room at the Westin, so I understood that they were safe.

The screenshots of our text message exchange illustrate my wife's immediate concern. Note that I sent my first text during my wheelchair ride at 12:45 p.m. MDT (2:45 p.m. EDT), just minutes before the first explosion:

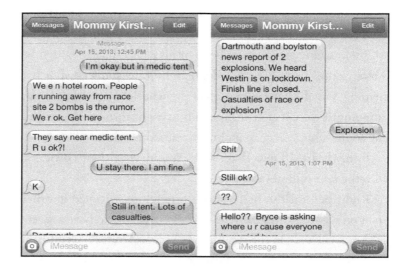

Later, I learned their story. Kirsta knew that the post-finish-line procession at Boston was extraordinarily long. Runners needed to proceed about four blocks past the finish line to collect their medals, Mylar blankets, water, bananas, checked bags, etc., before exiting the cordoned area. Knowing that, she gave Bryce two options after they saw me cross the finish line: stay in the bleachers and watch more runners, or go to the Westin hotel where the Alzheimer's Association reception was gathering and wait for Daddy.

Thankfully, Bryce chose option two. Kirsta made her way down from the top of the bleachers, carrying baby Teagan in one arm and holding the strap of Bryce's small backpack with the other—the big boy, of course, climbing down the huge stairs on his own. They were in the elevator of the Westin when the explosions occurred and didn't know anything had happened until they arrived at the 7th-floor conference room, where they found a room full of worried Alzheimer's Association staff staring at a TV that blared live news from the finish line. The screen showed the chaos, and through the hotel windows, they could see people running in droves away from Boylston Street.

After receiving Kirsta's concerned messages, I realized something *really* big had occurred. In the corner of the medical tent, I had the presence of mind to post on Facebook at 2:54 p.m., approximately ten minutes after I'd crossed the finish line and around five minutes after the first explosion. The post communicated everything that I knew at the time:

I am fine.

By now, the attendants paid more attention to the casualties entering the tent, and my group of fellow runners were left to our own volition. The runner beside me was a blonde woman with a worried expression. I asked if she needed anything. She was worried about her family and friends, but she'd put her phone in her checked bag at the starting line. I handed her my phone, but her hands shook, and she had trouble focusing on the numbers. I offered to message for her, and at 3:01 p.m. I sent a text to her out-of-state husband and to her fellow marathon friends, who were supposed to meet her at the finish line. "Julie is in medic tent. She is fine. Just from race, nothing from explosion."

Soon, I decided I'd seen enough. Emergency responders now controlled the situation, and I needed to get out of the way. Victims continued to be rolled into the tent from the north side while additional medical help arrived from the south side. Outside the tent, sirens blared as vehicles barreled to the scene.

I suggested Julie accompany me to the Alzheimer's reception, and she agreed. Later, she would tell me that I didn't give her an option. I wasn't going to leave her there, alone, with no way to communicate with her family or friends.

Amid the organized chaos, we exited out the south doors of the tent. Sirens blared through the clouds gathering in the sky. People with confused faces walked away from Boylston Street while others stood still, unsure where to go. Concerned officers and EMT officials hustled toward the finish line area.

Julie and I crossed diagonally to the Westin and entered the crowded lobby of the hotel. We exited the elevator at the seventh floor and walked unsteadily down the hallway. Limping into the conference room was like returning home from a long vacation with a bad ending.

To my left, Bryce played on the iPad at the table, and Kirsta sat in a chair against the wall calmly feeding Teagan. Yet, I noticed her thumb scrolling frantically on her phone, which had its cord plugged into an outlet, and I sensed that she was alarmed.

Other reception attendees stared out the window or at the TV, which showed coverage of the events occurring below us. Some punched away on their phones trying to connect with family and friends. A few days before the marathon, Alzheimer's Association organizer Angela Floro had asked each of us runners to provide her with emergency contact info. Now, Angela used her checklists and people's cell phone numbers to track down each of the team's runners.

I didn't know everyone in the room, so I didn't immediately recognize or understand the panic that many endured. I didn't know how many were unsure whether family members and runner friends had been affected. Nor could I tell from their expressions how deeply the shock had hit them.

Kirsta and the TV reporters quickly caught me up to speed on the news. Two bombs had exploded on Boylston Street. The marathon was over.

I introduced Julie to my wife and a few other people, and then, since we had a complimentary masseur in the room, Julie lay down for a rub-down on her legs, sore from her marathon run. Still recovering myself, I found more food and drink and a view from the window, which looked down on the medical tent, Copley Square, and Blagden Street. Ambulances still raced to the scene, but they lined up in an orderly fashioned—event organizers apparently were well-prepared.

Settling down with a plate of snacks, I finally got to hear the story from my wife's perspective. Only then did it hit me how close they had been to the action. Had Bryce not decided to wait for me at the hotel, my family would have been immediately across the street from the first explosion. At 3:25 p.m., I made another Facebook post to reassure our family and friends that we were *all* okay:

Kirsta, the kids, and I are fine. Explosion happened just after I crossed the finish line.

Soon after, I could sense Julie's anxiety—without her phone, she had no ability to communicate directly with her family and friends. I decided to head back out with her to see if we could retrieve our checked bags, and her phone. Her husband had responded to my text, but her friends had not, so I understood her worry. My bag mostly contained clothes of little value, but it also held my iPod, and I hated to leave town without that.

We caught an elevator to the Westin lobby and entered the distress that surrounded the hotel. Glancing at my phone, I saw it was still only forty minutes since the explosions occurred. Immediately outside the hotel, on the south side of the medical tent, streets were lined with ambulances, marked and unmarked police cars, and SWAT vehicles. For the second time that day, I was shocked by the sheer number of people around me.

By now, the medical tent and the area near the finish line had been blocked off by yellow crime-scene tape, so we detoured to side streets. I was slightly disoriented, but I knew the general direction we needed to go.

Emergency vehicles still swarmed to the scene and at least once, I recall taking control of a street as an ambulance approached. People stood in the street, apparently oblivious to anything around them. "Hey, we gotta move, people!" I commanded as the vehicle approached, unable to proceed. It sounded a bit bossy, I admit, but I was relieved to see people move out of the ambulance's path.

With some directions from others on the street, Julie and I had just found the appropriate school buses for our bags when a third blast occurred. Every person on the street jumped, cringed, and then stood still. What the hell was going on?

"Clear the area!" workers screamed. We later learned this had been a planned detonation of a suspicious device. But no one knew that then, and everyone was on edge, bracing for more explosions.

I wanted—no, I needed—to get back to my family. I dashed to the appropriate bus window, held up my bib number and a volunteer tossed out my bag.

Julie did the same just a few buses away and received her bag just as I did. The proximity was amazing—it may have been because our names, Kalkwarf and Kelada, were so close alphabetically, or maybe it was just God's will on that day. Knowing she now had her phone and could reach her friends, I called out, "I'm leaving you!"

She waved in acknowledgment, and I began a solo speed-walk back to the Westin. In a huge city so far away from home, I had never felt so alone. A shiver erupted over my entire body.

I wore my bright-blue Boston Marathon finisher's jacket that I had packed in my bag for the Westin, but it seemed to have lost the swagger and magic it contained the day before. I quickly realized that I had to stop to put pants on over my shorts. I was chilled and shaking—both from the cooling temperature and rattled nerves. A building security guard saw me struggling to pull my pants on over my shoes and graciously offered me a seat inside, but I waved him off. I wanted to get back to my family.

As I approached the Westin, yellow crime-scene tape cordoned off the primary entrance. I felt hopeless and looked the part, shoulders drooping and dried sweat from the marathon still lingering on my head and body.

I gestured to a state police officer standing guard on the right side of the yellow tape.

"I need to get into the hotel," I half demanded, half requested.

"Are you staying here?" he asked suspiciously.

"Yes," I lied, not taking any chance on getting turned down because I was just a reception guest. Kirsta had been through enough without worrying about me being on the streets any longer.

Thankfully, she didn't need to. The officer lifted the tape, and I ducked into the lobby, hustling forward on my tired legs before he changed his mind.

Inside the crowded lobby, two military personnel were attired in full combat gear with locked and loaded weapons, apparently trying to make their way to the roof. I breathed a sigh of relief as I stepped off the elevator, back securely on the seventh floor.

Within minutes of my arrival, my phone buzzed. Julie's friend responded to my text—the two of them had found each other.

From the conference room, we watched TV like millions of other Americans throughout the country, trying to decipher what had happened. The tension in the room abated somewhat as Alzheimer's representatives confirmed the safety of the running team members and family members. Race officials had stopped many of the runners at the intersection of Massachusetts and Commonwealth not far from the finish line.

Ambulances line Huntington Avenue on the southwest side of the Boston Marathon finish line area. I took this picture from a seventh-floor conference room in the Westin Copley Place in which the Alzheimer's Association hosted a post-marathon reception.

Below us, authorities scrambled in and out of the hotel. The Westin had become Command Central, attracting high-powered individuals like the Boston mayor and the Massachusetts governor. Not surprisingly, the Westin went into lockdown mode, trapping us inside.

CHAPTER 22

MEDIA

If I had to pick one thing at which I excel, it's communication. In this case, I knew I was part of the story, and I thought it was important to share my perspective.

As I looked at the time, just before 5:00 p.m. EDT, I realized that Denver approached 3:00 p.m.—time for "The Dave Logan Show" on radio station KOA, to which I listened on my drive home. I knew the sports-oriented program would be talking about the Marathon news. I found a phone number for the station, and within a few minutes, the show's producer had arranged an interview for me with the former NFL player and his sportswriter sidekick, also named Dave (Krieger).

From an empty conference room on the seventh floor of the Westin, I kept an eye on the scene below as I paced the floor, sharing my story with KOA listeners throughout Colorado. Unfortunately, or fortunately, the Boston Public Library blocked my view of the finish line, so I could describe what I'd witnessed in the medical tent and what I could currently see on the south and east sides of the library.

My voice remained surprisingly calm, though perhaps that was to be expected given that I'd been awake for somewhere around thirteen hours and had run and walked close to thirty miles. Regardless of any increased adrenaline from the intense situation, my energy was flagging.

In addition to being a former NFL player, Dave Logan is also a high school football coach with several state titles on his resume. If his coaching style is like his interviewing, I can see what makes him successful. He asked insightful questions about my experience, then let me tell my story without interrupting. Krieger was great, too, listening to my comments and asking follow-up questions. As I recounted the experience in full for the first time, I was surprised by how many details I remembered and how composed my answers sounded. However, as I listened to the interview later, I definitely noticed a few moments where I paused, or my voice broke.

After completing that interview, I realized that Will Ripley, the reporter who had shot from our house during last year's Lower North Fork Fire, would also be interested in an interview. After a tweet, we made arrangements to talk, and Will combined some of my comments with those of others from Colorado, including Jennifer Schubert-Akin, to compile a two-minute synopsis of our experience for television viewers.

I learned later that Jennifer, with whom I had exchanged emails just a few months earlier, had crossed the finish line only a couple minutes behind me. Her husband, Rick, didn't see Jennifer run past on Boylston and was still waiting patiently for her when the second bomb exploded 100 hundred yards away. After the incident, and a few panicked minutes, the couple reunited at their hotel in the Back Bay, both having avoided any direct harm.

I'm glad I brought my phone charger to the Westin because, during the three hours that we stayed at the hotel, my phone lit up nonstop—phone calls, text messages, Yahoo emails and Facebook notifications. The power of mass and social medias is absolutely amazing. During an eighteen-hour period, I received some sort of communication from nearly three hundred people. That's a lotta love!

Stuck at the hotel and with little food in my system, I devoured popcorn and chips that the Alzheimer's Association had provided in our room. Another charity group in an adjacent room shared cookies. But, I was still hungry, and Bryce would need dinner soon.

As six o'clock approached, the Westin staff offered to bring a pizza so we could eat some real food. But just then, we got word that we would be able to leave with no hassle, so we bundled up the kids in the stroller, said our farewells, and navigated through the madness in the lobby and out onto the street.

At 6:03 p.m. EDT, I posted on Facebook:

> *We are still safe. We are at a scheduled reception for the Alzheimer's Association at the Westin across the street, but now heading to our hotel, as it is no longer on lockdown. Thx for your prayers, emails, etc.*

The walk back to our hotel was brisk, eerily quiet, and, thankfully, uneventful. Military police lined each intersection of the now-restricted marathon area. The Common stood practically empty. Although, to our knowledge, whoever had committed this atrocity still ran loose, we plodded forward unconcerned. If something happened now, the response would be swift and fierce.

Not surprisingly, both kids fell asleep in the stroller, and Kirsta and I seemed ready to collapse, too. However, other media venues contacted me for additional interviews, asking if I would go on-air. Under the circumstances, I felt obligated to share my story.

Then, in the middle of our just-under-two-mile walk back to our hotel near Massachusetts General Hospital, my phone battery died. That sucked, but it didn't . . . I needed the emotional break. Modern technology makes it easy to keep in touch, and makes it challenging to be alone. I needed time to talk privately with

Kirsta and see how she was holding up.

We talked on the walk back to the hotel, trying to process everything that had occurred.

"So, Bryce is the reason you left the finish line?" I pried.

"Yes," Kirsta said. "He said he wanted to wait for you at the hotel reception."

"What if he had said he wanted to stay?"

"Yeah, I don't want to think about that." Kirsta turned her head away from me.

"You're a nurse. You could have helped treat the victims."

"Not with two kids on my hands. Besides, I'm not an ER nurse. I take care of babies."

"I know, I know. But I keep feeling like I should have done more."

"You had no way of knowing what was going on, and you had just run a marathon. Anyway, medical personnel were right there."

"Yeah, but still . . ." Guilt lingered on my shoulders. Feeling helpless, I could only thank God for taking care of my family.

Back in our room, I got another kind of break—a much-needed shower. The water cascaded down my head as my brain absorbed the incidents of the last few hours. "Somebody tried to blow us up!" ran through my head on repeat.

Processing the timeline, I flashed back to my thoughts while lying in bed earlier that morning. Had I run a marathon time of 4:04 to 4:06, Kirsta, Bryce, Teagan, and I would have been right there when the explosions occurred! Had we not secured the VIP passes, Kirsta, Bryce, and Teagan would have been right there next to the bomb!

Water steamed from the showerhead, but I shivered anyway.

After a few minutes, the water did more than wash off the sweat and stink; it cleansed my brain of the negativity. I focused on positive thoughts—because of my personal-record time, the VIP passes, and Bryce's decision, we were safe.

After the shower break and with my phone charged, I had another interview, this one on KOA's sister-station KHOW. The interviewer was former FEMA director-turned-radio-host Michael Brown—yep, the guy to whom President Bush said, "You're doing a heckuva job, Brownie" during the Hurricane Katrina mess in New Orleans. In a situation like this, though, I wasn't going to make any political judgments. I just wanted to tell my story.

Brown asked some terrific, probing questions related to trauma, my family, my response, the police response, and any photos/videos we took as potential evidence.

After thirteen minutes, I pushed the red "end call" button on my phone. Its battery had recharged, but mine was drained. The snacks at the hotel had provided some immediate energy, but all of us needed dinner—some real food. Although my body was dragging, I ventured outside to find a pizza place I knew of just one block away.

So, I ended up conducting my final interview on the street. This conversation was on television, with a host on the opposite side of the political spectrum from Michael Brown—Chris Hayes, who had a talk show on MSNBC. Again, not carrying about politics, I just wanted to tell the amazing story of the rapid response by the medical personnel.

As I strolled down Cambridge Street, the police presence was obvious outside Mass Gen, where many of the victims had been taken. I could only imagine what occurred inside the hospital, now nearly six hours after the explosions.

Security was tight around Massachusetts General Hospital when we returned to our hotel across the street in the Beacon Hill area of Boston.

I experienced a long delay on the phone to talk with Hayes. Kindly, a producer kept coming on the phone and apologizing for the delay. Sad and disappointed that my pizza delivery to Kirsta and the kids had been delayed, I alternated between pacing, stretching and hanging out on a bench in a pocket park across the street from the pizza restaurant.

Finally, after an interview with a former FBI agent, Hayes came on the phone and I was on live on TV sets across the country, and perhaps internationally. The interview was short with few questions, so I used my time to heap praise on the response team who dealt so capably and professionally with the disaster.

After hanging up, I crossed the street, exhausted, and entered the small restaurant. Maybe ten people sat inside eating. Though

I am sure they all had their own stories to tell from the day's tragedy, the scene looked so ordinary that it struck me as bizarre. I paused to ponder. "Hunh, I was just chatting on a national TV show, and now I am calmly ordering slices of pizza." It was just that kind of day.

I grabbed the food and walked back to the hotel. My legs were amazingly spry after all the miles they'd traveled. Those back-to-back runs at Pikes Peak had prepared me well.

I breathed a deep sigh of relief as Kirsta opened the hotel room door. I locked the door behind me and at last, it was time to eat and decompress.

As a parent, you don't want your child to watch bad movies or war scenes on TV. But there aren't really guidelines for how to cope when your children have experienced a terrorist attack first-hand. Baby Teagan remained blissfully unaware of anything. At age three, Bryce was more aware, but he remained cool—like a cucumber, as the saying goes. He knew there had been an explosion and he was confident that everyone was okay because they had gone to the hospital and gotten Band-Aids. Bryce made me very proud.

So, we kept the TV on as we ate, partially because we needed to know if the airport would be open the next day for us to fly home, but also because Kirsta and I desperately needed to know what was going on. A suspect remained at-large. We were safely in our hotel room, but we were near the city's largest trauma hospital and only blocks from the state capitol. It seemed premature to assume we were in the clear. Could something else still be planned?

At 10:36 p.m. EDT, we all finally settled down with the lights out, and I made a final Facebook post for the day:

Thanks to everyone for their prayers and wishes. I was in the medical tent when the explosions occurred, so I saw the carnage first-hand. Not going to describe. Kirsta and the kids had left the VIP bleacher seats across the street, so they were safe at the hotel, and we exchanged texts quickly. The parents and boyfriend of an EndAlz teammate had just left the area when she crossed the finish line. Scary. Please continue to pray for the victims, their families, and investigators.

CHAPTER 23

GETTING HOME

I slept solidly for six hours. I didn't even move until I woke up around six o'clock Tuesday morning. Kirsta and the kids still slept soundly. A fan in the corner provided a soft noise blanket over the room. After the commotion of the last twenty-four hours, the peace comforted me as I gently stretched my muscles, being careful not to disturb Bryce, lying next to me.

I couldn't help but smile. Not only had I run the Boston Marathon, but I had also cracked the magical four-hour mark—in front of my adorable little family. I allowed myself to be proud for a few minutes before the harsh reality of yesterday's events overcame me. Three people had died in the explosions, hundreds were injured, and thousands were reeling from the impact. My mind cycled through so many *what ifs*.

Worse still, whoever committed these atrocities remained on the loose. I looked down at Bryce's sleeping form, and for a moment I wanted never to leave the safety and comfort of our hotel room.

Nonetheless, because KOA wanted to interview me on their morning show, to which I listened on my drive to work, I slid out of bed, threw on some casual clothes, and snuck out of the room, easing the large door closed behind me.

My calf muscles had tightened overnight, so I eased down the stairs, hoping to find a quiet place to talk. The hotel's business center was empty, so first I logged on to an actual computer to do some real typing. My fingers were tired of tapping away at the tiny buttons on my phone.

I responded to the most urgent emails and changed my out-of-office email message to reflect our status. The exact words:

> *I am currently out of the office after having completed the Boston Marathon. My family and I are safe and hope to return to Denver on Tuesday. Thank you for your prayers and wishes.*

The interview with KOA's April Zesbaugh on Colorado's Morning News was terrific. They have some great hosts on that station, and I appreciated how they handled me professionally yet compassionately.

As I checked Facebook, I saw a message from James Kyhn, a Lincoln, Nebraska, morning-show disc jockey. He asked if I'd be willing to be interviewed on the radio. Kyhn, who goes by JP on air, is a fellow graduate of Crete High School and a former player on a baseball team I had coached. I was happy to oblige.

We quickly connected, and within minutes I was chatting with him and his sidekick Lauren on the radio. I felt honored to share my experience with listeners in my homeland of southeast Nebraska. Outside of family, this was my first post-marathon conversation with someone I knew, even if it had been a few years since we had last talked. I felt my tension ease away as I chatted with a familiar voice.

Then, two television stations in Denver wanted interviews, so I talked with their morning show hosts. I am pleased to say that in all these interviews, I plugged the Alzheimer's Association, so at least something positive came out of this horrible tragedy.

At some point during all of this, I discovered that a

representative from NBC's Today Show had texted me. She asked if they could send a crew to record an interview with me, but I declined. I was worn out, and I wanted to focus on my family.

Back in the room, the family had awakened during my sixty-minute absence. I finished my packing as Kirsta left for a final Dunkin' Donuts coffee. Like many buildings in Boston, our hotel was in lockout mode. To regain entry, she was required to show her photo identification, which, thankfully, she had in her pocketbook with her. The mood throughout town was still serious.

We weren't sure what the situation would be at the airport. So, though our flight wasn't scheduled to depart until 2:15 p.m., we arrived several hours early. To our surprise, we made it to the airport and through security with no hassles. We were shocked that we were able to do curbside baggage check, but it also felt good to see that authorities continued business as usual at such a high-profile location.

Once we cleared airport security, I had another phone interview to conduct—this one with Heather Draper, a reporter with the *Denver Business Journal*. Heather summarized my story in a succinct report that ran in the DBJ daily email. Her writing connected the Denver business community to the attacks in a manner few would have expected. While the explosions occurred nearly 2,000 miles away, one of those affected was a guy who worked in downtown Denver with other business executives.

Talking with another Denver person left me homesick, and I was ready to return to Colorado. First, though, we needed lunch. To get from our gate to the food court required navigating a large flight of stairs—probably about thirty steps total. I was so stiff that I had serious trouble getting up and down those stairs. After all that I'd encountered, those stairs served as my final Boston obstacle.

I found comfort at Burger King and devoured a double bacon cheeseburger and fries as Kirsta and Bryce ate their lunch. At last, we boarded our plane back to Denver. Even as I rejoiced to be going home, I hated to leave Boston when I knew the city was hurting, but it would have been foolish for us to miss our flight.

The return trip was uneventful, and in-flight I crafted the words I wanted to post on Facebook, which I did when we landed at 5:29 p.m. MDT.

Physically in Denver, heart still in Boston.

Upon arrival at DIA, I decided I would not go to the office the next day. In the terminal, I conducted an on-camera interview with the local Fox affiliate as we waited for our bags to arrive. Then we grabbed some food at an airport restaurant—Taco Bell, Bryce's favorite. After running so many miles and going through such a stressful twenty-four-hour period, I had no qualms about eating some not-so-healthy comfort food. After all, "I run so I can eat—more."

From the comfort of our home, I made a final Facebook post at 9:24 p.m.: "So, after several exhausting days, I am slowly catching up on phone messages, emails, texts, and Facebook comments. Thanks for your prayers, thoughts, and patience."

As I settled down for the night, my phone buzzed. Veteran Alzheimer's Association team member Ted Lombardi had crafted an email for the team, which read in part:

> *Thank you all for your commitment, your friendship, and your inspiration. Soon I'll remember those things much more than the evil that happened on Boylston.*
>
> *Peace,*
> *Teddy*

CHAPTER 24

LOCKDOWN

In the words of my wife, "Normal never felt so good."

A night in our own beds. Teagan rolling around on the floor, her eyes following big brother Bryce playing with his toys. Sunshine pouring through the windows of our mountain home on a beautiful Wednesday morning.

*Teagan watches Bryce play on the iPad on the floor of our home—
a nice, quiet break after the chaos of Boston.*

Miles away from Boston, I consumed the continuing coverage on the national news networks. I was concerned for the whole city, but especially for my teammates who lived in Massachusetts and had to go about their lives knowing that a terrorist remained among them.

As investigators released information, we saw that the FBI asked those who had been close to the scene to send any photos to a specially established email address. Somewhat humorous, and also frustrating, Kirsta had few photos because she literally had her hands full in the bleachers. The photos she'd tried to take of me crossing the finish line barely included the top of my head and part of my back. Also, the images focused on the finish line, and the explosions occurred just a few yards to the west.

Nonetheless, when I spoke with an FBI representative on the phone, she requested that we send the pictures to them because, "You just never know." That makes sense, especially now, knowing that videos and photos showed the terrorists walking toward the scene.

Then, later in the morning, Erica, my Boston teammate who had secured the VIP passes for us, sent this email.

Hi Greg,

I hope this message finds you home safely in Colorado. When I heard of the bomb while running on the course, my first thought was of your family in the bleachers. I was happy to read your email that everyone was ok and had left the bleachers before the explosion.

The FBI is asking for the names, phone numbers, and email addresses of everyone that had a pass to the bleachers. They are also asking additional details, such as if they were there during the explosion and if they are under age 12. This is not because anyone is a suspect, but part of the process of putting details together and seeing if anyone may have seen something.

When you have a moment, please email me everyone's full name and the contact info for your wife. I'm sorry to have to request this from you. I hope you understand that the request is coming from the FBI, as they are trying to find who caused such a dreadful event.

Best,
Erica

Erica is a humble and kind person, so she guffaws when I describe her as a lifesaver. Yes, we did eventually win additional VIP bleacher passes from the Alzheimer's Association, but it was her VIP passes that allowed us to make advanced arrangements for my family to be on the south side of Boylston. I know in my heart that if we had not had those passes, Kirsta, Bryce, and Teagan would have been on the north side near the finish line. That's how supportive my wife is.

I struggle to picture the scene: a woman carrying a baby and tethering a toddler on her arm when a bomb explodes feet away from them. Would have they been injured? Would they have been detained? Would Kirsta have been able to re-connect with me?

Even with the VIP passes, Kirsta and the kids could easily have been directly across from the first explosion. What if my stomach had not settled down, and I'd needed to use the restroom? What if Bryce had elected to stay in the bleachers instead of going to the hotel reception? What if I had not run with my phone, or if

Kirsta had not gotten my first text message?

Kirsta and I shudder at the thoughts.

I will remain forever indebted to Erica.

Erica and everyone else in Boston remained on high alert that Tuesday. The tension in the city was palpable. Various news reports indicated possible suspects and even stated some were in custody, but authorities emphatically denied this news.

Boston remained on edge into Wednesday. I tried to bring some normalcy back to my life by returning to the office. Of course, many people wanted to express their concern—coworkers stopping by and phone calls and emails from friends and business contacts. This made me recognize that I needed to write a full description of my experience, which I did in the days ahead—and which became the precursor to this book.

Wednesday, April 18, brought big news. At 5:00 p.m. EDT, the FBI held a news conference regarding the bombing investigation. Eyes from around the country tuned in as authorities released video of two suspects—one wearing a white ball cap, the other a black ball cap—walking down Boylston Street, each carrying a large backpack.

I'm not going to recount details of the investigation, but I will say it sparked an amazing forty-eight hours in Boston. When police located the two suspects, it was in Watertown—home of the Massachusetts/New Hampshire chapter of the Alzheimer's Association. As most people know, police shot Tamerlan Tsarnaev, who then was run over by a car driven by his brother. He died at the scene at age twenty-six.

His brother, Dzhokhar Tsarnaev, navigated past police officers and escaped into the community. Unsure of his status or plans, Boston authorities issued a shelter-in-place notification for Thursday, April 19. This essentially shut down the entire metro area. With few vehicles on the highway, no mass transit operating, and only a handful of people walking the streets, Boston looked like a ghost town. The Common, recently filled with thousands of people for the marathon, sat empty.

After an unsuccessful home-by-home search in the Watertown area, authorities lifted the shelter-in-place order at approximately 6:00 p.m. EDT. Soon after, a Watertown citizen noticed that the boat cover in his backyard was askew. While checking it a second time, he noticed blood—and a body moving slowly on the floor. He called 911, and law enforcement surrounded the younger Tsnarnaev brother.

I watched, horrified, as this all unfolded on TV. It felt like a Cops episode that went on for several days. But, I was shocked to hear that my Alzheimer's teammate Jeremy experienced some of it firsthand. Here are his words, captured from two separate emails that he sent to marathon team members:

Email after the marathon—

I am still in disbelief of everything that happened yesterday. Being 100 feet from the explosions and seeing the chaos I am so happy to hear that everyone is safe and sound. With the cell phones being shut down yesterday, It was a scary hour trying to locate my family as they were all at various spots along the finish line, but everyone is ok.

Email after the suspect was in custody—

For many of you who don't know, I live in Watertown. My house looks down Franklin Street, near the house with the boat. The suspect abandoned the hijacked Mercedes SUV close to my house, and probably ran through my yard to get to his place of hiding. Very scary to think about. You can only imagine what I witnessed/heard from 1 a.m. Friday morning until the capturing.

What an astonishing sequence of events. However, that night, for the first time in nearly one week, I relaxed for a peaceful night's sleep.

In the words of the Boston Police Department Twitter account, "The terror is over."

CHAPTER 25

COPING

I knew the phrase PTSD, but I only associated it with war veterans. After all, who would not experience Post-Traumatic Stress Disorder after seeing bombs explode, people covered in blood, and individuals with severed limbs? As I wrote my synopsis in the days after the marathon and the explosions, I realized I had PTSD.

On a scale of one to ten, with ten being the most intense, I would describe my stress level as three or four, at worst. I wasn't feeling PTSD 24/7, but even simple events would trigger a flashback. April has always been a favorite month since spring brings the return of baseball. But, as I sat in the Coors Field outfield celebrating 2014 opening day, fireworks exploded over my head during the singing of the National Anthem. My body trembled, and a tingling sensation lingered until first pitch.

Although telling the story of what happened that day was tough, I found it therapeutic. From emails and websites, I learned that other runners faced similar challenges; we were not physically injured, but we carried emotional scars.

A few weeks after the marathon, I participated in a webcast hosted by the Massachusetts Resiliency Center. It was organized by the Boston Medical Center to provide "a safe, welcoming space for survivors of the Boston Marathon bombing to heal and stay in touch with one another; a virtual hub for a widely dispersed community whose lives have been impacted by the tragic events of April 15th and the events that followed." While the webcast didn't offer any new information, it confirmed that my emotions were normal. Knowledge that felt well worth the sixty minutes of participation.

One of the blessings that developed from that April 15 marathon was my new friendship with Julie Kelada, the runner I had taken under my wing after the explosions. I hadn't heard from her since we parted at the bag pick-up buses. On April 20, I scrolled through my text messages—still trying to catch up—and noticed the messages I'd sent to her friend and her husband. Curious to know how Julie was doing, I texted George. I received a message back almost immediately:

"So glad to hear from you, Greg! Since Julie's been home I've had the chance to hear the full story of how you stuck by her as though she was a family member during the horrifying chaos after the bombs went off. She refers to you as her 'angel Greg.' We are eternally grateful for your calm strength, courage, and kindness. I learned of the explosions via your text (I thought your spell check had corrected the word exhaustion). Your text spared me the worry I would've otherwise felt had I learned of the attack before knowing Julie was safe."

I shared my written summary of the marathon and its aftermath with Julie and George, and Julie responded soon via text and email:

> *I am going to write down my own story soon. You are a key angel in my story. I am forever grateful you did not leave me, and I am looking forward to speaking soon. Thank you for sharing your story. I will look forward to talking to you and actually*

telling you my story. Your family forever will be in
my heart!!

Thank you!!!!!
Julie

I also learned that the Kelada family had a trip to Colorado planned for later in 2013. They were spending a week at a camp hosted by Young Life, a Christian organization that Julie participated in as a child. The camp was outside Buena Vista, about ninety miles southwest of our house.

The most direct driving route to the camp was via a highway past our house. On their way back to the airport on July 6, the Kelada family visited. Less than three months after Julie and I met under miserable conditions, we reconnected and had the honor of meeting each other's families on a beautiful summer day.

Kirsta made lunch, and after we ate, we shared our stories from April 15 as we stretched out in our living room. Their children, Wyatt and Elle (like ours, their first a boy and their second a girl), are more than five years older than ours. Despite their age differences, the kids played with each other like they'd been best friends forever. We bonded in a way that two terrorists could never imagine. Those two SOBs wanted to blow us apart; instead, they brought us closer together.

Julie Kelada became a friend for life after we met in the finish line medical tent. Kirsta and I were happy to host her and her family at our house in July 2013.—photo by George Kelada

Alas, the Kelada family had a plane to catch, so after photos on the deck, we said our goodbyes. While I still feel like I could have done more on April 15, I know that for one family, and specifically one individual, what I did do was more than sufficient.

Noises like those from fireworks and cannons can still alarm me. I notice unattended backpacks and do not hesitate to find a police officer to investigate. Paranoid? Yep. But I will do everything in my power to prevent others from experiencing what I did.

At the same time, I am going to live my life as free as ever. When we stop doing things out of fear, that's when the terrorists win. And I don't want the terrorists to win.

CHAPTER 26

LOOSE ENDS

I didn't get my finisher's medal.

Because I went to the medical tent after crossing the finish line, I didn't receive the honor of a volunteer placing the medal around my neck. For the first few days, I wasn't concerned.

But once the suspects had been arrested, my brain turned to unfinished business, including my medal. For the first time in my running career, I'd run a sub-4:00 and I wanted that important memento.

My teammates were aware of my situation and that I lived halfway across the country. So, on April 23, Dale Ann Eckert forwarded me an email from the Boston Athletic Association indicating that persons with proper identification would be able to pick up their medals and unclaimed checked bags. Teammate Erica, who lived close to the BAA office, offered to pick up the goods for both Dale Ann and me.

After picking up my medal, Erica joked about selling my medal on eBay. But she reassured me that she would to ship it to our house for free, courtesy of "Your Friends in Boston" (remembering what I had typed when I made the donation for the VIP passes). What a generous act from a kind person.

It took several weeks after I finished the marathon with a personal record, but I finally got my medal, thanks to my teammate Erica.

I still missed out on one thing. In the days just before the marathon, we learned that Joey McIntyre, of New Kids on the Block fame, would be joining our Alzheimer's Association team. Joey's mom was battling Alzheimer's (she has since died), and he ran the marathon in an Alzheimer's singlet. He was scheduled to stop by the reception at the Westin hotel, but after narrowly missing the explosions himself (he finished in 3:57:06), none of us got to meet him. Maybe a rematch, Joey? After all, I did beat you by a solid fifty-seven seconds!

Although I missed out on meeting a celebrity, my experience created ripple effects.

In the months following my participation in the Boston Marathon, my cousin Brian Reetz signed up to run his first marathon in Lincoln. He pledged to run the 26.2 miles to raise funds to battle Parkinson's, a disease affecting his mom.

Then, Iowa friend and school principal, Dominic Giegerich, landed a spot in the 2014 Boston Marathon as part of a team raising funds to conquer Rhett's Syndrome, which a girl in his school district was battling. Both guys said they were inspired by my run and efforts to raise money for the Alzheimer's Association. I felt like a high school coach witnessing one of his players advance to playing the sport in college—flattered and proud.

Also flattering was the article that *The Crete News* editor Jenn Lampila wrote in the April 23 edition of the weekly publication. I've often labeled myself as a naïve, small-town Nebraska boy, and this incident illustrated that better than anything. Of all the things that I expected and planned for during my Boston Marathon preparations, none of them included a terrorist attack. I am grateful to Jenn for sharing my story in my hometown— illustrating that anything can happen to anyone, regardless of where you're from. Of note: Jenn's article later won an award from the Nebraska Press Association.

I had not exchanged any information with the woman who bought one of our extra VIP passes, but I did with Jeff, whose wife also ran in wave three. The morning after the marathon, Jeff texted my cell phone, wanting to make sure that we were okay. His wife was approaching the twenty-six-mile mark when the explosions occurred—meaning that Jeff sat in the bleachers directly across from the first blast. Jeff later emailed me, "I always believe that meeting you most likely saved me from injury."

I appreciated his checking in with us and was horrified to see the pictures that he shared—visuals of what my family would have witnessed had Bryce elected to stay and watch more runners.

My shoes and bib from the 2013 Boston Marathon. After this photo, I now take a picture after each timed run of my shoes, bib number and medal from each competition.

We continued to hear how other runners and their family and friends were affected by the explosions. My Alzheimer's Association teammates shared their stories via an email chain, and this response from Trish Reske on Sunday, April 21, 2013, made me so proud:

> *Hi Greg,*
>
> *Wow, your story is incredible. I came in just minutes before you and hightailed it to the Westin (making a sneak exit out by the medical tents to save time).*

I was with your wife and kids in the room at the Westin. She seemed, in retrospect, amazingly calm, given your account of events.

For us locals, well, the drama continued, as you know. And the Alzheimer's Association, based in Watertown, was at the center of the manhunt.

I am thankful to have finished 15 minutes before my planned time—a new record. My family, like yours, left the finish area after they saw me pass.

Thanks again. I hope you will be back,
Trish

Within a few weeks of April 15, I knew it would be hard not to go back. Honestly, I'd planned for a one-and-done with the Boston Marathon. Our 2013 trip cost us several thousand dollars. But now, I couldn't end my participation with the bombings as my final impression. I needed more-positive closure, and I started the process one morning on my drive to work.

In the early morning hour, I was listening to radio station KOA, like I always do on my commute, when April Zesbaugh read a news report regarding Dzhokhar Tsarnaev. Anger surged up inside me at the sound of his name, anger at what he had done. But it hit me—what good would it do to maintain this hatred in my heart? Wasn't it hatred that caused him to create the bombs in the first place? There, in my truck, driving to Denver on Highway 285, I forgave him.

Tragedy comes in so many forms. For us, it had been a raging forest fire near our house, the sudden death of a family member, the diagnosis of a mind-changing, fatal disease in another family member, a bodily collision with a vehicle, and a terrorist attack during a fun, vulnerable event. It's too easy to live in fear of these events, or in sadness when they happen. Instead, my family and I overcome, persevere, and celebrate. Life is full of choices, and I choose to be happy.

Driving toward the northeast, I saw the sun peeking above the horizon. It was going to be a fantastic morning for a run.

GOING BACK

I had to go back.

In the weeks and months after the explosions, I paid more attention to the Boston news than I did to Denver's. I devoured the continued investigation into the why and how of the bombings. In the Mile High City, my friends and business acquaintances wanted to hear about my experience, and I retold the story over and over, each time trembling as I acknowledged how close we were to the situation.

Months later, I faced a dilemma. One of my favorite baseball teams, the St. Louis Cardinals, was facing the Boston Red Sox in the World Series. On a whim, I'd secured tickets, thanks again to my friends in the baseball world, and flown to St. Louis to catch Game Four of the showdown. When Kolten Wong was picked off first base to end the game, giving the Red Sox the victory and tying the series 2-2, I couldn't help smiling. As much as I wanted the Cardinals to win, deep down I knew that a Sox title would help Boston recover. Days later, tears brimmed in my eyes as the Red Sox team stopped on Boylston Street with the World Series trophy to honor the victims of the bombings.

Jason Kramer, a native of the St. Louis area, is an Alzheimer's Association teammate who is also Cardinals fan. He flew from Boston to St. Louis to meet me for Game 4 of the 2013 World Series, Red Sox at Cardinals.

Sadly, despite the fantastic (for me) Boston Marathon finishing time, I was nowhere near a qualifying time to return, so when the Alzheimer's Association sent the email in fall 2013 asking for 2014 applicants, I knew I would have to up my game—specifically, my fundraising goal—to stand out from what was sure to be a record number of applicants. Runners were mad that terrorists had attacked their turf, and we wanted to reclaim the finish line.

Having run 2013 in honor of my mother, I developed a new number and plan to return for 2014. I turned my children's birthdates (12/10/09 and 11/10/12) into dollar amounts ($12,100.90 and $11,101.20) and combined into my goal: $21,222.10. The Alzheimer's Association received many applicants, and I was elated to be one of twelve accepted for the team.

I received more than $24,000 in donations, which was only

good for fourth-place fundraiser that year since the team set a new record, raising more than $400,000. My family and I returned to the East Coast in April 2014, ready to bring joy back to the Boston Marathon.

After arriving in Boston late Friday night, I woke up early Saturday and met my new teammate Brady Hoover and his now-wife Grace to take the subway to the convention center to pick up our bib packets. Without thinking about where I was, I climbed the subway stairs to the street. The first thing I saw was the medical tent on Boylston Street. I started shaking as we walked down the street to the finish line.

At the location of the first explosion, I squatted and gently placed my fingers on the spot that had been covered in flesh and blood one year earlier. Brady took my phone and snapped a picture as I knelt, my eyes red and tearful. I spent a minute in prayer and reflection, still unable to comprehend how someone could cause so much harm to innocent people.

I have toured many memorials, but visiting the site of the first explosion of the Boston Marathon bombing was personal and overwhelming.

Thankfully, the 5K run started then, so we headed to the convention center to watch the runners pass as we waited for the doors to open. After exchanging lots of handshakes, hugs, and stories, we took a group photo and made our way to the packet-pickup tables. I spent a little time milling about the convention hall exhibits then hustled back to the hotel because Bryce and I were going to the Red Sox game, of course.

By coincidence, a promotion at the Red Sox game that
Bryce and I attended in 2014 allowed us to go on the infield warning
track before the game. Here we are in front of the famous Fenway Park
Green Monster, the huge wall in left field.

Finally, Monday, April 21 arrived. I woke at four o'clock to get to the Westin hotel for a 5:15 meet time with my teammates. Serendipitously, I took the same route as last year. The Common was already a flurry of activity, and security was tight in the area around the finish line and medical tent.

Although I sensed some apprehension after last year's bombings, the overall mood was lighthearted in the hotel conference room. The morning was beautiful, and we were ready to run a marathon. Promptly at 5:45, our bus left Boston, and forty-five minutes later we arrived in Hopkinton. Athletes' Village had an increased security presence, too, with metal detectors at entrances and police vehicles lining the perimeter.

Since I and most of my non-qualified teammates were not scheduled to run until eleven, we found ways to hang out for nearly four hours. I'd lined up a handful of media interviews, so that helped keep me busy. At last, ten thirty rolled around, and we headed to the starting line.

My running jersey again bore the names of my donors, and this year I had a special addition: a B-Strong patch, one like the Red Sox and the Kansas City Royals had worn in the first game at Fenway Park following the explosions in 2013. My baseball friend Chris pulled some strings and secured a patch for me. Waiting in the starting corral, I fingered the patch on my left chest, close to my heart, giving thanks for my supporters and praying for a safe, happy race.

After the countdown, we were off. Energy coursed through my legs, and I ran at a solid pace. The miles ticked off, and I reached the halfway point in 1:54. Once again, the Alzheimer's Association had a huge cheering section at 16.5, which inspired me as before.

Heading through mile seventeen, I was on track for a 3:48 finish when I realized the temperature was getting warm. I was getting warm. And people around me were starting to cramp.

I contemplated. *Should I run hard to try to break 4:00 again, and possibly end up in the medical tent like last year, or back off my pace and just absorb the Boston Marathon?*

Seconds later, I called my wife to tell her that I was slowing down, so my finish would be later than what I'd originally anticipated. Soon after, a spectator offered some potato chips, and I snarfed them down—the salt hit the spot. Then, I realized my Gu packets were nastily warm, and I was hungry for real food. When I called out to the crowd, "Does anyone have a cheeseburger?" a man greeted me at the end of his driveway with a turkey sandwich. I took half and munched for the next half-mile before I spotted a young lady eating frozen yogurt. When I asked for a bite, she kindly shoved a spoonful into my mouth.

The chocolate hit the spot, so I thought, *why not?* and asked the next group for a cookie . . . which I was photographed eating a few steps down the road.

As I munched on a cookie during the 2014 marathon, I could not believe photographers were ahead. So, I embraced the opportunity and proudly displayed my snack!

Finally, I decided to get a bit more serious and picked up the pace again. However, I still had fun, taking lots of pictures, including some selfies, and videos along the race course. The temperature continued to rise, so I dumped cups of water on my head at each water station. This washed off my sunscreen, so my hairless head ended up a bit red by the end of the day.

The final few miles of the Boston Marathon were, simply put, awesome. The crowd was incredible and, with my name on the shirt, chants of "Greg!" were inspiring and welcome. The jog down Commonwealth, past the location where many runners were stopped last year, was breathtaking. I pumped my fist as I made the turn onto Hereford and then the left onto Boylston for the final 0.2 miles. I stopped for a selfie with the finish line in the background, then turned on my phone's video recorder and moved it side to side to record this run forever.

As I neared the finish line, I checked behind me before coming to a complete stop in front of my family in the grandstands, almost exactly where they were last year, thanks again to teammate Erica. I signed an emotional "Love you" and then pocketed my phone for my venture across the finish line, roughly 4:27 after I'd started.

*After stumbling across the finish line in 2013, I finished the
2014 Boston Marathon at a slower pace but much more cognizant of
my surroundings, video recording my run down Boylston Street
and waving and smiling to my family.*

This year, I crossed happily, and instead of being rolled into the
medical tent, I exchanged high fives with attendants. I purposively
strolled to the medals where a volunteer placed one around my
neck.

I took a side exit for a shortcut to the Westin hotel, where the atmosphere was tremendously upbeat after last year's tension. Cowbells clanged and voices exclaimed as each team member entered the room, having reclaimed the finish line.

The morning after the race, my family and I met up with Julie, the North Carolina runner whom I'd befriended in the medical tent during last year's chaos. She and her friends had also returned to Boston, running 26.2 miles and reclaiming the finish line. This year, we celebrated.

ACKNOWLEDGEMENTS

The process of writing this book was about as challenging as the adventures in the book. I am eternally grateful to my wife for her patience in all of my crazy endeavors, and to my children, Bryce and Teagan, for surrendering time with Dad so I could write.

I was naïve heading into the publishing process and appreciate the guidance from fellow mountain author Kirstin Pulioff. Thanks for all of the advice, Ms. P!

Many thanks to Catherine Jones Payne of Quill Pen Editorial and Melinda Martin of Martin Publishing Services. This book would still be on my laptop without your assistance.

Thank you to the Massachusetts / New Hampshire Chapter of the Alzheimer's Association for selecting me (twice) to run the Boston Marathon. Thanks to the teammates who made my experience so awesome!

I remain appreciative to everyone who donated on my behalf to the Alzheimer's Association in 2013 and 2014 while I participated in the Boston Marathon. If we keep trying, we will EndAlz.

When I decided to publish this book, many individuals stepped up with contributions to defray much of the upfront hard costs. Thanks for helping make the book become reality.

Thank you to the staff of the Jefferson County Public Library. I am grateful for your immediate feedback when I was writing in your branches.

To the throngs of people who line the Boston Marathon route each Patriots' Day—we runners hear you and know you are there, even when we don't acknowledge you! Thanks for the amazing support.

For every bombing victim, survivor and their families—you are always in my prayers. May good prevail.

GREG KALKWARF

Was That Thunder? is Greg Kalkwarf's first published book. A Nebraska native, Greg has completed ten marathons in Colorado, Florida, Massachusetts and Nebraska.

Greg has a story for each run, and for many other of life's events. He is available to share those stories as a speaker for audiences of any size.

Learn more:

www.gregkalkwarf.com

Contact:

Email: gregkalkwarf@gmail.com
Twitter: @gkalkwarf
Facebook: @OfficialGregKalkwarf

As Carey examined the seam, his smirk of triumph faded to a baffled frown. "I don't understand. She hasn't mended it at all. Why I can still put my fist through the tear." He did so to prove his point.

The surcoat began to quiver, then to emit gruff choking noises. While they exchanged alarmed glances, Austyn turned the garment, displaying its back for all of them to see.

Sewn across the broad shoulders of the garment in delicate stitches that must have taken exquisite workmanship and an even greater surfeit of patience was an intricate border of glossy green ivy.

Austyn chuckled ruefully as he wiped his streaming eyes. "It never occurred to me that our definitions of *needlework* might vary to such a degree. God, if I'd have known having a wife was going to be so damned amusing, I'd have sought one long ago!"

Hugging the garment to his chest, he threw back his head and roared with laughter.

The others might have joined in had they not been stunned to silence by a shock even more keen than that they'd felt upon witnessing Austyn giving vent to that infamous Gavenmore temper he kept under such rigid control. They'd seen rare flares of rage before, but it had been twenty long years since they'd heard the music of their master's unbridled mirth.

Chapter 15

From that day forward, Sir Austyn was rarely seen in any other surcoat but the crimson one with the delicate chain of ivy emblazoned so boldly upon its shoulders. To Winnie's chagrin, he refused to let her mend the torn seam, preferring to expose the tunic beneath rather than risk offending his bride.

His extravagant praise of Holly's handiwork was so convincing that within a week, a majority of his tunics, his surcoats, and even his stockings, sported frivolous chains of daisies, plump bouquets of posies, and tiny pink butterflies flitting from hem to cuff. He finally begged Carey to help him hide the surcoat he wore in battle, fearing his industrious wife might embroider a meadow of hollyhocks on its padded chest while he slept.

Faced with the daunting challenge of becoming mistress of her husband's castle, Holly came to the humbling realization that she had been trained to be a bride, not a wife. She could sing a complicated round of "Sumer is Icumen In" in perfect pitch and dance a sprightly carol with nary a stumble, yet she was helpless to master the intricacies of baking a loaf of bread over the kitchen fire. Her flaming puddings fizzled. Her mulled wine soured. Her cream curdled.

Winifred took to keeping a bucket of well water by the hearth to extinguish the daily blazes ignited by her efforts. Emrys trailed behind her in the garden, digging up the hemlock and nightshade she inadvertently planted among the neat rows of sage and thyme.

Rather than reproving her for her incompetence, Austyn greeted all of her domestic tragedies with profound interest and a fond

144

tweak of her nose.

After soaking several pairs of her husband's hose in a vat of boiling water, shrinking them to the size of sausage casings, she earned a disbelieving bark of laughter from Carey upon informing him with a yearning sigh, "Your master must truly be a saint. He has no temper to speak of, does he?"

It was Winifred, desperate for a reprieve, who finally shoved a wooden bucket and a handful of rags into Holly's eager hands. Delighted to find something she could excel at, Holly devoted those first golden days of summer to restoring Caer Gavenmore to its former grandeur. She polished the brass torch holders until they gleamed, tore the cobwebs from every corner, and swept the flagstones clean.

'Twas a full fortnight before she screwed up the courage to attack the shadowy landing at the foot of the stairs winding up to the haunted tower. Her task brightened considerably after she broke out the rotted shutters that had sealed the gloom for nearly fifty years, flooding the landing with sunlight and sweetening the stale air with summer's breath. She batted her way through a dervish of dust motes, then dropped to her knees to scrub the wooden planking, thinking how her papa would chuckle if he could see his "wittle angel" now.

Her days were no longer filled with trivial amusements and desultory boredom, but with hard work and satisfying results. Instead of tossing restlessly in her bed at night, plagued by nameless yearning, she slept deeply, dreaming of the day when she would coax her husband to surrender his heart. She no longer felt like a canary trapped in a gilded cage, but like a graceful curlew gliding high over the river Wye at sunset, free to pursue its dreams.

Austyn was warming to her as slowly but undeniably as the black Welsh soil was warming to the summer sun. His boyish grins had grown more frequent, his silences less brooding. And even more promising, she'd not seen him slip his hand into his tunic to finger

145

that elusive token of his lady's love for nearly a sennight.

Charming a man without twirling a spiral curl around a crimson fingernail or puckering her rouged lips in an inviting moue had proved an even greater challenge than molding beeswax candles that did not go limp at the first kiss of flame. Yet Holly had embraced the challenge, savoring each tiny victory — each fleeting glimpse of the dimple that softened the rugged angle of her husband's jaw — as a herald of a more lasting triumph.

She sank back on her haunches to rub a trickle of sweat from her brow. Exertion had warmed her, only making the icy prickle at her nape more pronounced. She swiveled to peer at the yawning mouth of the stairwell. No amount of sunshine could banish the miasma of despondency that seemed to come rippling down the narrow stairs like a pool of tears.

Holly rose to her feet, sternly reminding herself that her disquiet was only a childish fancy. She'd already banished one of the legendary ghosts of Caer Gavenmore, proving the eerie rattling in the south corridor to be nothing more than the mischievous bobbing of an iron candelabra designed to be raised and lowered on chains for ease of lighting. She crept toward the stairwell, refusing to be cowed by a growing sense of unease.

Resting her foot gingerly on the first step, she peered upward into the shadows, knowing a door must be hidden just beyond the curve of the wall. Her spine tingled as a faint scraping sound reached her — like the desperate scrabbling of fingernails on wood.

"Mice," she muttered.

She climbed another step, brushing aside a veil of cobwebs. A musty breath of air, as fragile as a woman's sigh, struck her face, making her flinch.

"Naught but a stray draft," she pronounced, clenching her teeth to keep them from chattering.

As her foot came down upon the third step, a low-pitched dirge swelled around her, rising to a lamentation so keen it sliced Holly's tender heart to the quick. Clapping her hands over her ears to block out its sorrowful warning of broken promises and shattered hopes, she fled, kicking over the bucket as she went.

Austyn was in the solar, poring over a parchment scroll yellowed by age and neglect, when Holly went flying past the doorway, her face so pale she might have been one of the Gavenmore haunts. He rose from his chair, then forced himself back down.

He was getting as addled as his father, he thought, tempted to trail after his young bride like one of his own hounds besotted by a leg of mutton. He scowled at the mildewed plans for the completion of an outer curtain wall. His bride's unflagging exuberance must be wearing off on him. Not a stone had been lifted toward finishing Caer Gavenmore since that cold, rainy autumn of 1304, yet here he sat, daring to dream of castles in the clouds.

His restless gaze drifted to the door. Perhaps he'd do well to follow Holly and see what nonsense she was about today. He'd been reviewing the accounts with Emrys only yesterday morning when a shrill cacophony that sounded as if every demon in Christendom had been summoned down upon their heads had sent them all careening toward the south corridor. They had arrived to find Holly riding up and down on a rusted candelabra, squealing with glee at each dizzying ascent to the rafters.

Austyn had plucked her down the moment she came into arm's reach, choking his heart from his throat to deliver a stern lecture on the dangers of such reckless behavior. Her nose tilted at an unrepentant angle, she had vowed to take more care before offering the gentle suggestion that she might not have had to exorcise the ghost of his great-great-great grandfather's bride had the malicious old rogue not burned her at the stake.

Snapping the scroll shut, Austyn rose to his feet. He was not a man given to stealth, but it wasn't as if he were following Holly just to study the beguiling habit she had of tucking her little pink

147

tongue between her teeth when she was concentrating on some arduous task. Or to puzzle over the hint of gloss the morning sunlight evoked in her drab hair, as shimmering and elusive as a raven's wing.

Suppose she took a notion to ride the bucket down the castle well? Or curl up for a nap in the bowl of the catapult? Reassuring himself that a husbandly concern for his wife's well-being could hardly constitute spying, Austyn slipped from the solar, looking both ways before following in the path of Holly's rapid footsteps.

Some instinctive yearning for refuge drove Holly to the castle chapel. She dropped to her knees before the dusty altar and folded her trembling hands, offering up a wordless prayer for the restless soul of Austyn's grandmother. Apparently, the poor woman's plunge from the north tower window had failed to restore the freedom her vindictive husband had denied her.

Holly started violently as a hand came down upon her shoulder. "Praying for the soul of your pagan husband, my child?"

"Good Lord, Nate," she swore, scrambling to her feet to find the priest lurking behind her. "You frightened the devil out of me. What are you doing here?"

All it took was an acerbic roll of his eyes to make her realize the idiocy of her question. "I should have known you didn't come to seek me out. Why I'd almost suspect you've been avoiding me."

With his lean, wiry body blocking her retreat, all Holly could do was incline her head to avoid his eyes. "Please don't lecture me. I've no need of any more guilt to burden my soul."

"I've seen little enough evidence of a troubled conscience in the past fortnight. On the contrary, your behavior has been quite . . . shameless."

Holly lifted her head, unable to hide her hurt at the injustice of his accusation. Her retort died as the beams of sunlight slanting through the lancet windows revealed his haggard condition. His robes were rumpled, the hair around his tonsure disheveled. Shadows dwelt beneath his dark eyes.

She reached instinctively for his arm, distressed anew by the sharp angles of his bones beneath the nubby wool. "Have you been ill, Nathanael? You look terrible."

"Ah, but you don't, do you, child?" His benevolent smile chilled her. "Your lashes are growing. Your hair is beginning to curl. Your very teeth grow brighter with each besotted smile you bestow upon your lord." His gaze flicked to her bodice, lingering just long enough to make her face heat. " 'Twill be only a matter of time, I suppose, before even your tender young breasts begin to bud."

Holly withdrew her hand. "Don't be ridiculous. My new duties have consumed my attention. I haven't had time to darken my teeth or crop my lashes or . . . or —"

" 'Thou shalt not bear false witness!' " Nathanael thundered. "So cease your lying before you've more than just your unholy lust for a Welsh pagan to repent!"

Holly's first instinct to quail beneath his attack was supplanted by a stronger urge to lash out, to hurt him as he was hurting her. "What would you know of lust, *Brother?* Or of love for that matter? Of the tender devotion that can bind a woman to a man? A wife to her husband?" Holly had never meant to reveal so much, but the truth spilled over like a brimming teardrop, leaving her heart exposed and raw.

"Ah, 'tis worse than I feared. You fancy yourself in love with the churl when all you really desire is to feel his greedy hands pawing your naked flesh. To submit to the indignities of his animal lust!"

Holly's hand shot out, wiping the sneer from Nathanael's face with a single open-palmed blow. The color bled from his cheeks, leaving only the brand of her handprint. His eyes clouded with dazed hurt. His hands hung limp at his sides. The crumbling of his pious armor made him appear not only vulnerable but terribly young.

"Oh, Nathanael," Holly whispered, besieged by pity and remorse. She lifted a hand to his cheek as if the caress of her fingertips could somehow erase the damage they'd done. "Please forgive me. I'm so terribly sorry."

Neither one of them saw the man who slipped from the back of the chapel like an angel banished from the presence of God.

Chapter 16

Austyn rode.

The thunder of a man's rebuke. Fierce, impassioned words, pitched too low for his ears to decipher. A woman's response, her plea unintelligible, but trembling with fervent conviction. The unmistakable crack of a hand striking human flesh.

He had rushed forward then, prepared to do battle for his lady's sake, only to discover Holly, *his* Holly, with her palm pressed tenderly to a man's cheek. *His* Holly, begging prettily for a man's forgiveness. A man of God perhaps, but first and always, a man.

A veil of darkness had descended over his eyes. And he had flung himself on the bare back of his horse and rode.

Austyn rode until the silent bellow of rage trapped in his lungs subsided to ragged pants. He rode until his fists unclenched from their primal need to do harm. Until they surrendered the seductive temptation to smash and maim and utterly destroy the wall of sanity he'd labored upon for a lifetime, one heavy stone at a time. A wall so thick and so high that it was already completed before he realized too late that he had enclosed himself inside.

He rode until he could do nothing but slide off his winded mount and drop to his knees in the tall, coarse grass at the edge of the river.

The rising wind whipped his hair into a frenzy, stung his burning eyes, sang a mournful refrain over the rushing in his ears. Gray clouds scudded in from the west bringing with them a wistful hint of the sea that had birthed them. Austyn remembered laying on this very bluff as a small boy, his head pillowed by his mother's skirts

151

as she recited from memory one of the epic poems he adored. Tales of battle. Tales of valor. Tales of honor.

She had raked his hair from his brow and smiled down at him, her eyes alight with love. "Someday, my son, you'll be such a man as these. A knight. A hero. The pride of the Gavenmores."

Austyn doubled over, sickened by the memory. Sickened by the poison festering in his soul. He had thought Holly — his funny, homely little Holly — to be the one who would purge him of it. 'Twas utterly ludicrous that she would be capable of provoking even a shadow of the debilitating jealousy that had scarred the hearts of the Gavenmore men for generations.

He pressed a hand to his heart, feeling beneath his tunic the outline of the token bequeathed to him so grudgingly by the beauty he'd encountered in the Tewksbury garden. Now *there* was a woman to incite madness in the heart of a man! he thought. *There* was a woman worth surrendering his soul for! But when he closed his eyes to conjure her face before him, her exquisite features melted, reforming into a puckish grin and a pair of animated violet eyes. Her mane of sable curls vanished, disintegrating into springy tufts that bobbed like a nest of baby snakes, yet felt surprisingly silky to his touch.

Austyn groaned. What in God's name was he to do now? Rush back to the castle, drag that snide priest from the chapel by his cowl, and demand to know the nature of the man's impassioned quarrel with his wife? Corner Holly and bully her into a confession of wrongdoing?

He came to his feet, setting his lips in a grim line of determination. He wouldn't give that treacherous witch Rhiannon the satisfaction of doing either. 'Twas but a single stone of the wall around him that Holly had crumbled with her clumsy affections and artless attempts to please him. It could be easily enough repaired with the mortar of indifference. And what man would dare to judge him for refusing to count the terrible cost of that indifference?

As Austyn swung himself astride the horse and drove it back toward the castle, the first cold beads of rain struck his face like a baptism of his mother's tears.

Thunder rumbled over the black mountains like the purring of a giant cat. A cool breeze drifted through the oriel window of the solar, carrying with it the gentle pattering of the rain on the balcony. 'Twas the seventh day of rain and the gloom and damp were beginning to sorely vex Holly's nerves. She paced the cozy chamber, the defiant crackling of the fire on the hearth only heightening her restlessness.

Carey sat sharpening his arrows on the windowsill while Emrys, Winifred, and Elspeth played a muffled game of dice in the corner. Two yellow hounds drowsed before the fire. They lifted their broad heads to give Holly a doleful look as she swept past.

She stopped abruptly before the table, planting her palms firmly on its freshly polished surface. "Sir, I have strewn the floor of the great hall with new rushes and dried herbs — sweet-smelling tansy and lavender, basil and winter savory, even a sprinkling of wintergreen."

Her boast earned her only a taciturn grunt from the man behind the table. A man nearly buried behind a mound of ledgers and scrolls. A man who'd barely spoken to her for a sennight and who only endured her company when he could devise no escape from it.

Holly wracked her brain for more achievements to recite. "I've scrubbed the rust from all the manacles in the dungeon."

"Very industrious of you," he said, refusing to grant her even the boon of a glance. His voice was as cool and distant as the silvery web of lightning arcing over the river.

Elspeth crooked a sympathetic eyebrow. Winifred and Emrys stared fixedly at the dice. Carey scowled at Austyn's back.

Holly straightened, her back rigid. If she could no longer please

153

her husband, perhaps she could anger him. Any stamp of emotion upon the impassive beauty of his countenance would be a welcome variation.

She reached up to tug a lengthening curl, her eyes narrowing with a hint of temper only Elspeth recognizd. "I've asked Winifred to prepare pickled lamprey for your supper tonight."

Nothing. Not even the threat of pickled eel could induce a shadow of his crooked grin, a petulant twitch of his chiseled lips. Lips that had once praised even her smallest effort with extravagant charity.

Holly folded her arms over her chest and tapped her foot on the floor. "I fear I accidentally spiced your porridge with hemlock this morn. You should succumb to the throes of a convulsive death by nightfall."

"That's very nice," he murmured. Snapping a ledger closed, he rose in one crisp motion, directing his words at Carey. "I'm off to the north fields to see how long the rain will delay the haying. I shall return at eventide." He brushed past her as if she were invisible, leaving her standing empty-handed and hollow hearted before the table.

Carey unfolded himself from the windowsill. "My lady, you mustn't take his brooding to heart. The Gavenmore lords have always been prone to black moods. They harden their hearts and —"

Holly lifted a hand to silence him, forcing a tremulous smile. "I fear that one must first possess a heart before one can harden it."

Terrified that Carey's compassion would entice her hurt and frustration to spill over into tears, she turned and fled blindly from the solar.

Holly wandered the castle like a restless wraith, pondering how she was going to endure the next thirty years of Austyn's indifference. Had he treated her with such callous apathy from the beginning, she might have been left the comfort of blaming her unsightly

154

appearance or her churlish behavior. She might have resigned herself to a marriage between two strangers who were destined to remain thus until death parted them.

But Austyn had given her a taunting glimpse of something more. Of stories shared before the fire after an exhausting, but exhilarating, day of labor. Of a crooked smile and a deep rumble of laughter, made all the more precious because they were bestowed with such rarity. Of a strong masculine hand that reached to rumple her butchered hair as if it were yet a cascade of sumptuous curls. He had given her all that, then snatched it away without even a clue as to what terrible transgression she had committed to lose his favor.

Had she known what sin to confess, she might even have humbled her pride to seek Nathanael's ear. The priest had apologized for their quarrel, vowing that it was only concern for her soul that had prompted his outburst, but relations between them remained strained and guarded. He spent most of his days poring over the musty Gavenmore histories he had discovered in a chapel vault.

As Holly passed an arrow loop, a watery swath of sunlight informed her the rain had ceased at last. Too late, it seemed, to dispel the gloom of her spirit. Each time she rounded a corner, her pathetic attempts to prove herself a fit wife for Austyn mocked her: the fresh coat of whitewash covering the cracked plaster of the buttery walls, the pungent aroma of the herbs crunched beneath her shoes, the tubs of scarlet poppies perched along the battlements. She had left her cheerful stamp on every chamber of the keep, abandoning only the north tower to its cobwebs and ghosts.

Holly could bear it no longer. She snatched up a woolen shawl and fled the castle by an outside staircase. Escaping the enclosed courtyard, she trudged through the wet grass of the inner bailey, paying more heed to the clouds scudding across the sun than to the shy footfalls behind her.

"Gwyneth."

Holly sighed wearily. She was not in the mood to be mistaken for anyone's wife, dead or otherwise. "No, Father Rhys," she said, glancing back over her shoulder at him. "I'm not Gwyneth. I'm Holly." She could not quite banish the wistful note from her voice. "Austyn's Holly."

He shook his head. "Gwyneth," he repeated with stern conviction, pointing at the knoll just beyond her.

A phantom of a shiver caressed her nape. The breeze teased gooseflesh to her arms as she drifted toward the stone cairn nearly smothered by a blanket of ivy and weeds.

She stopped at the edge of the unmarked grave. "Gwyneth?" she whispered, hugging the shawl tight about her.

The wind bore the echo of Austyn's baritone, its gruff timbre softened by an edge of yearning. *I remember everything about her. Her voice. Her smile. The angle at which she tilted her head when she was singing.*

Gwyneth. Rhys's wife. Austyn's beloved mother. Holly swallowed around the lump that rose unbidden to her throat.

She glanced back at the keep, frowning in bewilderment. She could understand why the castle had fallen to neglect without a mistress to maintain it, but she could not fathom the disgrace of this untended grave. Her own mother's tomb was kept dusted and polished, lit day and night by costly beeswax tapers, decorated with armfuls of fragrant yellow jonquils each spring on the anniversary of her death.

A stray beam of sunlight slanted full across Holly's face, warming her for the first time in days. Perhaps 'twas not too late to win her husband's favor, she thought. Perhaps she had sought to impress him with trivial domestic accomplishments when all he really required was a simple gesture of her devotion. A gift from the heart.

Turning, she clasped the old man's gnarled hands in her own. "Father Rhys, would you care to help me?"

He nodded eagerly, the slant of his smile tugging at her heart with its familiarity. A gust of wind parted the lingering clouds as they both fell to their knees and began clawing the ivy away from the cairn.

Holly sank back on her haunches to rub a smudge of soil from her cheek. Dirt encrusted the abbreviated crescents of her fingernails. Her lower back ached. The wind had chapped her face. She grinned, as delighted as she was exhausted by her afternoon's labor.

Her shawl lay abandoned on the grass beside her. A tangle of weeds and ivy was heaped a few feet away, begging the touch of a torch. A profusion of transplanted anemones crowded boldly around the neatly piled stones of the cairn. As Holly gently poked the last plant in the dirt, Austyn's father marched over the crest of the hill, cradling a freshly cut armful of red hyacinths. They were to be Holly's special gift to her husband — a fragrant blanket to guard Gwyneth of Gavenmore's eternal slumber.

Between one step and the next, the old man's eager smile faded. His feet faltered. The flowers fell from his arms in a crimson shower.

Holly turned to gaze behind her, shading her eyes against the lowering sun. The earth beneath her knees vibrated with the thunder of approaching hoofbeats. Her heart began to race, beating in time to the frantic rhythm.

Austyn slid off his destrier before it could come to a complete halt, stalking toward her with deadly grace. She came to her feet in instinctive defense. 'Twould seem her efforts to coax a response from her husband had succeeded beyond her wildest hopes. He was in nothing less than a murderous rage.

He stopped less than a foot from her, his broad chest heaving, his nostrils flaring with each ragged breath. "How dare you? Is there no corner of my life you won't scrub or sweep or befoul with your childish attentions, your ridiculous flowers?"

A bellow of rage would have been less wounding than his low

157

snarl of contempt. He was gazing at her as if she were a vile thing — a profanation of the holy ground on which they stood.

Holly could do nothing but summon the queenly composure Nathanael had taught her. Clasping her hands in front of her, she tipped back her head and said, "I sought only to please you. Your father told me his beloved Gwyneth was buried here."

"Gwyneth," he spat. As if seeking a fresh target for his fury, he stormed past her and grabbed his father by the front of his tunic. "Did you tell her, old man? Did you tell her what your *beloved* Gwyneth did? Did you tell her what *you* did to your *beloved* Gwyneth?"

At seeing a helpless creature so abused, Holly's fear was supplanted by reckless anger. She snatched at Austyn's arm, tugging the rigid muscles with all of her strength. "Stop it! You're frightening him!"

Austyn freed his father and wheeled on her. For one terrible moment, Holly thought he would strike her. She recoiled, not in anticipation of physical harm, but of the irreparable damage such a careless blow would do her heart. At her blatant flinch, shame flickered in his eyes, so intense as to be almost self-loathing.

Holly reached for him, this time in tenderness, but he jerked his arm out of her reach and strode back to the cairn. Dropping to his knees, he dragged off his gauntlets, then began to tear up the tender anemones with his bare hands, hurling the ripe gobbets of earth as far as they would go.

Holly felt as if her heart was being wrenched from her chest with each snap of the fragile roots. She came to kneel on the opposite side of the grave, not bothering to wipe away the tears trickling steadily down her cheeks.

"I don't understand how you could defile her memory," she said softly. "She was your mother."

Austyn's eyes blazed cold blue fire as he threw back his head and roared, "She was a faithless whore!"

158

Chapter 17

"Aye, a more treacherous harlot never lived! As cunning as Eve. As wanton as Jezebel. Enticing decent, God-fearing men to her bed like bees to a honey pot."

It took Holly a dazed moment to realize the damning denouncement had come not from Austyn, but from his father. The old man waved his arms for emphasis as he strode toward the grave, all traces of uncertainty banished from his step. The fire had been restored to his rheumy eyes. Sanity flirted with their depths, somehow more dangerous than the vague madness that kept him occupied most of the time. Having never heard him utter more than two words at a time, Holly could only gape.

"A weak, willful woman my Gwyneth was, given over to sins of the flesh. She could never be satisfied with only one mortal man to quench her insatiable lusts. Nor with two. Nor with . . ."

'Twas as if the floodgates of silence had parted to loose a river of virulence. As he ranted on, Holly became aware that his impromptu sermon was collecting an audience. Emrys, Carey, and a white-faced Winifred clustered at the garden gate. Nathanael watched from the chapel door. Other castle inhabitants came creeping out from the brewery, the mews, the smithy, their curiosity overcoming their trepidation. Holly kept her eyes averted from Austyn, fearing he would judge her just another leering witness to his anguish.

'Twas Carey who came forward and gently took the old man by the arm. Holly suspected it was not the first time he had done so. Nor would it be the last.

"Come, sir," Carey said. " 'Tis time for your evening meal.

Pickled lamprey, you know. Your favorite." The others retreated as abruptly as they'd appeared, as if Carey's simple act of kindness had shamed them.

Rhys of Gavenmore pointed a condemning finger heavenward as he marched alongside the man-at-arms. "Strumpets, every last one of them! Panting for a man's rigid staff like bitches in heat. Only too eager to spread their thighs and milk him of every last drop of God-given vigor —"

A door thudded shut, mercifully cutting off the vivid recital. If Holly could not look at her husband before, she certainly couldn't look at him now.

"I've never seen you blush before. 'Tis quite becoming."

Austyn's quiet words confused her. They gazed at each other over the chasm of his mother's grave. Unnerved by his steady perusal, Holly ducked her head, worrying her bottom lip between her teeth. Since he'd began to stare *through* her instead of *at* her, she'd grown rather careless about mangling her appearance.

"I've never seen you throw flowers before, sir. 'Twas quite unbecoming."

"I should have warned you. All the Gavenmore men are cursed with" — he hesitated, as if uncertain how much to reveal — "unpredictable tempers. By Gavenmore standards, that was but a mild tantrum."

"Then I should hate to see a severe one."

"As would I." Austyn rose and wandered to the crest of the hill. He stood with hands on hips, gazing over the crumbling curtain wall to the swollen river. The bruised lavender of twilight framed his rugged profile.

"My father's Welsh loyalties weren't always as pure as he pretends them to be," he said. "When he heard the English king. Edward was attempting to ensure peace with his contentious neighbors by building several castles along Welsh rivers and strategic byways, he volunteered Gavenmore as a site. He knew the king would bestow

160

extravagant rewards of land and wealth to each lord who swore his fealty to such an undertaking."

"Nathanael taught me of such castles." She did not add that Nathanael had also taught her that Edward's dream had never been fully realized. That the Welsh continued to stage sporadic rebellions against the sovereignty of Edward's son to this very day.

A wistful smile played around Austyn's lips. " 'Twas a magical time to a boy of nine. The place swarmed day and night with master builders, carpenters, diggers. Carey and I managed to get ourselves into some abominable mischief. You can imagine our excitement when we learned that Edward himself was to honor us with a royal visit. We'd never seen a real king before."

Austyn's expression darkened. " 'Twas a rainy autumn eve when he and his entourage arrived. Edward was getting on in years, but he was still a virile man. I was a rather plump lad, but he lifted me as if I weighed no more than a feather."

Holly could not help but smile at the image. There was certainly no hint of lingering baby fat on Austyn's well-honed physique.

"They sat up late into the night — my father, my mother, and this English king. Laughing, talking, jesting with one another. The king was charmed to distraction by my mother's singing."

Holly shivered as the ghostly echo of some long forgotten melody seemed to play across her nerves.

" 'Twas almost midnight when they retired. My father awoke later to find the bed beside him empty."

Suddenly, Holly didn't want him to go on. Would have done anything to stop him. Even thrown her arms around his neck and smothered his words with her mouth. But she was paralyzed, her limbs weighted by dread of what was to come.

All emotion fled Austyn's voice, leaving it cold and distant. "He searched the castle for his Gwyneth, just as he still does. But that night he found her. In the king's bed."

"What did he do?" Holly whispered.

161

Austyn shrugged. "What could he do? 'Twas not uncommon for an ambitious lord to permit his liege the pleasure of his wife's favors. He simply closed the door and returned to his own bed.

"At dawn the next morning, he bid Edward a gracious farewell, swearing his eternal fealty. Then he climbed the stairs and strangled my mother to death."

The stark beauty of Austyn's profile was stripped of humanity, so impenetrable it might have been carved upon a tomb. "I found them there on that bed, on the same rumpled sheets where she had lain with another man. Father was cradling her lifeless body in his arms, rocking back and forth and weeping. He kept kissing her face, begging her to wake up. All the while her limp neck was swollen and purple with the marks of his fingers, her face black with death."

Holly clapped a trembling hand over her mouth, appalled that she had come to Rhys's defense. Had allowed him to follow her about the castle like a harmless puppy. Had gently clasped his frail hands in her own, those very hands that had squeezed the life from Austyn's mother.

"When Edward heard of her death," Austyn continued, "he withdrew his builders and his favor. He stripped my father of his title and all his holdings, drove all of his finest fighting men to desert him until only the most loyal of his peasants remained."

Holly understood now why she'd witnessed no squires or knights training in the list. Why the castle was guarded not by skilled men-at-arms, but by farmers and bakers and beekeepers.

"Edward's son continues to hound us, seeking to tax us until we have no choice but to surrender even this barren rock. All because of the treachery of a woman. Because she betrayed us." Holly heard in his bitter whisper the echo of a wounded child, a child forced too soon to bear the somber responsibilities of manhood. "Abandoned us."

162

"Abandoned *you?*" She shot to her feet, her compassion smothered beneath a maelstrom of churning emotions. "I think not, sir, for 'tis you who have abandoned her."

Chapter 18

Austyn would not have been surprised had he been forced to endure his wife's pity. Or had she shrank from him in disgust. Or bowed her head in shame at his family's disgrace. But he was flabbergasted by the petite virago who leaped to her feet to challenge him. He'd faced less daunting opponents on the jousting field. Had she been a cat he had little doubt she would have been hissing and spitting in his dumbfounded face.

"Abandoned you?" she repeated. "The way I see it, the poor woman had very little choice in the matter."

The sheer volume of her attack jolted Austyn out of his brooding. He raised his voice to match hers. "She could have chosen to remain in her husband's bed! To honor her wedding vows!"

"And your father could have chosen not to choke her to death! I can't help but notice that he didn't strangle his precious king."

Austyn fell back a step at the well-placed blow. Every soul at Caer Gavenmore had been tiptoeing around the subject of his mother's death for decades. The incident had stained all of their lives the color of blood, yet no one dared to speak of it. Until Holly. Ugly, courageous little Holly.

She was without mercy, his Holly. "Was your father's crime a less terrible transgression than your mother's infidelity? You coddle him as if he were an invalid, yet deny her even a humble flower to honor her memory. She has only cold rocks to mark her resting place."

Austyn strode over to Holly and snatched her up by the shoulders, dragging her rigid body against his own. "Every one of which was

164

placed there by my hand!"

Her violet eyes blazed with a passion that surpassed his own. Instead of hanging limp in his harsh embrace, she clung to his arms, refusing to be cowed. Her fierce expression betrayed not even a hint of a flinch. Austyn could not have said how much that pleased him.

"How generous of you," she said, softening her voice to a scathing rebuke. "Tell me, did you truly hate your own mother so much?"

"I adored her!" The declaration, pent up inside of him for twenty years, burst from his chest with the force of an explosion. He dropped his gaze to Holly's lips, suddenly so soft, so inviting, and whispered, "I adored her."

Holly was only too willing to bear the brunt of Austyn's anger, but the bewildered yearning in his eyes threatened to dissolve her. She wanted to melt into his arms. To draw his head gently down to her breast and . . .

She remembered with a painful shock that his head would not encounter the nurturing softness of her breasts, but the stiff strips of her bindings. Panicked by the realization, she pushed against his chest. For a dizzying heartbeat, he held her as if he would refuse to let her go, then his arms fell away without protest.

She backed away from him lest she fall prone to some other, even more dangerous, temptation. "So your mother was not the harlot your father painted her to be?"

Austyn's frown reflected his conflicted memories. "She was a beauty, aye, but she was also modest, devout. She could bear no more children after me, so she knew I was to be her only son and my father's only heir. She taught me to read and write, encouraged me to develop the manly skills that would make me worthy of becoming a knight and lord of these lands. She taught me to pray." His dark thicket of lashes swept down to veil his eyes. "I haven't prayed since she died."

Holly gathered up her shawl and wrapped it around her shoulders.

"Then perhaps 'tis time you did."

She turned, determined to leave him to make peace with his memories.

"Holly?"

She paused. "Sir?"

He shook his head with a wry wonderment that squeezed the remnant of her breath from her chest. "You're enough to tempt me to trust my heart to a woman's care."

Holly had no answer for him that would not condemn her for the wretched liar she was. She could only hasten her steps toward the castle.

When she dared to steal a look back by the light of the rising moon, Austyn was kneeling beside his mother's grave, his big, blunt hands gently patting the earth around the bowed stem of an anemone.

Holly was lost. Running headlong through a shadow-laced forest, blinded by mist and tears. No, she realized. She wasn't lost. Someone was lost to her. Someone dear. Gnarled branches whipped at her face, clawed at her gown, seeking to stop her from finding who she sought.

Her frantic flight ended when she slammed into an iron-banded door. She beat upon it until her fists were bloody, but still it would not yield. She sank into a despairing heap, weeping and pleading for mercy from her faceless captor on the opposite side of that door. Her hot, salty tears ignited a tiny flame at the hem of her gown. She beat it out with her hand, but another sprang into its place, then another, until her entire skirt was ablaze.

A shadow fell over her, extinguishing not only the flames but her last hope of redemption. A man's face emerged from the darkness, harsh with contempt and accusation. 'Twas a face she had once caressed in tenderness, a face she had adored with both her lips and her heart.

The worst of it was that she loved that face still, loved him.
Reached to draw him into her embrace even as his powerful hands
closed around her throat.

Holly sat straight up in the four-poster bed, her heart thundering
in her ears. The moon had dipped below the arrow loop, abandoning
her to the cloying darkness. She touched her quaking fingertips to
her cheeks, surprised to find them damp with tears.

Casting aside the tangled sheets, she fumbled to light the tallow
stub at her bedside. Its feeble flicker did not completely exorcise
the ghosts of those other Gavenmore brides, but it at least drove
them back to the shadows writhing along the plastered walls. She
could not say if they had come to warn her or if her dream was
nothing more than the tormented ramblings of her own conscience.

She slipped from the bed and padded over to the chest. Dropping
to her knees, she picked up her mother's hand mirror and slowly
turned it to capture her reflection. Relief slowed her heartbeat to a
dull thud. She had feared the poison of her own guile might have
transformed her into something even more monstrous than her disguise. She watched her brow crinkle in a bewildered frown as she
realized she was instead gazing into the face of a stranger.

Her features had lost their haughty cast. The tension around her
mouth had softened. The yearning in her eyes deepened them to
misty violet pools. She lifted a hand to her sun-burnished throat,
gliding it downward until her splayed fingers encountered the tingling swell of her unbound breasts. A sigh escaped her parted lips.
'Twas no longer the face of the fairest lady in all of England
reflected in the mirror. 'Twas the wistful face of a woman in love
with her husband.

She laid the mirror aside, no longer able to bear the transparency
of her reflection. Did she dare go to Austyn now? Confess all and
cast herself upon his mercy? Would he turn her away from his bed?
His heart? His life? Would he believe she betrayed him, just as his

mother had betrayed his father?

Perhaps 'twould be better if she did not trust her plea to the inconstancy of words. If she simply slipped into his bed in the darkness. Burrowed against the crisp fur of his chest and coaxed his big, warm body to cover hers. The vision left her breathless, terrified, exhilarated.

Surely with his heart softened in the aftermath of their lovemaking, he would forgive her deceit.

But what would she have proven? she asked herself. That she could beguile a man with her touch? Bewitch him with the velvety softness of her skin? Charm him with the sumptuous plumpness of her breasts? She'd been confident of those powers before she wed Austyn. The faceless lover he still pined for had surely offered him no less.

You're enough to tempt me to trust my heart to a woman's care.

In truth, Austyn's hoarse confession, wrung from his throat in the bloody aftermath of battle, meant more to her than any honeyed words he might whisper in the dark. If she crept beneath his sheets with shadows for her shield and beauty as her sword, she might never know if he would have succumbed to that temptation. If he would have dared to trust his heart to a stocky, flat-chested, crop-curled little minx who adored him.

One day, Holly vowed to herself. She would give him one more day. If she could coax from him some gesture of affection for the woman he had married, then tomorrow night she would go to him. She would scoff at the warnings of those other Gavenmore brides and take the risk of laying her heart at his feet.

Her resolve strengthened, Holly danced back to the bed, feeling as lithe as a Welsh faerie without her padding to hinder her.

"Good morn, Winnie," Holly called out as she passed the woman bent over a laundry tub in the courtyard. "I'm off to gather some wildflowers from the riverbank."

168

"And a good day to you, Lady Holly." Winifred straightened to rub her lower back, envying the spryness of her young mistress's step.

Holly swung the basket draped over her arm in cheery rhthym, humming beneath her breath a melody ripe with hope. The azure sky sprouted blossoms of cloud as white and fluffy as chrysanthemums. 'Twas as if the rain had baptized the earth, then sent the sun to shine full upon it to fulfill the promise of its salvation.

The crisp sparkle in the air had coaxed most of the castle residents to turn their talents to chores that could be undertaken away from the gloom of the keep, such as gathering honey from the castle hives or trimming the hooves of a placid donkey. They offered Holly jovial greetings and shy smiles as she passed. The twin yellow hounds capered at her heels for several steps before being lured away by the aroma of ham being cured over an open fire.

Holly was relieved to find Rhys of Gavenmore nowhere in sight. She had no desire to sort out her conflicting feelings about Austyn's father on such a delicious day.

She waved at Carey as she passed the list, laughing merrily when her distraction forced his arrow to miss the target painted on a moldy hay bale. He shook his fist at her in mock anger, then blew her a teasing kiss.

Holly's steps slowed as she passed the grave of Austyn's mother. Much of the earth surrounding it still bore the raw scars of warfare, but at uneven intervals, scraggly anemone plants had been rescued and embedded in the dirt in clumsy splashes of crimson and purple.

Holly's throat tightened as she saw scratched upon a large, flat rock in an unsteady hand the words *Gwyneth of Gavenmore, Beloved Mother.*

The moment was nearly spoiled when Nathanael came flapping after her like an overgrown crow, a sheaf of papers rolled in his fist.

She hastened her steps, starting down the hillside toward the river. "I've no need of your pleas for atonement this morning, Nate.

169

I chose to share my prayers with God in the privacy of my chamber and I can promise you that my soul is as shiny as a new coin." Or it soon would be, she amended silently, after she confessed her duplicity to Austyn.

Nathanael slid after her, his sandals finding little purchase in the rocky soil. "You must listen to me, Holly. 'Tis not your soul that concerns me. 'Tis you. You're in danger. Terrible danger."

"I'm in danger of rolling down this hill and breaking my neck if you don't cease trodding upon my heels. Do you know what a challenge it is to toddle about in these skirts?"

Her gentle scorn fuled to deter him. He shook open the papers. They rustled with a life of their own in the sinuous breeze. "In my extensive study of the Gavenmore history, I've come upon irrefutable evidence that your husband may very well be cursed."

Holly sighed. "Cursed, eh? Eternally damned and all that rot? Tell me, does he sprout horns and cloven feet during the full moon? Cavort with demons and sacrifice maidens to his lust on a blood-stained altar?"

"Worse. Listen to this. These were purported to be the words of the faerie queen Rhiannon after she was falsely accused of infidelity by one of Austyn's forebears." He stumbled over the uneven turf as he read, " 'Let love be your mortal weakness and beauty your eternal doom.' "

That those melodramatic words could actually cast a chill over the glorious summer day only exasperated Holly further. "For God's sake, Nathanael, you're a priest! Surely you haven't come to believe in pagan curses."

"The curse may not be a pagan one. 'Tis written this Rhiannon called the very wrath of God down upon the unfortunate fellow's head."

"Then I give you leave to wave a crucifix over Austyn while he naps." Holly wiggled her fingers. "Or sprinkle some Holy Water in his porridge."

The priest skidded to a halt as if realizing his surrender would be more effective than open pursuit. "Don't you think it odd that so many of the Gavenmore brides have met gruesome ends at their husband's hands?"

Holly stopped and stood with hands on hips for a long moment. Then she turned and marched back to Nathanael, stabbing a finger at his chest. "You may believe whatever superstitious nonsense you like, Brother, but I'll tell you what I believe. That there's no curse that cannot be broken by the blessing of true love."

She left him standing there, his expression forlorn, his robes tossed by the wind. As the ancient scrolls crumbled in his grip, he whispered, "God go with you, Holly, and may He in His infinite mercy prove you right."

The river was sluggish and calm today, but Austyn's wife, it seemed, was not. He watched from beneath the sprawling branches of an elm as she waded through thigh-high weeds, snipping and snatching to fill a basket with a colorful profusion of wildflowers, muttering beneath her breath all the while.

Austyn grinned. She was so funny, so charming, so damnably bold. Graceless and yet so full of grace it made his eyes sting just to look at her.

Yestereve in the fading twilight with her eyes sparking violet fire and her mouth taut with challenge, she had been almost comely. Sunlight banished that illusion without remorse. She waddled about like a brown little butternut with legs, pausing only to swipe a stray grasshopper from her listless hair. Austyn shook his head, chuckling with amazement that he could still want her so badly. To be his wife. To bear his children. To warm his bed.

She had given him a glimpse of a different kind of beauty yesterday. A beauty comprised of courage and brutal honesty. A beauty unselfish enough to restore to him his loving memories of a mother he'd spent the last twenty years despising. A beauty that had little

171

to do with a creamy complexion or a cascade of sable curls that required five-hundred strokes of the comb at bedtime.

Austyn reached into his tunic, drawing forth his memento from its hiding place. He recognized it for what it was now — a token of his empty infatuation with a woman he had never truly known. A woman who would have doubtlessly proved to be his damnation just as Holly had proved to be his deliverance.

Tucking it carelessly back into his tunic, he started down the riverbank toward his wife with eager strides.

Holly was popping the heads off a cluster of marigolds with spiteful satisfaction when a wry voice behind her said, "I hope you're not pretending I'm one of those flowers."

She looked up from her kneeling position, her heart doubling its rate. Austyn was leaning against the trunk of a willow, garbed all in black except for his crimson surcoat. The sun-bronzed skin around his eyes had crinkled in a slanted grin. That frivolous dimple flirted with his jaw. He was so devastatingly handsome that she had to look away.

She nervously ripped one of the marigolds to shreds. "In truth, I was pretending they were a certain pesky priest I know."

Austyn's tones were carefully measured. "And have you and the young Brother Nathanael been quarreling again?"

"Brother indeed! He nags me like the older brother I never wished I had. The man is insufferable. He thinks that just because he was once my tutor, he is entitled to instruct me for the rest of my life."

"And what did your Brother Nathanael teach you?"

Holly glanced up, startled by Austyn's sudden nearness, the odd light in his eye — half resignation, half amusement. Before she could reply, his callused palms were cupping her forearms, guiding her to a standing position. The basket slipped from her arm, spilling her floral treasures over their feet in a fragrant shower of crimson and gold. Even in her unwieldy disguise, Holly felt very small next

172   •

to him, as frail and delicate as one of the wood hyacinths huddled around the trunk of the willow.

Her voice sounded faint to her own ears, as if it were coming from leagues away. "He taught me to chew each bite of food fifty times."

Austyn crooked an eyebrow and Holly blushed, remembering how she had wolfed down the cold meat pies on the journey from Tewksbury.

"He taught me never to speak above a polite murmur." Her husband's expressive eyebrow shot higher.

Holly knew she was revealing too much too soon, but she could hardly think with Austyn's warm hands gliding up her arms, seeking the naked flesh beneath her slashed sleeves.

"Have I ever told you what entrancing elbows you have, my lady?" he murmured against her ear.

Her voice was fading faster than her reason. "Nathanael taught me to rub cut lemons on them," she whispered. "And he taught me never to speak with my mouth occupied by anything other than my tongue."

Austyn leaned forward until his lips were a heated breath away from hers. "What about your husband's tongue?"

His lips brushed hers then, as feathery and beguiling as a butterfly's wing. Holly moaned softly, eager for more. He rewarded her with a fiercer, sweeter press, molding her lips beneath his own as if he might sculpt their malleable contours anew for his pleasure. It seemed only fitting that they should part to beckon him inside. His tongue accepted her shy invitation, its rough satin stroking deep to claim her yielding mouth with exacting mastery.

When Holly swirled her tongue to joust in kind, he captured her nape in the cup of his palm, a growl of pained delight rumbling deep in his throat. He kissed her until she could not speak at all. Or breathe. Or stand without the bracing support of his arms wrapped around her lower back. 'Twas different from his kiss in the garden somehow. Less tentative. More possessive. Less a culmination than a prelude to a more exquisite rapture. When he finally drew away, she was clinging to him, utterly overwhelmed by the desire that had risen between them, hot and fragile.

His eyes sparkled with pure devilment, yet she could feel his massive body battling a tremor, as if the earth beneath his feet was no steadier than the earth beneath her own. "Tonight, my lady," he whispered against her brow, " 'twill be your husband who teaches you."

With that husky vow, he brushed his lips across the bridge of her nose, then turned to go, leaving her limp, trembling, damp with wanting. It was through a haze of bliss that she saw the wisp of ebony tumble from his tunic and blow across the grass.

"Sir?" she called after him, pointing at the grass. "You dropped something."

A sadness too brief to be reckoned passed over his face before he shook his head. " 'Tis nothing of any import."

He had barely crested the hill before Holly was scrabbling through the tall grass on hands and knees. She let out a muffled whoop of triumph as her questing fingers found what they sought. 'Twas a brooch woven of black thread so fine as to be almost gossamer. She held the curious object up to the sun, mystified.

She tugged first one thread, then another. Her heart began to pound faster as the brooch unraveled, leaving her holding what had once been a single glossy curl. A curl severed by the unsteady hand of a surly knight who had mocked its owner for her vanity, yet sought to preserve this one memento of it with a care that bordered on obsession. Holly lifted the shimmering tendril to her cheek, having nearly forgotten what it felt like to have her face caressed by such bounty.

Astonishment paralyzed her. It seemed she had been the only rival for her husband's affections all along — Lady Holly of Tewksbury, that shallow, selfish girl who had branded him a crude barbarian because he dared to speak with a different accent from her own. She had fled his company like a frightened rabbit rather than linger in that moonlit garden and face her own desires.

Holly's spirit soared. She could only imagine the wonder that would light Austyn's face when she revealed that he had been wed to the woman of his dreams all these weeks. With her husband's kiss as a pledge of his present affections and the brooch as proof of his past devotion, her heart brimmed with hope for the future. A future she simply could not wait until tonight to begin.

As she scrambled to gather her scattered flowers, her happiness overflowed in wordless melody. When her humming could no longer contain her joy, she broke into song, absently crooning the haunting ballad that had first summoned Sir Austyn of Gavenmore to her side.

Austyn marched along beside the unfinished curtain wall, struggling to convince his ravenous body that his sweet wife deserved more than a boisterous tumble among the weeds of a riverbank. She deserved a fluffy feather mattress on a luxuriant four-poster draped in pleated silk. She deserved silver goblets brimming with spiced wine to ease her maidenly shyness. She deserved scented tapers to cast flickering light over their entwined limbs.

Austyn groaned aloud. It seemed his truculent body was not to be persuaded. It clamored more insistently and with far more cunning than his besotted brain. After all, what need had husband and wife of silk and feathers when the bounty of God's green earth was spread beneath them? He could lay her gently down upon his surcoat, sprinkle her naked flesh with fragrant petals of hyacinth and heartsease.

What need had he of wine to ease her shyness when he possessed the skill to intoxicate her with pleasure, to coax her to shed her inhibitions with nothing more than a nimble stroke of his fingertips?

And were not tapers but a pale reflection of the splendor of God's

175

sun? Did he dare affront the Lord himself by implying 'twould be preferable to bed his bride in the warm glow of beeswax than partake of her innocence beneath the benevolent rays of the sun?

Austyn made an abrupt about-face, marching back toward the river.

He was nearly to the top of the hill when the first haunting notes of the melody came wafting to his ears on a jasmine-scented breeze. His steps faltered as the warm summer day went as cold and black as the deepest winter night.

Chapter 19

Holly had just tossed the last flower in her basket when a dark figure came sliding over the hill. She shaded her eyes against the sun, fearing Nathanael had hunted her down to plague her further with his proclamations of impending doom. A tremulous smile softened her lips as she recognized her husband's imposing shoulders and mane of dark hair. It seemed he was as eager to begin their future as she was.

Her smile died as she caught a glimpse of his burning eyes, the only hint of life in a face as still as death. She took an involuntary step backward. Austyn kept coming, the lumbering grace that had once seemed so endearing now a terrible and relentless thing. She backed away from him, driven by some primitive instinct for survival. She stumbled, sliding the last few feet down the muddy bank into the shallows fringing the river.

The current sucked greedily at her skirts, yet she continued to retreat until the chill water swirled around her ankles, her calves, her trembling knees. Her cowardice did not deter him. He plunged in after her, closing the distance between them in two splashing strides. Tangling his fist in her scant hair, he jerked her head back, baring her face to his merciless scrutiny much as he had that long ago night in the garden.

Fear seized her as he searched her features. His eyes seared her tender skin, scorching away the layers of her deceit with the flame of truth. Open fury would have been preferable to his icy composure. His silence terrified her more than any bellow of rage.

"Please," she whispered, tears welling in her eyes.

Unmoved by her entreaty, he captured her jaw and forced apart her lips. Lips he had kissed only moments before with aching gentleness. His thumb penetrated her mouth, scrubbing at her chattering teeth with rough efficiency.

When he had examined the results, he freed her hair to study his other hand, finally wiping the dull film of ash coating his palm on his surcoat as if it were the vilest filth.

Holly hugged herself, trying to still the shudders that wracked her body. "Please, Austyn, I never meant to deceive you. I was going to tell you. I swear I was. If you'll just let me explain —"

Her fractured litany was cut short as he seized her in his powerful hands and shoved her head beneath the river's surface. Dank water rushed into her mouth and nose, strangling her hopes. Believing he intended to drown her, Holly's soul died a tiny death, but her body refused to give up the fight. She was still clawing and pummeling when he jerked her from the water.

Even as her desperate lungs struggled for air, she saw reflected in the smoldering chasm of his eyes a cap of sodden curls as black and glossy as the wing of a raven.

By the time he drew the misericorde from the chain at his waist, Holly had grown wise enough to know he had no intention of killing her. Killing her would have been quick and merciful and not a drop of mercy lingered in this man's soul. She choked back her pleas, knowing they would be to no avail, but not even her tattered pride could staunch the tears flowing in a river of regret down her cheeks.

He shredded the padded fabric of her skirts, cutting them adrift and leaving her shivering in her thin chemise. The dagger made even quicker work of her bodice, cutting its laces to expose the crude linen of her bindings. Holly stood as rigidly as a statue while the cold blade skated over the fluttering pulse in the hollow of her throat in a mocking caress. Then with a single downward slash, Austyn — her kind, loving, patient husband — severed her bindings, baring her naked breasts to the uncompromising sunlight and the dawning hell in his gaze.

Holly's pride crumbled. With a sob of anguish, she sought to cover herself, but Austyn caught her wrists and forced her arms apart, his eyes drinking their fill of her as if it were their sacred right. Trembling with humiliation, she searched the unearthly beauty of his face for a crumb of compassion that might have escaped the ravening beast feasting on his humanity.

When her search yielded nothing, she bit back her sobs to try again. "Austyn, you must grant me the boon of an audience. 'Twas never my intention to anger you. Or hurt you. I sought only to —"

"Cease your babbling, woman!" he roared.

Austyn felt the tremor that wracked Holly's body at his rebuke, but the part of him that might have felt shame for his bullying had been seared to a crisp by her betrayal. She was no better than his mother, he thought bitterly, his grandmother, all the beautiful women through the ages who had brought ruin to his family and his name.

He gazed down at the pale, exquisite globes of her breasts, struggling to fathom that she was the same creature he had once pitied for her ugliness. Her generous breasts were crowned with circles of the softest peach and tipped with ripe nipples that pebbled beneath the brutal caress of his eyes. Not in desire, he knew instinctively, but in fear.

Her chemise clung to every swell and hollow of her slender body, rendered almost sheer by the treacherous kiss of the water. He lowered his gaze, allowing it to linger with deliberate insolence on the teasing hint of shadow at the juncture of her thighs. She moaned, a soft, broken sound that enticed rather than convicted him.

Austyn tightened his grip on her wrists as he battled a mingled lust and fury so desperate it made a mockery of every constraint he'd exerted over his temper since boyhood. He wanted to drag her to the riverbank, force her to her knees in the weeds, and do things to her that a man would do to no decent woman. Things he wouldn't even do to a whore.

But how long would it be before fury overcame his lust? How long before he fastened his hands around her fragile throat and began to crush the life from . . . ?

Austyn started as a single tear splashed the back of his hand. He lifted his gaze to Holly's pleading eyes. Violet eyes that would soon be fringed by lush sable lashes. His wife's eyes.

When Austyn grabbed her arm and began to drag her toward the castle, Holly had no choice but to stumble along behind him, desperately clutching the tatters of her bodice over her naked breasts. Mortification scorched her cheeks as they passed a pair of shepherd lads who could only gape at the curious sight of their master hauling a scantily garbed stranger over a break in the curtain wall.

As they approached his mother's grave, Austyn's steps never faltered. He dragged her right across its rocky surface, crushing the tender anemones beneath his boots.

His relentless strides carried them past other inhabitants of Caer Gavenmore, their puzzled faces nothing more than a blur to Holly until the first astounded cry went up.

"Good Lord, 'tis Lady Holly!"

Then with the grim clarity of a nightmare, it all came into focus. Their appalled cries as they realized the exquisitely beautiful wraith stumbling along behind Austyn was indeed their mistress, their apprehensive glances at his resolute face, the chill burn of their stares on her face, her exposed body.

A withered old man shouted, "What is this dark enchantment? Mayhap she is a witch!"

They began to recoil from her after that, some in fear of her, others in fear of Austyn's wrath. Worse than their unspoken condemnation was the bewildered hurt Holly glimpsed on Winifred's round face. She ducked her head for the first time, shamed by her own deceit.

The hounds capered after them, barking at their heels. Emrys and

Carey came running from the list to seek the source of the commotion, swords in hand. Carey slid to a halt, his jaw dropping in naked shock. His father followed suit, his own ruddy face darkening with dread.

As their grim procession neared the chapel, a man slipped from its doors to plant himself firmly in their path. Holly began to mumble a spasmodic litany of curses and prayer. At first she feared Austyn would just run right over Nathanael, forcing her to trample him, too, but her husband stopped several paces away, drawing her in front of him like a shield. He slipped one arm around her waist, the mock tenderness of his embrace an affront she could hardly bear.

"Stand aside, priest," Austyn commanded, "unless you care to hear your own last rites."

Nathanael's eyes were dark and hollow, but his voice rang with a conviction Holly had never heard in any of his Candlemas masses or Ascension prayers. "I'll not stand aside and allow you to mistreat this lady."

"She's no lady. She's my wife. Or have you forgotten that you were the one who united us in unholy wedlock?"

" 'Tis not I but you, sir, who seem to have forgotten your vows." Nathanael stood his ground, staunch as always in his pious arrogance.

"You test my patience, *Brother*." Austyn snarled, his arm tightening around Holly's waist until it nearly cut off her air. "Are you truly concerned with my wife's well-being or are you just protecting your lover?"

Holly's was not the only gasp to go up at such blasphemy. Could Austyn truly believe such a terrible thing of her? And why not? she wondered wildly. She'd given him little enough proof of her fidelity.

Nathanael's gaze dropped from Austyn's face to her own. Holly's mumbles escalated to a frantic murmur of, "Oh, God, Nathanael, don't do it. Not now. Oh, please, not now," as she saw humility in his eyes for the first time, coupled with the dangerous knowledge of what she had always known, but denied, even to herself. The crowd held its breath in anticipation of his reply.

"She is not my lover," he said softly.

Holly breathed a sigh of relief.

"But I do love her!"

Groaning with despair, Holly collapsed over Austyn's arm.

" 'Tis God's truth!" Nathanael shouted. "I love her! She's bright and beautiful and talented and charming and you, Sir Austyn of Gavenmore, are not fit to lick the soles of her slippers!"

Holly slowly straightened, bracing herself for Austyn's reaction. When it finally came, it was far worse than anything her feeble imagination could have conjured. He threw back his head and laughed. 'Twas a black sound that rolled through the courtyard in mirthless waves even as he set Holly firmly behind him and pried Carey's sword from his hand.

Nathanael's courage faltered as Austyn stalked toward him, broadsword in hand. The bell of his voice tolled with a smidgen less zeal. "I'm not afraid of you, so you needn't think I am." He took two steps backward to match each of Austyn's, but Austyn just kept coming. He fumbled for an appropriate scripture. " 'F-f-fear not them which kill the body, but are not able to kill the soul, but rather fear him which is able to destroy soul and body in hell.' "

Holly winced as he stumbled over his own robes and sat down abruptly on the cobblestones. Austyn's shadow fell over him like a messenger of death. Holly knew what she had to do. Knew even as she flung herself forward that it was both the worst thing she could do and the only thing she could do. She had no choice but to reward Nathanael's foolish gallantry by striving to save both men's souls.

Austyn was already drawing back the sword when she fell across Nathanael's body, still clutching her bodice, but spreading her free arm in a protective gesture as old as Eve. Nathanael poked at her, but she refused to budge.

She glared up at her husband, allowing him to witness the birth of the first spark of defiance in her eyes. "Need I remind you that I saved your life once, sir? I ask in return the life of this humble priest."

For a chilling moment as the gleaming blade hung poised above them, she thought he would drive it home through her breast, bidding them both a gleeful fare thee well.

Then his lips quirked in a crooked grin more sneer than smile. "Humble indeed. How touching! Would that I could ever hope to inspire such devotion in a woman's heart!"

He reached down, grabbed her wrist, and hurled her aside with one hand. She stumbled to her knees as his fist struck Nathanael's jaw with a resounding crack. The priest melted into a limp puddle on the cobblestones.

Through a haze of shock and relief, Holly became aware that Carey knelt beside her, his deft hands gently assessing her for injury. She might have told him that only her heart was bruised had Austyn's voice not cracked like a whip in their ears.

"Move away from her."

Her husband stood over them, every trace of grim humor stripped from his face. The crowd was deathly silent, the tension so hot and thick even a broadsword could not slice it.

"She fell," Carey said. "I was simply seeking to —"

"Take your hands away from her."

Carey gazed up at him disbelievingly.

"Now," Austyn said, touching the tip of Carey's own sword to his friend's throat. Holly's agony multiplied a thousand fold to be the cause of such.

His mouth taut with resentment, Carey rose to his feet, surrendering her to her husband's mercy.

When Austyn withdrew his gaze from her in that moment, Holly somehow sensed that he had done so for the last time. 'Twas far

183

worse than when he had recoiled from her in the garden at Tewksbury or avoided glancing at her homely visage during the tournament. Worse even than enduring his icy loathing at her betrayal. This was a dissolution of every bond, both holy and earthly, a separation more absolute than death. Grief pierced her heart, loosing a fresh flow of tears.

"Whore! Jezebel!" The triumphant cry rose from the sky, borne on the wings of insanity. "May God punish the harlot who dares to tempt the righteous man!" Rhys of Gavenmore stood on the parapet with arms outstretched, calling the wrath of God down upon her poor, damp, rumpled head.

Holly had had enough. This time when Austyn reached for her, she resisted. His grip was no longer tinged with violence, but was as implacable as an iron manacle clamped around her wrist. Ignoring her spirited struggles, he marched her into the castle, past a sobbing Elspeth, and up the first set of winding stairs to a landing drenched in sunshine.

When Holly saw where he meant to take her, she began to fight in earnest, hammering at his broad back with her fists, clawing at the sun-bronzed skin of his arms. He remained as impervious to her blows as a stone golem. Her curses rose to frantic screams as panic seized her, so dark and consuming it verged on madness. By the time they'd reached the ancient oak door, she was begging, despising herself, but begging all the same, promising anything if he would not lock her away in that terrible place.

He shoved open the door and dragged her inside. Shadows masked his expression. Where before she had struggled to escape him, now she clung to him, pleading with him not to go, not to leave her alone. Tearing her arms from his neck, he thrust her away from him.

Holly stumbled and fell, but was already lurching back to the door when it slammed in her face. A bolt fell into place with the finality of a death knell. Bracing herself with splayed hands, Holly slid down the door, no longer able to summon the will to hammer and scream and plead. All she could do was hug her knees to her chest and pray that if she curled herself into a small enough ball, she would disappear altogether.

part 2

And, like another Helen,
fir'd another Troy . . .
Could swell the soul to rage,
or kindle soft desire.
JOHN DRYDEN

None but the brave deserves the fair.
JOHN DRYDEN

part 2

Chapter 20

'Twas a dark eternity before Holly emerged from that shadowy netherworld between madness and stupor. She knew a vague surprise to find herself still alive. 'Twas inconceivable to her that her battered heart could go on beating as if nothing had happened. As if Austyn still loved her.

She uncurled her stiff limbs. Dried tearstains had hardened the tender skin of her face. She did not mind, preferring its expressionless mask to any vain twitch of sorrow or hope. She found the numbness a blissful relief, especially when she realized it had crept all the way to her bones.

She rose to face the chamber. She would not have been surprised had Austyn abandoned her to total darkness, but freshets of moonlight streamed through the cracks in the wooden shutters hanging askew from their hinges.

The circular tower defied her expectations. She found no horde of rats nibbling on a fresh carcass. No bleached bones rising to dance a clattering jig. Not even a chorus of Gavenmore brides wailing their mockery at her for failing to heed their warnings. She had anticipated the spartan horrors of a dungeon, but instead found herself in the most luxuriously appointed chamber in the entire castle.

Decades of neglect had left their stain of decay, yet the room still possessed the faded elegance of an elderly woman who clung to her velvets and silks to maintain her fragile illusion of beauty. The thick fall of cobwebs only added to its unearthly air, billowing from the rafters of the vaulted ceiling like veils of ermine.

Holly drifted farther into the chamber, her footsteps muffled by the heavy tapestries surrounding the walls. A massive four-poster bed crowned a gilded pedestal in the center of the room. Not even the moth-eaten condition of its hangings could disguise their brocaded splendor. Tattered velvet ribbons hung from each of the thick, carved bedposts. Holly reached to caress one absently, wondering at its purpose. A magnificent chest resting on four carved claws perched at the foot of the bed.

She ran a finger over its dust-furred surface. A pot of dry, crumbled rouge lay beside a silver comb and an empty scent bottle, reminding Holly with stark clarity that another woman had once occupied this opulent prison. A woman accused of infidelity by her husband, then cut off from his company with ruthless finality, leaving her only these mocking mementos of his former affections.

She lifted the lid of a squat silver box, half expecting to find a severed finger or some other such horror. Her breath caught as the grudging moonlight sparkled over a king's ransom of gold and gems. She buried her fingers in the tangled treasure, sifting through an emerald-studded fillet, a diamond brooch, a ruby-encrusted pendant on a gold chain thicker than her smallest finger. Why in God's name hadn't Austyn sold them to sate Edward's greedy tax collectors? she wondered. Surely it wasn't out of respect for his poor dead grandmother.

Dropping the jewels as if they were a nest of snakes, she went to the window and tore open the shutters. No stingy arrow loop here, but a generous rectangular window framed by stone window seats. 'Twould have to be a large window, she thought bitterly, large enough for a woman to hurl herself out of.

Wind battered Holly, scorching the barren dryness of her eyes. The dizzying height offered her a panoramic view of the surrounding countryside bathed in a silvery quilt of moonlight, but little more than a slice of the solitary courtyard below. She gazed down at the cobblestones, wondering if any trace of blood remained to stain their pitted surface.

A sigh grazed her nape, faint yet audible enough to make the fine fleece there stand erect. She closed her eyes, fearful the ghostly echo would awaken her from her benumbed state. The sigh escalated into a bereft moan that mirrored her suppressed grief so exactly she feared the sound had come from her own throat.

The shutters began to flap wildly on their hinges. Holly backed away from the window, stricken by terror. The moan rose to a piercing wail, a keening protestation of wronged innocence. Her heel caught the edge of the hooded hearth and she fell hard on her backside. She clapped her hands over her ears, but the lamentation swelled until it vibrated the very marrow of her bones to aching life.

Tearing her hands away from her ears, she screamed, "Stop it, damn you! Stop it, I say!"

The shutters slammed shut. The howling ceased as abruptly as it had began, leaving her in silence. Quaking like a dormouse, she searched the shadows, fearing an even more dire visitation.

The shutters swung open with a creak. A dank gust of breath stirred her hair. She swiveled to stare into the fireplace, finding nothing but cold ashes and the tiny skeleton of some unfortunate rodent.

A shrill whistle assailed her ears, escalating to a tormented shriek as a musty draft poured from the gaping jaws of the fireplace.

"The wind," Holly whispered in dull astonishment. " 'Tis only the wind whistling down the chimney flue."

An abashed giggle escaped her, then another. She cupped a hand over her mouth, but the torrent of mirth refused to subside. Soon she was laughing aloud, laughing until her sides ached and tears streamed down her cheeks.

She was utterly alone now. Without Austyn. Without even the ghost of his grandmother to share her exile. Holly doubled over, gasping for breath, never even realizing when her laughter deepened into broken sobs.

Carey found Austyn standing atop the battlements on a completed section of curtain wall, gazing over the molten pewter of the river by moonlight. The balmy wind whipped the dark veil of his hair from his face, revealing features as soulless and foreign as an infidel's. He bore little resemblance to the man Carey had called friend through sunny days and stormy battles and none at all to the bright-eyed boy with the ready smile and rollicking laugh he remembered from childhood.

"The priest is secured," Carey said softly, folding himself into a sitting position between two merlons, "but I cannot coax her nurse to stop weeping. I fear the woman's tears will flood the hall before she's done."

"Let them," Austyn replied, his face betraying not even a flicker of pity. "My father?"

"Sleeping at last. He was quite excited. It took several spoonfuls of mead to calm him."

They were both silent for several moments before Carey dared to ask, "Did she tell you why?"

Austyn gave a harsh bark of laughter. "Shouldn't the question be 'Did I bother to ask?' "

Carey already knew the answer to that. "What will you do with her?"

"Why? Do *you* want her?" At first, Carey feared his friend did not speak in jest, then a humorless smile quirked Austyn's lips. "What are my choices? Had he not gone to such pains to be rid of her, I could send her back to her father. Given her talent for mummery, I could sell her to a band of passing troubadours. Or I could just keep her locked in the north tower until her hair grays and her pearly little teeth fall out one by one."

"And if she chooses to escape captivity as your grandmother did?"

192

Austyn shrugged. "Then I shall once again be without a wife. 'Twould be almost a pity though." His voice softened to a musing purr, his eyes taking on a speculative gleam Carey did not recognize. "Do you know that she promised me anything if I would not lock her away? Pleaded quite prettily for her freedom, she did. Fires the imagination, does it not? The temptation of having a beauty like that on her knees before you, eager to do your bidding . . ."

"Stop it!" Carey jumped to his feet, no longer able to bear Austyn's taunting. "She's still your wife, man, not some London-town whore. Have you no shame?"

Austyn's icy indifference shattered with a roar. "Aye, I have shame! I burn with it. Shame for being such a fool! Shame for being so blinded by her charms that I couldn't see through her ridiculous disguise! Shame that I was ready to offer the deceitful little creature my love." Austyn turned away, gripping a stone merlon until his knuckles whitened.

Carey reached for his friend's shoulder, then let his hand fall back to his side, sensing his comfort would be neither welcomed nor accepted. "You were no more fool than the rest of us," he said.

When Carey's soft footfalls had faded, Austyn threw back his head, savoring the roar of the wind in his ears. He had hoped its savage clamor might drown out the haunting echoes of Holly's pleas, her pathetic screams as she begged him not to leave her, to stay by her side even if he would extract a terrible price for doing so. He could still feel the weight of her fragile arms clinging to his neck, the plush softness of her breasts pressed to his chest.

He gritted his teeth against the primal urge to howl with loss. He wanted to go to her. To batter down the door that stood between them with his bare fists. To draw her beneath him and rut her like a ravening beast, as if to prove to them both that that was all he ever would be. All any Gavenmore man could be.

He had not shared his darkest shame with Carey — that he had locked away his wife not to punish her, but to protect her from himself.

He searched the indigo sky, finding in its star-tossed sweep no warmth, but only a frigid beauty that chilled him to the marrow.

"You heartless bitch," he whispered hoarsely, unable to say if he was cursing Rhiannon or his wife.

At a muffled thump outside the door, Holly awoke from a stupor nearer to death than slumber. She did not remember crawling to the bed or curling up on the tattered ermine coverlet. She unfurled her stiff limbs, sneezing as her movements stirred up a cloud of dust.

The sound came again, the unmistakable thud of someone fumbling with the bolt. Holly sat straight up. Some cynical demon had already convinced her that Austyn would pack up his household and ride away without a backward glance, leaving her to starve. But as the door swung open, her heart lurched with a hope she despised, but could not help.

Her pulse ceased its expectant thundering when a crown of flaxen braids appeared, but her disappointment was quickly squelched by joy at the sight of Winifred's familiar face. She jumped down from the bed and ran over to her.

"Oh, Winnie, you cannot know how glad I am to see you. I knew you wouldn't desert me."

Winnie's plump cheeks had been robbed of their ruddy glow. Puffs of flesh hid her eyes as she rested the tray she carried on a table and turned back toward the door.

Holly could not believe she was going to go. Without a glance. Without a word.

She trailed behind the mute woman, her desperation swelling. "Please, Winnie. Has Austyn forbade you to speak to me? Are you afraid he'll punish you if you do? If you could just convince him to come here. To grant me a few meager moments of his time so that I might explain . . ." Winnie reached for the door handle. Holly clutched her arm, starved for the warmth of a human touch. "If Austyn refuses to come, then send Carey. Austyn will listen to Carey. I know he will!"

"Have you lost your wits, girl?" Winifred hissed, jerking her arm from Holly's grip. Holly recoiled from the wounded virulence in her eyes. "Do you seek to have my son cast into the dungeon with that rash young priest of yours?"

Holly felt a flare of shame that she hadn't even paused to consider Nathanael's plight. For all she knew, Austyn might have returned to the courtyard and whacked off his inflated head.

"Of course not," she replied. "I would never wish Carey harm. He has been naught but a friend to me."

"Aye, and I see how you repay him. How you've repaid us all."

Kind-hearted Winifred's derision was even harder to bear than Austyn's. Holly's lower lip began to quiver; her eyes welled with tears.

As Winifred stared at Holly's rumpled chemise, her matted curls, her grubby, tear-streaked cheeks, the woman's broad face slowly crumpled in horror. "Oh, God," she whispered, "you're so beautiful." Staggering over to a stool, she sank down and buried her face in her hands.

Holly crept near to her, longing to pat her shuddering shoulder, but fearful of being rejected. She dropped to one knee at the woman's feet. "Please don't cry, Winnie. I never meant to make you cry."

"Don't you know what a terrible thing it is you've done?" Winifred lifted her head; her Welsh accent was thickened by grief. "We thought you were different. That you might be the one to finally break the curse." At last Holly understood their open-armed welcome of Austyn's new bride, their unabashed delight in her ugliness. "And now 'tis happening all over again. The lies. The jealousy. The accusations. Half of them calling you a shape-shifting witch and begging the master to burn you at the stake. The other half

195

blaming him for locking you away."

"What do you think? Do you think I'm a witch? A monster?" Holly could not have said why Winnie's reply was so vital to her.

Winifred studied her from beneath her damp lashes, then shook her head. "I think you're a foolish girl who's played a nasty trick on a man as much son to me as my own. Don't ask me to help you. For I won't."

Holly straightened as Winifred brushed past her. "I still love him," she said defiantly before the door could close.

"Then may God have pity on your soul," Winifred murmured before shutting the door and dropping the bolt into place.

Winifred came twice a day after that, bearing hearty meals of stew and fresh baked bread, ewers of steaming water for bathing, and crisp linen sheets, but never again did Holly shed a tear or utter a single plea for help. She sent most of the trays back untouched and left the clean sheets piled on the chest, preferring to curl up each night on top of the moth-eaten coverlet.

When Winifred stiffly told her, "The master wants to know if you require anything else for your comfort — extra blankets or perhaps a fire to warm you at night," Holly burst into peals of merry laughter, their shrill edge sending the woman fleeing from the tower.

For Holly knew that no measure of blankets could warm her. No fire could banish the chill from her soul. She might have been deprived of the company of Austyn's grandmother, but she still felt a keen kinship with the woman. She finally understood that 'twas not being falsely accused that had driven her to that window or the tedium of her own company. 'Twas the anguish of being torn from the arms of the man she loved. Knowing she would never again see his crooked smile or watch the way his eyes warmed when they beheld her.

But there the similarities ended. For Austyn's grandmother had

196

been innocent of wrongdoing and Holly knew herself to be guilty, guilty of a cruel deception. If Austyn left her there for a month or a century, she would be no less deserving of her punishment.

She roamed the tower in her frayed chemise as the minutes melted into hours, the hours into days. The wind wailed its melancholy refrain and she found herself standing more often than not at the tower window, gazing down at the courtyard below with an emotion akin to yearning.

Nearly a fortnight had passed when she began to envision her body there, pale and broken on the cobblestones, and to wonder what Austyn's reaction would be when he discovered it. Would he cradle her across his lap and repent his harshness as his father had done, or would he be relieved to be rid of her so tidily, sparing him the embarrassment of seeking an annulment from the king?

Holly stepped up on the window seat, then onto the narrow sill, bracing her palms against the cut stones that framed the opening. The warm wind pummeled her, molding the thin garment to her shivering body, bearing on its wings the ripe scents of summer and life and freedom. She lifted her eyes from the cobblestones and gazed across the Welsh countryside, drinking in its rugged beauty. A beauty so wild and sweet it hurt her eyes to look upon it, yet so compelling she could not bear to look away and forsake all of its unspoken promises for the morrow.

Holly's knees collapsed. She crawled back on the window seat, clamping a hand over her mouth, ill with the thought of what she might have done had the bullying wind not snapped her out of her haze of despair. Feeling as if she'd just awakened from an enchanted sleep, she gazed around the tower, seeing it with crystalline clarity for the first time. Her father might have pronounced her selfish and wayward, but he would not have wished such a heartless penance upon her. Despite what her husband might have chosen to believe, she was guilty of idiocy, not adultery.

The wind whined down the chimney flue, no longer a comfort

but an irritant. Holly sprang off the window seat, snatched the wad of pristine sheets from the chest and stuffed them up the flue. Her stomach growled its approval. Marching over to the table, she grabbed an untouched loaf of bread, then sank down cross-legged on the floor. As she tore off fat hunks of bread and tossed them in her mouth, she felt a blazing surge of something in her belly. Something even more dangerous and wonderful than hunger.

Anger.

When Winifred came to deliver supper and fresh water for bathing to the tower that night, Holly informed her that she required only two things: pen and paper. Although fearing the girl would scribble some maudlin, tear-smeared missive Sir Austyn would refuse to read, Winnie dutifully delivered both items the following morning.

When she returned at twilight, Holly presented her with a ten-page list of articles she required from the master for her comfort. The words *master* and *comfort* were underlined with a scathing flourish.

Winnie and two wide-eyed maidservants trundled in the next morning, staggering beneath their assorted burdens of tub, towels, sheets, embroidery frame, thread, fragrant oils, fresh apples, harp, beeswax tapers, broom, bedclothes, books, and various other treasures that would make Holly's captivity tolerable, if not pleasant.

The girls continued to gape at her, even as Winifred shooed them out and shut the door in their faces. Winnie awkwardly cleared her throat. "The master wishes to know if you require any lemons to rub on your elbows, or perhaps a Nubian slave to comb your hair five hundred strokes before bedtime."

Holly snapped a crisp bite from a fat red apple. "Tell him that given the current length of my hair, two hundred and fifty strokes should be sufficient."

When Winifred had gone, Holly surveyed her plunder with a calculating eye. She had chosen few items that could not be used as a weapon against her husband. She'd already pillaged the chest

198

at the foot of the bed for her armor — brocaded cottes woven of samite and cloth of gold, twin cloaks lined with the softest sable, sendal chemises so sheer they appeared more suited to a harem than a noblewoman's bedchamber. Most were in need of only minor repairs and a healthy airing.

Holly carried cloaks, thread, and needle to the window seat and curled up in the sunshine. A devilish smile played around her lips. If Austyn thought he was going to just lock her away and forget her existence, he had sorely underestimated his opponent. 'Twas here while she prepared for battle that she would wield her most lethal weapon of all.

Tipping back her head, Holly began to sing.

Chapter 21

Holly sang.

She sang while she swiped the dust from the furniture and swept the timber floor. She sang while she replaced the moth-eaten coverlet with the wedded cloaks, creating an inviting nest of plush sable. She sang while Winifred and the maidservants carried in buckets of steaming water for her bath. She sang while she soaked her weary muscles in the tub and afterward, while she rubbed oil of myrrh into her neglected skin, restoring its pearly glow. She sang while she combed her flourishing curls and each night when she lay down upon her pillow, she sang herself softly to sleep.

She sang cheery May songs and wistful ballads. She sang stirring Crusade anthems and complex rounds, alternating the parts of the different singers. She sang children's rhymes and bawdy ditties. She sang liturgical chants, spinning songs, lays, and laments. And one evening at sunset, she stood at the window of the tower and warbled a hymn so full-throated and magnificent that even Nathanael in his dungeon cell lifted his eyes heavenward, seeking a choir of celestial angels.

Austyn suffered no such delusions. 'Twas no heavenly visitation, this scourge of melody, but a demonic infestation. Each note pricked his tortured flesh like a tine of Lucifer's pitchfork. There was nowhere he could flee to escape the compelling sorcery of Holly's voice. He could ride to the ends of the earth and still it would pursue him.

He did not know if she sang in *her* sleep, but by God, she sang in *his*. In his fevered dreams, she sang only for him while he coaxed

200

her to a climax of flawless rhythm and perfect pitch.

'Twas not her soaring hymns that disturbed him most, but the simple lullabies she sang at night when her voice had grown weary with just a hint of a husky croak. 'Twas then that he found her most beguiling. 'Twas then that he had to brutally remind himself that the sirens had sought only to lure Ulysses to certain doom.

Then one twilight eve when he thought he was going to have to beg Carey to tie him to one of the pillars in the courtyard just as Ulysses had been bound to his own mast, the singing ceased. Just like that. No hint of hoarseness. No fading. It simply ceased.

The silence was more terrible than anyone had anticipated. A pall of dejection descended like a black cloud over the castle. When Austyn strode into the great hall, all conversation lurched to a halt and he felt the gazes of everyone in the hall settle on him. He'd grown accustomed to their weight in the past month. Grown accustomed to Carey's furtive glances, Winnie's nervous stares, Emrys's unspoken question of, "What monstrous thing will he do next?" Gone were the days when they had looked upon him with pride and admiration instead of fear.

Most damning of all were the swollen eyes and perpetually reddened nose of his wife's nurse. Austyn suspected the old woman would have fled for help long ago if she hadn't feared to leave her mistress at his mercy.

Even his father, who had not uttered a single word since his harangue from the parapet, blinked up at him with the wide, frightened eyes of a child. With his soul so recently stripped of melody, Austyn felt naked and raw beneath their probing scrutiny. Suddenly, he could bear it no more.

"What ails the lot of you?" he bellowed, whirling around to glare at them. "Are you never going to smile again? Laugh again? Speak above a godforsaken whisper?"

With a heart-wrenching sob, Elspeth threw her apron over her face and burst into tears. But not before Austyn had caught a glimpse of himself through her eyes — a towering brute, more ogre than man.

The deafening hush only made the music of Holly's voice clearer, more seductive. She beckoned him with her crystalline silence, driving him to stride blindly toward the stairs, determined to confront the enchantress who had bewitched him into such a beast.

Austyn's treads slowed as he neared the north tower. The silence was no longer pristine, but haunted by the echoes of Holly's screams and pleas as he had dragged her up the winding stairs beneath his feet. 'Twas as if the ancient stones had absorbed her piteous cries. His wrists and forearms still bore the fading marks of her scratches, but he feared the deeper scars of her betrayal and his abandonment would never heal.

His hands shook as he lifted the heavy bolt from its iron brackets. He had no idea what he might find. Each time Winifred had dolefully displayed an untouched tray for his inspection, he had hardened his heart to images of Holly's vibrant flesh wasting from her bones.

The door creaked open beneath the coaxing of his hand. A cobweb drifted across his face; he swiped it away, fighting a shudder. The chamber was bathed in the gathering shadows of dusk. Fading light drifted through the open window.

There was no sign of Holly. A chill of dread caressed Austyn's spine as the abrupt cessation of song took on a more sinister cast. He stood transfixed by the gaping maw of that window. The window Carey had begged him to fix an iron grate over. The window overlooking the enclosed courtyard he had forbade anyone to enter. The one man fool enough to scale the wall and try to steal a glimpse of his captive bride had been exiled from Caer Gavenmore with naught but the tunic on his back.

Austyn took a hesitant step. Then he was hurling himself toward the void, leaning out just as a honeyed voice behind him said, "I wouldn't give you the satisfaction."

Sparrows twittered and hopped on the cobblestones below, mocking him with their serenity. Austyn slowly turned as a woman brushed aside a veil of webs and emerged from the shadows around the bed.

"Sorry to disappoint you so sorely," she said, "but I've not made a widower of you yet."

He folded his arms over his chest, much as he had done the first time they met. "A pity. I thought perhaps you had sang yourself to death."

The lit taper Holly carried cast a flickering halo around her, giving Austyn his first true look at her since she'd stood trembling and debased by his brutal perusal in the river.

She was slender, aye, but hardly wasted. Her breasts swelled against the brocaded bodice of her cotehardie as if seeking to overflow it. Her skin had lost its sun-burnished hue, but its translucence only made her look more fragile, more alluring. He fought the urge, but his gaze drifted to her face of its own volition.

If she'd thought to ruin her appearance by cropping her hair, she'd sorely miscalculated. The dark cap of curls framing her face only enhanced its heart-shaped purity. The missed meals had sculpted beguiling hollows beneath her cheekbones. If anything, she was more beautiful than she'd been in the garden at Tewksbury. She'd been naught but a shallow girl then. Now her violet eyes sparkled with the complex depths of a woman.

Austyn narrowed his eyes, seeking any hint of the awkward, charming girl he had called wife for a few idyllic weeks. He found nothing of her in the exotic creature standing before him. 'Twas her loss that both wounded and enraged him beyond bearing.

"Why?" he asked hoarsely. "Did you and your father think it a fine jest to play upon an ignorant Welshman?"

She rested the taper on a stone corbel jutting from the wall, but lingered near enough to remain bathed in its lambent light. " 'Twas never meant as a jest at all. My father sought to wed me to a

203

stranger. I believed I had no other choice than to try and stop him. Have you never felt powerless?"

Powerless to resist you, Austyn thought, but he would have died before uttering the words. "Powerless? With your father's wealth at your disposal? Your own beauty a sword to drive into any man's heart?"

"You see where beauty has gotten me. It has been naught but a curse since the day I was born." She widened her eyes in mock innocence. "And you, of all men, should understand curses."

Austyn scowled at her, admiring her boldness against his will.

"I sought only to repel my suitors," she continued. "How was I to know you'd be so pigheaded as to pursue me despite my ugliness? Or so greedy, I might add?"

"Greedy?"

She tilted her delicate chin to a defiant angle. "Aye, greedy! You dare to cast shadows on my own motives while yours were none too pure. You sought not a wife, but a fat purse to swell your coffers. As I see it, sir, you are no better than I."

'Twas all Holly could do to stand her ground when Austyn came swaggering toward her. She had spent the lonely days and interminable nights plotting schemes to summon him to her, not what to do with him once he arrived. As he entered the spill of candlelight, she bit back an involuntary gasp.

He was dressed all in black with the shadow of a new beard darkening his cheeks. He looked younger, more gaunt, yet somehow larger and infinitely less manageable.

He circled her like a wary raptor, his eyes narrowed to frosty slits. "You've had ample time to concoct such a cunning tale. Why should I believe you? How do I know your father didn't seek to marry you off to some unsuspecting jape because you'd been ruined?" His gaze flicked to her taut belly, then back to her eyes. "How do I know that even as we speak your womb doesn't thicken with another man's babe?"

Holly choked back her outrage and managed a sneer of her own. "And I suppose you believe this imaginary lover of mine followed me here to Gavenmore in the guise of a priest?"

At the murderous flare of his eyes, Holly feared her sarcasm might cost both she and Nathanael their heads. But Austyn swung away from her, flexing his fingers as if to keep them from curling around her throat.

Mustering her courage, Holly moved to stand within his view. If her beauty was his only weakness, then she would exploit it to her full advantage.

"Since you're determined to believe me a harlot, regardless of the truth," she said softly, "what will you do with me, Austyn? Will you beat me?" Taking a terrible chance, she reached for his hand. He flinched at her touch, but did not pull away. She cradled his knuckles in the cup of her palm, gently folding each finger until they formed a mighty fist. " 'Tis well within your rights as my husband. Or will you burn me at the stake, laughing as my tender flesh melts in the flames?"

She surrendered his hand to splay her palms against his chest with reckless abandon, whispering over the erratic thunder of his heart. "Or will you simply turn around and leave me here? Walk away and bolt the door behind you as your grandfather did. Forget you ever saw my face, heard my voice, kissed my lips . . ."

His ravenous gaze caressed her face. Holly moistened her lips, nearly breathless with hope.

Austyn tore away from her with a harsh laugh. "Is that what Winifred told you? She always did have a gift for glossing over the more sordid aspects of the family history."

Holly's confidence faltered. "What do you mean?"

With one fleet step, he jumped up on the pedestal supporting the bed. Holly would not have recognized the cynical quirk of his lips as a smile were it not accompanied by a diabolical flash of his dimple.

"Oh, my grandfather did imprison my grandmother in this tower for ten years. But he never forgot her. On the contrary, legend has it that he returned to rape her nightly. With unflagging enthusiasm." Austyn reached out to finger one of the frayed ribbons still attached to the bedpost, shooting her a naughty glance from beneath his dark lashes. " 'Tis whispered he was quite imaginative in his . . . punishments." The ribbon slipped through Austyn's deft fingers. " 'Twas only after he bored of the sport and sought solace in the arms of another that she hurled herself to her death."

A shiver of shameful anticipation coursed down Holly's spine as Austyn stepped off the pedestal. She took an involuntary step backward, wondering too late what manner of predator she had engaged.

He strode right past her, making for the door.

"Austyn?" she said.

He turned, the sensual curves of his mouth robbed of any hint of humor.

"I'm innocent."

He sketched her a mocking bow. "That, my lady, remains to be seen."

As the bolt thudded into place, Holly groped blindly for the nearest stool. Even as she pressed her fingertips to her lips to still their trembling, she felt a spark of triumph. For she had seen the indisputable truth in her husband's eyes. He would return to her.

One night passed. Then three more. By the end of a sennight, Holly's hopes were beginning to wane. Perhaps, she feared, her goading had only driven Austyn further from her embrace. Perhaps he, like his grandfather, had chosen to seek his pleasures in the arms of another.

Her eyes clouded at the image, her throat tightening with a sense of loss as keen and poignant as anything she had endured since her mother's death. She tried to sing, but found the melodies would not come. Even the most soulful of ballads failed to convey the depth of her yearning.

As a sennight melted into a fortnight, she ceased to don the elaborate cottes each day, ceased struggling to arrange her unruly curls into some semblance of elegance.

Late one night, she curled up on the window seat in her chemise and watched a summer storm batter its way across the sky. The far horizon vanished as black clouds billowed toward the castle. Thunder rumbled and jagged forks of lightning crackled over the roiling cauldron of the river. Holly hugged her knees, paralyzed by the inevitability of the approaching maelstrom. 'Twas a kindred spirit, prowling the sky with a hunger as wild and restless as her own.

'Twas only when the wind began to drive sheets of rain against her skin that she rose to latch the shutters, unable to bear the elusive scent of freedom. She paced the tower, lighting every taper to cast a fragile pall of brightness over the gloom.

The wind hammered the shutters with angry fists. Holly curled up on the bed and struggled to focus her torn attentions on an illuminated manuscript detailing the spiritual ecstasies of Mechtild of Magdeburg, bride of Christ. Perhaps Austyn had sent it so that she might prepare her own wicked soul for its future in the nunnery, she thought bitterly.

Between one sullen growl of thunder and the next, the door crashed open and Holly jerked up her head to meet the smoldering eyes of her earthly husband.

Chapter 22

Austyn had envisioned Holly in many guises in the past fortnight: haughty lady sneering down at her patrician nose at him; malicious harpy berating him for his greed; bewitching temptress taunting him with a flutter of her burgeoning lashes and a flick of her moist, pink tongue. But as he gazed at her curled on the bed of sable like a small, contented cat, he realized each of those women were only illusions contrived to distract him from who she really was.

His wife.

The thin chemise had puddled around her hips, baring her slender legs. 'Twas impossible for a man to look upon such legs and not envision them wrapped around his waist. As if Holly had divined his thoughts, she tugged the chemise down to shield them from his gaze. Her modesty pricked his conscience, stirring his conflicting desires to protect and possess.

He tore down the veil of webs that separated them with a savage swipe. "Rather enjoying playing the captive princess, aren't you, sweeting? Would you like me to fan you with peacock feathers or pop grapes in your mouth?" His sarcasm betrayed him, battering him with images of Holly's succulent lips parting to receive whatever he would give her.

Holly moved to a sitting position, warily eyeing the savage stranger she had once called "husband." His hair was unkempt, his eyes red-rimmed and wild, as if he hadn't slept since their last encounter. He'd been seething with icy anger then, but now an edge of desperation sharpened his expression. Holly longed to reach out to him, but did not dare. She knew with a conviction beyond faith that if she drove him to abandon her this night, he would never return.

She hid her distress behind a mask of scorn. "If you think I take any pleasure in my captivity, then you're sorely mistaken. I'd gladly trade my lavish cell to lay in a meadow of fresh cut hay or feel the cool rain beat on my face. But I suppose you wouldn't understand that, being the sort of man who locks up a lady and allows a murderer free roam of his castle."

Austyn's faint flinch told her she had struck well and deep. "You, my lady, committed your treachery willfully. My father had no choice."

Had Holly not been convinced that Austyn believed every word he was saying, she would have given vent to the hysterical laugh that welled in her throat. "Ah, the dreaded curse of the Gavenmores! Refresh my memory. Was it cast by a temperamental mermaid offended by some clumsy fisherman?" She wiggled her graceful fingers at him. "Or some fat little Booka infuriated because one of your ancestors stepped on his toadstool?"

A becoming flush crawled up Austyn's throat. Holly doubted that anyone had ever dared to question the veracity of the Gavenmore curse. At least not to his face. " 'Twas neither," he strangled out. " 'Twas the faerie queen Rhiannon, a cruel and heartless witch."

"A heartless witch falsely accused of infidelity." Holly twined a curl around her finger, pursing her lips in a thoughtful pout. "If a man refuses to trust a woman he claims to love, then tell me, husband, who between them is the faithless one? Has it never occurred to you that your father might be cursed with nothing more than a savage temper? Perhaps 'twas his own wretched jealousy that drove your mother into the arms of another man."

"Enough!" Austyn roared. "You know naught of what you speak. Perhaps you seek only to justify your own infidelity."

Holly sat up on her knees, eager for any opportunity to defend herself. "If you believed that, Nathanael would be dead instead of

209

rotting away in your dungeon. You are a knight, sir. 'Twas I who wronged you; therefore, honor should demand that you free him."

Austyn's caustic smile never reached his eyes. "See how prettily she pleads for her lover's freedom."

"He is not my lover!" Holly yelled, pushed beyond endurance by her husband's stubbornness. "I am innocent!"

Austyn's voice softened to a velvety rasp. "There's only one way to find out, isn't there?"

A fearful hope quickened in Holly's heart. If her husband required proof of her innocence, then she was only too willing to provide it. As he stalked toward the bed pedestal, she scrambled off the other side, provoking him to pursue her with deliberate insolence.

"Did you think Nathanael my only lover? How naive of you! There were scores of others. Dozens! Hundreds!" She ran to the window and wrenched open the shutters. A violent gust of wind and rain extinguished every taper, whipped the webs into a dancing frenzy. Holly refused to cower from Austyn's inevitable approach. "They visit me here in my bed every night." She gave her riotous curls a shake. "I just lower my hair and up they climb!"

Wrapping a muscular arm around her waist, Austyn drove her against the sill, parting her legs with the breadth of his hips. Cold raindrops pelted her back in stark contrast to the rigid heat pressed to the vulnerable hollow between her thighs. He tangled his free hand in her curls, bending her head back until his lips hovered above hers, a sigh away from possession. Each desperate catch of his breath throbbed in her ears.

If only he would kiss her, Holly thought frantically, she might be able to reach the man she had married.

"Why do you hesitate?" she whispered hoarsely. "Is it the curse you fear?"

"The curse has no power over me."

"Why not?"

Holly's world narrowed to the feral gleam of his eyes in the

210

darkness, the note of savage despair in his voice. "Because I would have to love you first."

She knew then that he wasn't going to kiss her. Knew it even as he wrapped an arm around her hips and lifted her to the bed. Knew it as he laid her beneath him on the plush sable, shoved up her chemise, baring her to the waist, and nudged her knees apart.

She reached for him, desiring nothing more than to caress his bearded jaw, thread her fingers through his hair, wrap him in her embrace. But he caught both of her wrists in one hand, his grip a gentle manacle that sought not to bind her in cruelty, but to deprive him of a tenderness that might destroy them both. Shivering with reaction, Holly braced herself for the worst.

Her entire body convulsed as if seared by lightning as one of his deft fingers parted the fleecy down between her thighs.

She turned her face to the pillow, aflame with shyness at his perverse gallantry. He might deny her the kisses and caresses of lovemaking, but he would not brutalize her. Broken gasps escaped from between her clenched teeth as he probed the tender cleft, his big, blunt finger burrowing deeper with each stroke, making her ready to receive him. Devastating tingles of pleasure spread from his touch. When his one finger was joined by another, she could not resist the foreign urge to arch against his hand.

Austyn knew he'd erred the instant his hand breached Holly's silky nether curls. He'd had every intention of bedding her urgently and crudely, as if she were nothing more than a jaded harlot he had laid down his coin for, but the feel of her delicate body shivering beneath his own had stirred some lingering remnant of decency in his soul.

When his finger sought to prime her for his possession, he bit back a groan to discover the fragile cup of her womb already overflowed with nectar for him. 'Twas a bitter sweetness he had not entreated and did not deserve.

It tempted him to graze his thumb across the sensitive nub buried in her own sable pelt. Tempted him to suckle her magnificent breasts through the gossamer sendal of the chemise until she writhed with pleasure beneath him. Tempted him to part the tender petals of her lips with his tongue. But how long would it be before that tongue betrayed him? Before he began to murmur hot, hoarse words against her mouth, the curve of her throat, the satiny cream of her belly? Words of tenderness. Words of love. Words of doom.

His reckless musings cost him dearly. Holly's hand escaped his and twined around his nape, scorching him like a red-hot brand.

Ruthlessly quenching every longing but his most primal one, Austyn unfastened his hose, linked his fingers through hers and pressed her hands back on each side of her head.

Holly clung to Austyn's strong hands, all she knew of substance in a shadowy universe of torrential rain, crashing thunder, and howling winds. When terror threatened to overwhelm her, she reminded herself that this was no stranger looming over her, but her Austyn — big and warm and smelling of mint and the musk of his need.

A flash of lightning illuminated the tower. Their gazes locked for a brief eternity, then he drove himself between her splayed legs with a guttural groan, cleaving the fragile barrier of her innocence.

Holly's fingers arched along with her back as a bright lance of pain consumed her. Austyn's hand could have ravished her for hours and not prepared her for this fulsome weight inside of her. He seemed overwhelming to her, so massive she did not know how her slight body could contain him. Yet somehow it did, adjusting magically to welcome the length and breadth of him into her melting core.

As the pain subsided, she squeezed his hands until their palms were mated as tightly as their bodies. He ground his hips against her own, wedging himself as deep in her throbbing sheath as she could take him, then withdrawing to do it again. His hands held her captive to his will while his body bludgeoned her with waves

212

of dark pleasure until she could hardly recognize the sound of her own voice, entreating him with broken moans and hoarse whimpers for some shimmering reprieve he alone could deliver.

His only reply other than the harsh rasp of his breathing was to double the intensity and rhythm of his earthy siege. She gasped with pure delight as every muscle of his powerful body went as rigid as the part of him buried to the hilt in her. Lightning sizzled through the tower, gifting her with a glimpse of the savage beauty of his features as he threw back his head in exultation, breaking his silence at last to roar her name in an incantation of pure ecstasy.

He collapsed against her, burying his face against her throat. Holly slipped her hand from beneath his limp one, thinking only to curl her fingers in the damp silk of his hair. He rolled off of her with nary a word, adjusted his hose, and went striding from the tower as if a legion of demons nipped at his heels.

Holly lay there in the dark with her bare legs sprawled apart, her chemise crumpled around her waist, her tender body still overflowing with the scalding bounty of her husband's seed and murmured, "Oh, my."

Austyn's steps grew heavy as he descended the winding stairs to the great hall. The cavernous chamber was deserted, the dying embers of the fire in the central hearth its only light. A tankard of ale and an abandoned goblet sat on the table. The storm's threat had subsided to a distant rumble of thunder and the muted patter of rain on the battlements.

At the discordant strum of fingers against lute strings, Austyn nearly jumped out of his skin.

"What ails you, man? Guilty conscience?"

Austyn scowled into the shadows fringing the hall, finally making out the luster of Carey's fair hair. " 'Tis fortunate I'm unarmed. I might have mistaken you for a Viking raider and whacked off your pretty head."

213

Carey plucked a few saucy notes in reply, then tilted his head to study him. "That didn't take nearly as long as I thought it would."

For a searing moment, Austyn hated his friend for knowing him so well. It took little more than his heightened color to betray him to Carey. He strode over to the table, poured a strong splash of ale in the goblet and drank it down in one swallow. "I didn't rape her, if that's what you're thinking."

"Would I imply such? I have no doubt that she simply succumbed to your gallant charms. What did you do? Growl some poetry at her?"

Austyn clenched his teeth to suppress a growl. "There is no need of such nonsense between us. She is my wife. I had every right to determine if she had lain with another man before me."

Carey's tone was as light as his fingers dancing over the strings. "And had she?"

"No," Austyn replied, despising his own sullen tone.

"But that didn't stop you, did it?"

Nor could Austyn stop himself from reliving that moment when he'd primed himself with Holly's copious balm and breached the taut cocoon of her body. She'd fit him like a silken gauntlet. Even as guilt assailed him at the memory of her muffled whimper, his insatiable body stirred to life.

He slammed the goblet on the table, paying it no heed when it overturned. "What would you have had me do? Withdraw and apologize? Say 'Forgive me, my lady, for piercing your maidenhead. I can promise you 'twill never happen again.' " He paced over to the stairs, sank down on the lowest step, and rested his aching head in his hands. "God forgive me, Carey, I used her like a common whore," he confessed hoarsely. "I kissed neither her lips nor her breasts. I offered her not a word of kindness or solace. I swear I did not deliberately seek to hurt her. I left no bruises to mar her beautiful skin." He raked his fingers through his hair, lifting his despairing gaze to Carey's face. "At least none you can see."

214

Carey only strummed a thoughtful chord.

Austyn shook his head. "I had such tender courtesies plotted for my wife's seduction before I discovered her treachery. Scented tapers and spiced wine. Gentle kisses and honeyed words. Yet I offered her none of those tonight."

The lute fell silent. "And she accepted your brutish attentions with open . . . um, arms?"

Austyn nodded.

"Then perhaps you should ask yourself why."

As Carey rose and strolled from the hall, his fingers plucking a pensive melody, Austyn stared into the glowing embers on the hearth. He had bedded Holly without grace or tenderness, fearing that if he allowed his hands to explore the extravagant curves of her breasts or given his thirsty lips leave to sip the honeyed nectar of her mouth, his soul would be eternally lost.

Yet as he buried his face in hands still scented with the wedded spices of musk and myrrh, he felt more damned than ever before.

Chapter 23

Holly was drowsing in the sunshine of the window seat the following morning when she saw the donkey appear in the distance. She had slept late, overcome with a delicious languor that had yet to subside. As she recognized the robed figure astride the donkey, she sat up on her knees, wincing as her tender muscles twinged in protest.

Even from her dizzying perch, the dejected slump of the rider's shoulders was evident. Nathanael must know what his freedom had cost her. Even if Austyn hadn't been so vindictive as to enlighten him, the priest was bright enough to realize that if her husband still harbored the faintest suspicion that he'd been her lover, he would have been carried away from Caer Gavenmore on a burial litter, not a donkey.

As she watched, he slowed the animal and glanced back over his shoulder.

She lifted her hand in a farewell salute, murmuring, "God go with you, brother."

Nathanael did not return her wave, but stared up at the tower for a long time before plodding on. Troubled by mingled affection and regret, Holly watched him fade to a tiny speck on a vast canvas of moor and mountains still damp from last night's storm.

"Austyn should never have sent him alone," she muttered to herself. "The man has a wretched sense of direction. He'll probably ride straight into the sea or incite some hot-headed Scot to martyr him."

She had little time to fret over Nathanael's fate for the dull clatter of the bolt being lifted warned her invasion was imminent. She lifted her chin, unable to stifle the expectant flutter of the pulse in her throat.

'Twas not her husband, but Winifred and a flock of tittering maidservants who entered, each one of them bearing an urn of steaming water. Winnie kept her head bowed, more reticent even than before, but Holly noted that poppies once again blossomed in her cheeks. Her mouth was compressed to a stiff line, as if she might burst into giggles herself at the slightest provocation.

Her darting gaze managed to ricochet off everything in the tower except Holly's face and the bed. "The master thought you might enjoy a hot bath this morning." She nodded down at the crisp bundle in her arms. "And some fresh sheets."

The girls ceased pouring water into the tub long enough to nudge each other and steal sly glances at the rumpled bed. Winnie gave the one nearest to her a warning swat to her generous backside.

Holly stood to greet them, inclining her head as if her chemise was a mantle of ermine and her disheveled curls a crown. If they thought she was going to blush and stammer with shame over the long overdue consummation of her marriage, they were sorely mistaken.

However, she could not quite banish the note of irony that crept into her voice. "How very considerate of him. Do convey my most humble gratitude for his largesse."

"He thought ye might enjoy a bit o' my company as well, my lady."

At the familiar croak, a warm rush of tears blurred Holly's vision. Elspeth emerged from behind Winnie, her wizened little hobgoblin face one of the dearest sights Holly had ever seen. As the nurse scampered into Holly's arms, sobbing joyfully, Winnie and her disciples tactfully withdrew. The hollow thump of the bolt falling into place jarred Holly and Elspeth from their tender reunion, reminding them that Elspeth now shared her mistress's captivity.

Elspeth blotted Holly's cheeks with a license born of long habit

217

before wiping her own eyes. "Oh, my lady, ye cannot know how afrighted I was for ye. With Sir Austyn stalking 'bout the castle like a madman, ne'er sleeping nor eating for days at a time. All of us tiptoeing 'round him, a-whispering 'neath our breaths, lest he turn his temper on us. When he came for ye last night, I thought to stop him, I vow I did. I would have thrown myself on his blade if need be, but Master Carey clapped a hand over my mouth and held it there until 'twas too late."

Holly narrowed her eyes thoughtfully. It seemed Nathanael had not been her sole champion at Caer Gavenmore. Even Winnie had appeared secretly pleased that their union had been consummated. Perhaps the woman had not yet given up hope that Holly might be her master's salvation.

Elspeth shot the decadent disarray of the bed a wide-eyed glance. A shudder rocked her bony shoulders. "Oh, child, was he a terrible beast to you?"

Holly hoped her impish smile would quiet her nurse's fears. "Quite ferocious. But most bears are when they've been cornered in their own dens." She drew herself from Elspeth's embrace and wandered to the tub, leaning over to trail her fingers in the steaming water. "I'd almost dare to venture my beast is suffering rather human qualms of remorse this morn. He frees Nathanael. Sends you to nurse my wounded feelings. Provides a luxurious bath to soothe my . . . um . . . spirits." Holly turned to the bed, beset by misty images of the wondrous act that had taken place there in the darkness. A tingling ribbon of delight curled through her belly. "And clean sheets so that I might whisk away all memory of his debauchery."

"He rode out before dawn," Elspeth volunteered, "his face so fierce I'll wager he's not coming back. And a good riddance to him, I say, for daring to lay a finger on my lady!"

"Oh, he'll be back," Holly said softly, but with grave certainty. She only wondered what his tormented conscience would expect to find. His wife pale and weeping in the window seat, her skin scrubbed raw of his touch, her red-rimmed eyes shadowed by reproach? Or perhaps cowering in the bed with the pristine sheets drawn up over her head?

A slow, dangerous smile curved Holly's lips. "Elspeth, darling, would you mind helping me with a bit of laundry while you're here?"

'Twas near nightfall when Sir Austyn of Gavenmore returned to his castle in utter defeat. He had battled his way through steep, stony gorges, forded streams and rivers swollen by the previous night's rain, and driven his steed over countless leagues of windswept moor. Where once he had sought only the challenges of war to test his mettle, now he sought that most elusive of all prizes: peace.

His quest had been fruitless. The perfume released by the wildflowers crushed beneath his mount's hooves was but a wan imitation of the fragrant bouquet of Holly's skin. The wind tousled his hair, sifting through the damp locks at his nape just as Holly's fingertips had sought to do. The whisper of the breeze in his ears echoed her soft, broken gasps as the silken petals of her untried body had flowered to receive him.

He could not know if they were gasps of pleasure or pain since he had taken neither the time nor the care to find out.

Biting back a fierce oath, Austyn drove the destrier over a crumbling section of curtain wall. Both he and the animal were lathered with sweat and near to trembling with exhaustion. He had hoped he might ride his insatiable appetite for Holly out of his blood, but he feared there was only one way to do that. Desolation tinged his dark hunger. He wondered if his grandfather had dreaded climbing those stairs as much as he did, had known even as he did so that each step carried him nearer to damnation.

Austyn walked the horse past his mother's grave, refusing to honor it with so much as a glance. He could not help but remember the days when he had returned to Caer Gavenmore in triumph, when not even the specter of his father's madness could spoil his pride at returning victor from some tournament or bloody skirmish in which he'd been allowed the privilege of proving his worth in battle. His people would line the courtyard, waving green and crimson kerchiefs and cheering his victory as if it were their own.

A ghost of a cheer reached his ears. Austyn jerked up his head, wondering if impending madness had somehow given substance to his memories. But, no, there it was again — a lusty roar of approval, underscored by a smattering of applause. The sound baffled him. There had been little cause for celebration at Caer Gavenmore since Holly's unmasking and none worthy of such glee since the night he'd brought his ill-favored little bride home to present to his people. His brow clouded at the memory.

He glanced up at the battlements, but all he could see over the roof of the abandoned gatehouse was a thin slice of ivory dangling from a corner merlon. Odd, he thought, narrowing his eyes against the fading light. He could not remember there being a gargoyle perched on that particular embrasure. His eyes widened with astonishment as the gargoyle in question spotted him and went scampering over the parapet to disappear behind a stone chimney.

Besieged by curiosity, he hastened his mount's steps toward the inner bailey. An excited crowd milled beneath the battlements. As they spotted him, their cheers swelled to a roar of acclaim.

A burly beekeeper clapped him on the thigh as he passed. "The purest honey is always worth waitin' for, sir."

An ancient beldame bobbed him a girlish curtsy and crooned, "I'd be pleased if ye'd offer Master Longstaff my regards."

Austyn didn't have the faintest idea who this Longstaff fellow was, nor did he appreciate the rogue getting his castle into such an uproar.

As he dismounted, a freckled lad trotted up to relieve him of his mount. "Might I have a strip of it when ye cut it down, sir? My ma says if I sleep with it 'neath my pillow 'twill increase my p-p-pot'ncy."

Utterly baffled, Austyn followed the direction of the boy's pointing finger and rapt gaze to a square of ivory fluttering like a pennon from the highest rampart. The cheers died to a wary, but expectant, silence.

'Twas not a pennon, Austyn realized with a nasty shock, but a rumpled bedsheet, its fine linen stained with the unmistakable evidence of his wife's innocence. He swayed as every drop of blood drained from his face, then rushed back to suffuse it with a blazing heat.

Austyn had been a knight for ten years — long enough to know that the harmless looking sheet flapping in the breeze was not a flag of surrender, but an open declaration of war.

Chapter 24

Austyn took the winding steps to the tower three at a time. He briefly entertained the notion of shattering the bolt with a kick, but decided not to waste his violence on such trifles. He did allow himself the gratification of hurling the wooden bar aside and sending the door crashing open into the wall. 'Twas only then that he realized he had been fool enough to march unarmed and unarmored into his enemy's camp.

Holly had girded her own exquisite loins with a flowing emerald cotte shot through with shimmering threads of cloth of gold. A plump ruby glimmered like a teardrop of blood in the pale hollow of her throat. A diamond-studded pomander ball dangled from the woven girdle resting on her slim hips. She had cast a net of thinly beaten gold over her lustrous curls, but they resisted capture, preferring to coil and frolic in saucy rebellion.

She stood before the window, so beautiful and brimming with grace that it was all Austyn could do to keep from falling to his knees at her feet and surrendering his heart and soul to her dominion.

Her impeccable poise made him painfully conscious of his own sweat-dampened tunic and disheveled locks. With his fists clenched and his chest heaving with thwarted fury, he must appear little more than a savage to her. He'd certainly done nothing to supplant that notion last night. She probably thought all Welshmen rutted their wives like stags mounting a doe in season.

Both angered and shamed by his lack, Austyn averted his gaze from her, taking in the slender beeswax tapers, the feast spread for two on a linen-draped table before the hearth, the round tub emitting enticing little curlicues of steam over its rim, the delicate harp propped against a nest of pillows on the floor.

The opulent bed, its pristine sheets and sable coverlet folded back in brazen invitation.

His eyes narrowed as he realized his wife must have enlisted some very powerful allies indeed. 'Twas as if his possession had somehow elevated her from princess to queen and she was demonstrating no qualms whatsoever about ruling *his* castle from a locked tower.

"Good evening, sir," she said, her voice as melodious as a hymn. "I've taken the liberty of having supper prepared and a bath drawn for you."

Austyn could not help but think how he might have welcomed such tender attentions from the wife he had once believed Holly to be. "I'm not hungry," he growled. He could hardly claim not to be dirty with the same conviction.

"A pity. I had Winifred prepare all of your favorites. Not a pickled lamprey in sight. I wanted to assure you that your efforts to please me did not go unappreciated." At first Austyn thought the minx bold enough to remind him that he had made little effort to please her during his last visit, seeking only his own crude satisfaction, but her beatific expression lacked any trace of cunning. "After all, you were kind enough to free Nathanael and send Elspeth to spend the day with me."

He pointed a finger skyward. "That wouldn't be the same Elspeth I just saw cavorting about the ramparts."

A maddening smile played around Holly's lips. She glided to the table and seated herself, the pomander ball jingling against her shapely thigh. "I'm surprised you didn't have Carey draw his bow and shoot her."

"Had I known what mischief she was about, I might have considered it." Austyn folded himself warily into the opposite chair. "Of course, I'm sure you knew naught of her mission. As you hasten to remind me at every opportunity, you are, above all things, innocent."

She poured mead into two goblets and handed him one, refusing to allow so much as a blush to betray her. It galled him that she could still look as pure and serene as a violet-eyed Madonna. "Not this time, I fear. A confession is forthcoming and since you've sent my priest away, I am thrust into the unenviable position of casting myself upon *your* mercy."

He arched his eyebrow in a skeptical invitation to proceed.

She took a dainty sip of the mead. "It has occurred to me, sir, that you might attempt to rid yourself of me by having our marriage annulled and sending me back to my papa in disgrace."

Austyn caught himself staring as her luscious tongue darted out to dash a golden drop of mead from her lower lip. "Why would I do that? So you can gather more hearts to break?"

She shot him a reproachful look from beneath lashes that seemed to be growing even as he watched, but continued as if he hadn't spoken. "As I see it, you can accomplish such an end in one of two ways — by claiming our marriage unconsummated or by swearing that I was no virgin when I came to your bed. 'Tis why I chose that perfectly honorable, if rather barbaric, custom to display proof of my chastity to your people."

Austyn leaned back in his chair to survey his wife through narrowed eyes. He had to admire her shrewdness, but in doing so, he discovered his horror of loving her was nearly equaled by his horror of liking her.

He twirled the stem of his goblet between two fingers. "Had I known you craved an audience, my lady, we could have invited them into our bedchamber. Then you wouldn't have been forced to enjoy their accolades from afar."

"I heard the cheers. 'Tis gratifying to know that not every man at Caer Gavenmore equates beauty with harlotry."

Austyn started to protest, but knew his words would ring hollow

224

when compared with his deeds. In truth, Holly appeared more angel than harlot. His clumsy pawings might have robbed her of her virginity, but innocence still shimmered around her like a novice's veil. Disturbed by the image, he slammed the goblet down on the table and rose from his chair.

As Austyn paced behind her, Holly's nape prickled. In truth, she had welcomed his decision to decline a bath, for he smelled of sunshine and freshly cut hay and all the sweet summer aromas she'd been denied for too long. She longed to nuzzle her lips against the crisp froth of hair at the throat of his tunic, to lick the salty tang of sweat from his bearded jaw.

When he strode back into her line of vision, a helpless scowl had claimed his features. " 'Tis not that I believe you inclined to infidelity purely by virtue of your appearance. 'Tis only that I find you a . . . a . . ." He seemed to be having difficulty looking directly at her. ". . . a disappointment. You're hardly the woman I bargained for as a wife."

Holly lifted the goblet to her lips to hide how deeply his words wounded. Her entire education had been devoted to molding her into an engaging mate for her future husband. She could not help but wonder if he had found her as keen a disappointment in his bed. A treacherous lump welled in her throat.

She washed it down with a swallow of mead. "We seemed to suit well enough before you discovered my trickery."

"That's because I thought you were . . ."

"Someone else?" she gently provided.

He slammed a palm on the table, rattling the dishes. His eyes blazed with a frigid fire. "Aye! Someone else! A plain, ordinary girl who would entice no man to challenge her husband for possession of her. A lady a knight could trust the care of his people and his castle to when he was summoned to battle without being tormented every second he was away from her with visions of her succumbing to the seduction of some lusty rogue." The sharp edge

225

of Austyn's voice was blunted by a yearning more piercing to Holly's heart than all of his ranting. "A woman I'd always know would be waiting to welcome me when I returned. A devout wife and mother to my children."

Knowing that he had examined her and found her unfit for such a virtuous task as motherhood cut Holly to the quick. 'Twas hardly the first time someone had addressed her as if she had no feelings. As if her beauty were a shell of pretty armor that somehow made her impervious to their slights. But only with Austyn did she discover how fragile that shell could be.

She rose from the chair to face him, praying he would attribute the uncommon sheen of her eyes to the flickering candlelight. "If my beauty renders me unfit to be your wife, then what did you seek to make of me last night? Your paramour? Do the whores of the Gavenmore men fare any better than their wives?"

"They tend to live a hell of a lot longer." Austyn's restless strides carried him to the window where he stood gazing out into the deepening night. "As I see it, you should be begging me to send you back to your father. *Especially* after last night."

She forced a brittle laugh. "Don't be ridiculous, sir. I'm not some mewling child bride ready to flee back to papa because her husband chose to assert his carnal rights."

He turned to face her. "But an annulment would grant you freedom. Freedom from this tower. Freedom from my demands."

Holly was wise enough to know that if Austyn exiled her from his life, she would never be free of this tower. It would enclose her heart, stone by stone, until it smothered her.

She drifted toward him, cocking her head to gaze her fill, but not daring to touch. "Are your demands so unreasonable, my lord? Loyalty? Truth? Fidelity?"

"Those aren't the demands I spoke of and you know it." His voice was harsh, but his hands as they clasped her shoulders flirted with gentleness. "Shall I send you back to Tewksbury or would you rather remain imprisoned in this tower at the mercy of my every whim, forced to endure what my grandmother endured night after night after night?"

Holly met his desperate gaze boldly. "I am not your grandmother. Nor are you your grandfather. You may bluster and growl all you like, but I haven't the faintest fear that you're going to rape me. Or strangle me," she added out of spite for the hurt his candid words had caused her.

A disbelieving bark of laughter escaped him. "Do you honestly believe if you had denied me last night, I would have begged your pardon and taken my leave?"

"Aye, 'tis exactly what I believe. Which is why I'm denying you tonight." Her words tumbled like pebbles into a bottomless well of silence.

Austyn released her shoulders and backed away from her, as if realizing too late that he had stumbled not into an enemy camp, but into a trap. His heel came up against the edge of the harp; it collapsed with a discordant thunk.

He drove a hand through his hair as his bemused gaze raked the chamber. "Are you trying to tell me that had I partaken of your delicious supper, allowed you to recline at my feet and enchant me with a lullaby, then given you leave to strip my weary body and bathe me from head to toe with those exquisite hands of yours, you still had absolutely no intention of taking me to your bed?"

"None whatsoever."

"Why you shameless little . . ." He took a menacing step toward her.

"No," she said firmly.

He did not curb his dangerous charge until a mere inch of air sizzled between their bodies. To keep from shrinking in his shadow, Holly forced herself to remember the husband who had cradled her across his lap while he sponged her tears away. The warrior who had spared Eugene de Legget's life when vengeance demanded he

227

take it. The knight who had leashed his mighty strength to cup her nape in his broad palm and stolen her mouth's virginity with nothing more than the gentle persuasion of his tongue. If she had miscalculated that man's honor, the price would be very dear indeed.

She could almost see the unholy war being fought behind the glittering palisades of Austyn's eyes. A war between temptation and honor. Lust and mercy. Passion and compassion.

Just when she feared his dark desires might emerge the sole victor, he stroked the backs of his fingers down her cheek with a bewitching tenderness she had thought never to feel from him again. "You've chosen your weapons well, woman. Now I shall choose mine."

With that cryptic warning, he turned on his heel and left her.

When the bolt had fallen into place, Holly sank down on the window seat, trembling like a reed in the wind. Austyn might never return to her, but by proving to him that he wasn't the monster his grandfather had been, she had at least sent him on his way with his soul intact. She touched her fingertips to her tingling cheek, wishing wistfully that she could say the same of her heart.

Sleep eluded Holly. She squirmed and tossed in a bed that seemed to have swelled to twice its normal size since she had shared it with her husband, however briefly, the night before. The feather mattress threatened to swallow her whole. The coverlet and sheets tugged at her ankles until she kicked them away. Even the flimsy chemise sought to bind her, twisting its way around her throat in a perverse noose. She finally dragged it off and cast it to the floor, preferring to sleep as she had since childhood.

But the caress of the cool night air against her naked breasts only served to remind her that she was child no more.

Sleep came to her in fitful spurts and fevered dreams. She awoke from a sojourn into wrenching loneliness to find a dark shape poised above her. Her rational mind warned her that she should be afraid, but some more primitive instinct welcomed this shadowy manifestation of her longings.

Her womb quickened with expectancy as he descended on her, a swaggering satyr — half angel, half demon — in the darkness. He would not kiss her mouth.

This loving Austyn forged from stardust and shadows brushed his lips against her temple, traced the delicate shell of each ear with his tongue, nibbled the curve of her jaw, then coasted lower to nuzzle his lips against the throbbing pulse in her throat. She sighed her delight.

His delectable wooing enticed her to touch him, but she curled her hands into fists, fearing that if she succumbed to the temptation, he would melt back into the mists of yearning from which she had summoned him.

A shudder of pleasure convulsed her as his cunning tongue flicked out to lash one of her nipples. She arched her back, unable to resist the accomplished devilment of his mouth. The generous globes of her breasts had been both leered at and praised, but they'd never been debauched with such reverence. He licked and nipped and teased until she'd dropped every defense, then suckled her hard and deep, coaxing a surge of hot, thick nectar from between her thighs.

He would not kiss her mouth.

He rained tender kisses on the quivering skin of her belly. His tongue delved into her navel in a sinuous swirl, as if to warn her there was no secret hollow of her body he would not brand with his touch. He did not have to use his powerful hands to urge her legs apart. At the tingling scrape of his beard against the downy skin at the inner curve of her knee, her thighs melted into acquiescence, shyly inviting him to sate his darkest appetites in a sweet, forbidden feast.

Holly would never forget the first sensuous tickle of his mustache. Her fingernails drew tiny pearls of blood from her palms as she fought the desire to curl her fingers in the coarse silk of his hair.

At her soft whimper of mortification, his tongue both soothed her and maddened her, flicking her swollen flesh with devilish skill to whip her into a frenzy of incoherent pleasure, then lowering to lap gently at the bounty of his ministrations.

He would not kiss her mouth.

He drove her to the very brink of ecstasy once, twice, three times, but her choked pleas for deliverance only seemed to prolong the taut circles of his tongue. Just when she thought she would surely perish from want if he did not fill that melting hollow aching for his attention, he added his deft hands to her sensual agony, ravishing her tenderly, but with exquisite thoroughness, with his longest finger, then with his broad, spatulate thumb.

Holly writhed, desperate to wrap her arms and legs around him. Besieged by thick, throbbing waves of pleasure, she reached up and grasped the velvet ribbons dangling from the bedposts, placing herself in willing bondage to save herself from drowning in a sea of rapture. 'Twas then that he reached beneath her with his other hand and gently stroked the tip of a single finger down the fragile, cloistered valley between her buttocks.

That touch, so primal, so provocative, shuddered her to the soul. A low moan tore from her throat, so feral she did not recognize it as her own.

His voice was woven of the darkness itself, both hoarse and silken. "Would you deny me now, my lady? Shall I beg your pardon and take my leave?"

He had ceased to touch her, but even the kiss of his breath scorched her eager flesh. She could feel the flames roiling off his artful tongue, his big, graceful fingers, as they awaited her breathless leave to probe and stroke and possess. He had chosen his weapons with the diabolical skill of a mortal enemy, but Holly still had enough faith in him to know he would abide by her wishes. If she denied him, he would abandon her without so much as a growl of protest, leaving him bereft of release and herself teetering on the precipice of some wondrous discovery.

Gripping the velvet ribbons so tightly they cut into her palms, she uttered the one choked word that would seal both of their fates. "Stay."

He stayed. His fingers plundered every vulnerable cleft they could reach while his mouth suckled her with devastating tenderness. Holly cried out as ecstasy pulsed through her in surge after indescribable surge.

Before the last of those shivery frissons could cease to wrack her womb, he was sliding his turgid staff past the quivering petals of her sex, stroking deep with a dreamy, deliberate cadence that bore little resemblance to what had passed between them the night before. That had been a brief, roaring conflagration; this was a slow burn that threatened to incinerate her very soul. 'Twas as if he had all night, all eternity, to claim her for his own.

He would not kiss her mouth.

His brutal tenderness made Holly want to claw at his back, to beat at his muscled shoulders with her fists. She turned her face to the pillow with a hoarse sob, helpless to do anything but lay beneath him with her legs sprawled wide and her throbbing core uptilted for his pleasuring. Pleasure her he did, reaching to fondle and stroke the tiny nubbin sheltered by the damp nest where their bodies were joined until cry after cry of surrender was wrung from her throat. 'Twas as if he sought to turn her into the very thing he feared the most — a piteous, mewling creature ruled by her darkest, most sensual, impulses.

She lost track of the number of times he urged her to that dark peak and hurtled her over its edge. 'Twas a sweet infinity before his surging rhythm and straining muscles told her he had joined her in the fall. He came and went in equal silence, leaving Holly sweat-drenched and shivering in the empty bed.

Yestereve her husband had fled her company as if to linger would be to forfeit his soul, but this night he had torn away a jagged fragment of her soul and taken it with him.

Without ever once kissing her mouth.

There was but one door leading to the walled courtyard below the north tower. Austyn battered it open with his fist and staggered into the blessed chill of the Welsh night. He collapsed against the stone wall, tilting his face to the sky to let the misty air bathe his fevered flesh.

Holly might have been a fool to toss down the gauntlet of her denial, but he had proved himself an even greater fool by taking it up.

He could not have said what had possessed him to believe he could touch her in every manner, both sacred and profane, in which a husband could touch a wife, yet remain untouched himself. She had wooed him with nothing more than her soft sigh of welcome when she had discovered him standing over her bed. Yet he had forced himself to maintain his maddening charade of restraint until the bittersweet end, clenching his teeth against a roar of ecstasy that would have betrayed him for the fraud he was.

Austyn groaned. How in God's name was he to keep Holly at arm's length when he could still scent her on his beard, taste her on his lips? Never before had any woman, plain or comely, bought with coin or offered freely, so cut his heart to the quick. He feared her bewitching surrender in this initial battle might very well cost him the war.

"Are you satisfied, Rhiannon? Is this how it begins?"

His hoarse query was not greeted by the echo of mocking feminine laughter he expected, but by the muffled notes of his wife's weeping.

Austyn gazed at the darkened tower window for a tortured moment, then buried his face in his hands, unwittingly blinding himself to the stooped figure who cast himself from the shadows and went scrambling over the wall.

232

Chapter 25

Holly's days soon settles into a predictable routine. She lacked for no luxury but freedom.

Her invisible jailer sent Winifred to deliver armfuls of freshly cut flowers — late-blooming jasmine and morning glory, wood hyacinths and blood-red roses that sent the haunting fragrance of the waning summer wafting through the tower.

As she tossed them out the window in a shower of lavender and crimson, Holly compressed her lips to a bitter line and wondered what his offerings would be in winter when the fecund earth slumbered beneath a shroud of snow. Perhaps he would have tired of her by then and would be bestowing his floral tributes on a more appreciative lover.

Her harp was joined by a newly strung lute and a carved flute flawlessly molded to the contours of her lips. Illuminated manuscripts followed — rare pieces of music suited only to the ripe soprano of a woman's voice.

The instruments sat in forlorn silence; the manuscripts remained untouched.

He was even so generous as to send Elspeth to keep her company during the languid hours of daylight. Dear Elspeth who possessed the gift of chattering cheerfully about nothing at all, but could not quite hide her troubled glances at the smudges of exhaustion beneath her mistress's eyes.

Perversely enough, Holly thought the interminable days of captivity might have driven her mad were it not for the tempestuous liberties allowed her in the darkness of night.

For after she'd sent Elspeth on her way and extinguished the candles, Austyn would slip into her bed to cast his tender sorcery over her body. He had ceased being her husband to become a phantom lover in the darkness, stealing another precious splinter of her soul with each nocturnal visit.

He would not kiss her mouth or allow her to caress him in tenderness. He broke his fierce silence only to whisper what wicked magic he was going to work until it took little more than the husky rasp of his voice in her ear to bring her to the brink of fulfillment. Had there been even a hint of brutality in his attentions, Holly might have brought herself to hate him, but his accomplished hands cherished her flesh as if it were his own private altar. She'd never known such unbridled ecstasy. Or such misery.

He left no fragile hollow of her body unexplored, storming the last remaining bastion of her innocence with such wrenching tenderness that even as she buried her face in the mattress to muffle her sobs, her body was wracked by shudders of dark, exquisite rapture.

'Twas that night, when he withdrew from her without so much as a grunt of satisfaction, donned his hose, and padded heavily to the door, that she broke her own stubborn silence.

"Are you going to leave nothing of me, sir?" she cried, clenching her teeth against a belated chill of shame. "Have I given you cause to hate me so much?"

He hesitated for no more than a heartbeat. Then the door shut and the bolt fell gently in place, sealing her in with only her fading hopes for company.

Elspeth shot her mistress an apprehensive glance as Holly paced the tower, the slashed sleeves of her cotehardie rippling with each stride. She paused each time she passed the window, as if compelled to watch the daylight die. Her exquisite features were cast in bitterness and her eyes had a wild look that had never boded well for anyone, least of all herself.

"I care naught for the gleam in yer eye, child," Elspeth said, laying aside her sewing. " 'Tis the same gleam ye had when yer papa forbade ye a pony when ye were only six. Ye hid yerself in that tinker's cart and ran away during a snowstorm. 'Twas nearly two days later when yer poor papa found ye curled in the hollow o' that elm like an innocent sprite. Drove him half out o' his wits with worry, ye did, but all he could do was smother yer grubby little face with kisses."

A brief wistful smile softened Holly's lips. "Perhaps if he had thrashed my naughty little rump instead, I wouldn't now find myself in such a predicament."

The door swung open and Winifred poked her round face inside. " 'Tis time to go, Elspeth."

The nurse hesitated, reluctant to leave her mistress in such bleak solitude. Holly's pallor and glittering eyes made her look both fragile and dangerous, as if she were possessed by some exotic fever that might burn both her and anyone she touched to ashes.

"Sleep well," Holly said gently.

Elspeth cast Winifred a helpless look, but the Welshwoman shook her head, her fretful expression mirroring Elspeth's own. They had spoken bluntly about Holly's plight, but were at a loss as to how to break this cycle of destruction. 'Twas as if their master and mistress were locked in some dark dance of the soul, both determined to carry it to its grim conclusion.

Having nothing else to offer Holly, Elspeth gave her a fervent hug. "God keep ye until the morrow, my child," she whispered, wishing she could shake off her chill of foreboding.

When Elspeth had gone, Holly glided about the chamber, the jagged edge smoothed off of her restlessness by a growing sense of purpose. Instead of pinching the flame from each taper as she usually did, she retrieved the candles she'd been hoarding for days

235

and lit every feathery wick until the tower was bathed in a luminous glow.

If Austyn would come to her, then let him come to her in light. She would no longer offer him a shield of darkness to hide his heart behind. She would face him boldly in the candlelight, even if doing so made her blush to remember what had passed between them in the shadows.

She would have the truth from him. And if he vowed to her upon his honor as a knight that he could never love her, she would humble herself before him for the last time and entreat him to return her to Tewksbury. A spasm of anguish gripped her heart, but she squelched it without mercy.

As in the nights before, there was little she could do but wait. She drifted to the window, breathing deeply of the bittersweet incense of the flowers decaying on the cobblestones below, never feeling the sly caress of the eyes that watched from the gathering darkness.

Tonight would be the night he would keep himself from her.

Austyn strode up the moonlit hill, knowing himself a liar even as he made the vow. She burned like a molten fever in his blood. He was as helpless to resist her as the tides were to resist the siren tug of the moon.

The stones of the unfinished curtain wall gaped like ivory teeth in the jaws of night. He vaulted over a low section, welcoming the shadows and the sweet anonymity they would bring. 'Twas only in darkness that he dared reveal himself to her.

He slipped past the deserted chapel and into the inner bailey, skirting the rushlights like the predator he could feel himself becoming. He had nearly reached the refuge of an outer staircase when a fair-haired figure disengaged from the shadows and sauntered into his path.

Austyn halted and rested his hands on his hips. "You might not have as much leisure to act as my conscience were you to seek a wife of your own."

The cocky flash of Carey's smile should have warned him. "Now why would I go to the trouble when I was hoping you'd grant me a tumble on yours?"

At the furtive creak of the door opening and closing behind her, Holly squared her shoulders, girding herself to do final battle for the man she loved. She drew in a bracing breath as she turned. It escaped in an exclamation of surprise at the sight of the man huddled against the door.

"Father Rhys?"

Her father-in-law was the first man aside from her husband allowed entry to the tower since her captivity had began. Alarm tinged her bewilderment as she remembered his thundering denouncement from the parapets on the day Austyn had discovered her ruse.

He touched a finger to his lips to beg her silence, looking bashful and almost childlike. "Father forbade me to come. But I slipped away while he was with his doxy."

Holly's confusion mounted. "Your *father* forbade you? I don't understand."

"He said you were wicked, but I don't believe him." Tears puddled in his pale blue eyes — eyes so like Austyn's that it hurt Holly just to gaze into them. They only served to remind her of all the darkness had robbed her of. "I miss you, Mama. I miss you terribly."

Comprehension dawned. In all of her empathy for the woman who had inhabited this tower prison before her, Holly had never once cast a thought for the woman's child. A small boy forbidden his mother's love by a cruel and vengeful father. For the first time since learning how Rhys of Gavenmore had murdered his own wife in a jealous rage, Holly felt a twinge of pity for the man.

Sympathy gentled her voice. "I'm sure your mama missed you, too, sir. Very much. But I am not her."

He cocked his head to the side, as if listening to an echo of a long forgotten melody. "I hear the two of you, you know. When Father thinks I'm sleeping, I sneak into the courtyard and listen." Cunning crept in to banish the shyness from his expression. "I hear you moaning and panting. Sometimes you scream as if he's hurting you, but then you beg him to hurt you more. You fancy the lewd things he does to you, don't you? Perhaps you are wicked after all."

Holly clapped a hand over her mouth to smother a gasp of horror. 'Twas distressing enough to imagine a small boy hearing such noises between his parents, but even more appalling to realize he must have been eavesdropping on her and Austyn from the beginning. He made her feel violated in a way that his son never had.

He advanced on her, his voice swelling from the plaintive tones of a child to the dangerous vigor of manhood. "Perhaps you're nothing but a deceitful harlot." He raked her with a lascivious gaze. "How many men have you welcomed between those milky thighs of yours, Gwyneth? A dozen? A legion?"

"I am not Gwyneth! Nor am I your mother." Only too aware of the yawning chasm behind her, Holly sidled away from the window, realizing too late that she was backing toward the bed. "I am Holly, Father Rhys. Don't you remember me? You helped me carry tubs of poppies up to the battlements. We planted flowers on Gwyneth's grave together." When her frantic words failed to halt his pursuit, she cried out, "I'm your son's wife, for God's sake! Austyn's wife!"

Even to her own ears, her avowal lacked conviction. In truth, Austyn had not claimed her as his wife since that dark day by the river. How was she to convince this madman she was more than just a contemptible harlot if she could not even convince herself? Hadn't Austyn proved her as weak and wicked a creature as Rhys described, panting with eagerness to abandon her body and soul to torrid nights of carnal revelry?

Blinking back tears, she groped behind her for a weapon. A discordant twang provoked her hopes even as the backs of her knees struck the bed pedestal.

"Lift your skirts, love," he snarled, the endearment a profanity on his lips, "and we shall see if you find me as robust a satisfaction as you found the king when you enticed him to your bed."

He took his eyes off of her to fumble with his hose, his palsied hands betraying his delusion of youth. Holly swung the lute in a wide circle, aiming for his head.

The instrument shattered against his temple. He staggered backward, shooting her such a wounded look that it might have been comical under less dire circumstances. But before Holly could celebrate her triumph, he shook off the blow and rushed her. He tore at the rich damask of her cotte with a strength born of madness, leaving her only one weapon with which to do battle.

Austyn could not think of a single reason why his man-at-arms would seek to provoke him to murder. Especially with himself as the most likely victim.

He stared at Carey through narrowed eyes. "Have you lost your wits?"

Carey hiked one shoulder in a lazy shrug and began to circle him, affecting a swagger that was a creditable imitation of Austyn's own. "I haven't lost my wits, man. I've come to them. And I must say 'tis really not like you to be so selfish."

"Selfish?"

"Aye! Or greedy either. You've never begrudged me a taste of choice pheasant or a sip of your finest wine. So why should you be so grasping as to hoard a treasure like Holly all for yourself?" He elbowed Austyn in the ribs, shooting him a leering wink. " 'Twouldn't be the first time we'd shared a woman."

A scarlet curtain of rage unfurled over Austyn's eyes. He snatched

Carey up by the tunic and slammed him against the nearest wall. "How dare you? You're not talking about some ha'penny whore. You're talking about my wife!"

Carey looked far more nonchalant than he should have with Austyn's brawny forearm pressed against his windpipe. "Then you'll have to forgive my insolence for 'twas my impression that a man doesn't lock his *wife* in a tower. Nor does he creep into her bed by night to steal her favors like a thief."

"She brought that on herself. She should never have betrayed me!"

Carey's gray eyes glittered with challenge. "Aye, and if you snap my fool neck this very minute, you'll find a way to blame that on her, too, won't you? After all, isn't that what wicked women such as your mother and Holly delight in? Setting husband against king? Brother against brother? Friend against friend?"

Austyn sucked in a breath through clenched teeth, glowering down into the flushed face of a man who had been more brother to him than friend. A man willing to risk his life to make him see reason. The harsh rasp of their mingled breathing slowly dwindled.

The taut fabric of their silence was torn by a sound Austyn had heard only once before. A sound so terrible he wanted to drop to his knees like the terrified nine-year-old he had been and clamp his hands over his ears.

A full-throated scream stifled in mid-note with brutal efficiency.

Chapter 26

As Rhys's gnarled hands closed around her throat to mangle the life from her, Holly thought ruefully that at least there would be less of a mess for Austyn to mop up than if his father had hurled her out the window. By this time tomorrow night, she'd be just another Gavenmore ghost.

'Twas a pity she did not believe in ghosts. If she did, at least her spirit might have lingered to watch over Austyn and wreak mischievous havoc if he dared bring home some plain, docile bride to replace her. She would sing off-key in their bedchamber and shove tubs of poppies off the battlements on the woman's dowdy head. Holly might have giggled at the vision had she been able to suck any air into her tortured lungs.

The tower was dimming around her. 'Twould be full dark soon. Holly welcomed the gathering shadows. Austyn always came in the dark. 'Twas the one place where his touch promised love even if his lips would not. A single tear slipped from her eye. A tear of longing. A tear of regret. But she refused to surrender her hope. For Austyn would never abandon her to face the dark alone.

Jesus, God in heaven, it was happening all over again.
Austyn's knees had buckled at that ghastly cry and for a heartbeat of hesitation, 'twas only Carey's grip that kept him standing. They exchanged a frantic glance before Austyn tore himself from his friend's grasp and went racing for the castle.

He could hear Carey at his heels as he thundered past the stark white faces in the great hall and shoved his way through the men who had already started up the first set of stairs.

Please, God, he prayed, *don't let me be too late. Not this time.*

He reached the landing beneath the north tower in less than a dozen steps, yet felt as if he were wading through a silence as thick and viscous as death. He flew up the narrow, winding stairs, numbed to the sparks of pain that exploded through his brain when his shoulder slammed against the door.

He stumbled into the tower only to be engulfed by a swell of desolation so intense it threatened to submerge him.

Images came to him in fragments: the splinters of the lute scattered across the floor; his father straddling a woman; her slender fingers hanging limp over the side of the bed, just as his mother's neck had hung limp when he had carried her down the stairs to bury her.

'Twas the stubborn twitch of those fingertips that jerked Austyn from past to present. Crossing the chamber in two strides, he caught the back of his father's tunic and hurled him off the bed. He snatched Holly up in his arms, terrified he would find her beautiful face blackened by death.

Her wheezing gasp was the sweetest melody he'd ever heard from her lips. "Breathe deep, love," he begged, his own voice the hoarse rasp of a stranger. "Oh, please breathe. Breathe for me."

He rocked her in his arms, supporting her head with his palm until her nostrils lost their pinched look and her face faded from purple to white. His father's fingerprints marred the pale palette of her throat.

Rhys had collapsed in a flaccid heap, his lower lip quivering, his rheumy eyes puddling with tears. Blood trickled from a gash on his temple. "I'm sorry, Mama," he whispered plaintively. The anguished timbre of his voice deepened as he buried his face in his hands. "Oh, dear God, Gwyneth, I'm so sorry."

Not a drop of pity would have lingered in Austyn's heart had he not possessed the grim knowledge that he might yet be gazing into his own future. He would have risen to deal with his father then and there, but his arms refused to relinquish Holly's precious weight.

A blessed hiccup drew his hungry gaze back to her face. A hint of rose had bloomed in her cheeks. Her eyes fluttered open and she blinked up at him earnestly. "Am I a ghost, sir?"

Austyn tightened his embrace, shivering as he contemplated how close she'd come to achieving such a spectral state. He buried his mouth in the softness of her curls. "No, love, although I suspect you might be an angel."

She snuggled deeper into his arms. " 'Tis just as well I s'pose," she whispered in an endearing croak. "I should have been a very naughty ghost. I was going to sew the legs of your hose together and rip all the seams out of your surcoats."

Her eyes flew open. She glanced down, as if just remembering that Rhys's attack had torn her cotte. The damask had parted to offer a teasing glimpse of one creamy breast. Her gaze shot to the door to find Carey standing in the doorway, an anxious crowd hovering behind him.

Trembling like a child in his arms, she snatched the shredded bodice together to shield her nakedness and turned her pleading eyes on Austyn. "Oh, please don't be angry at Carey. 'Twasn't his fault. I enticed him to look at me. I swear I did."

Her teeth began to chatter with delayed reaction. Tears welled in those extraordinary eyes, spilling over to scorch Austyn's skin like droplets of boiling oil. His massive body shuddered as he felt the invisible wall around his heart collapse. How ironic that he should labor on it for twenty years only to discover too late that it had been forged not from stone, but ice! It had taken nothing more than the bittersweet warmth of Holly's tears to melt it to a heap of useless rubble, leaving his heart raw and exposed.

He had to do no more than cast Carey an agonized glance. His man-at-arms gently shepherded his father and the others from the tower, leaving Austyn and his wife to their privacy.

Austyn ran his hands briskly over Holly's icy arms, seeking to warm them. "Aside from trying to strangle you to death, did the wretch hurt you?"

Holly shook her head. "I shouldn't have hit him. I know he's naught but a frail old man, but he said such ugly things to me. When he began to untruss his hose . . ." She bowed her head, leaving Austyn to gaze helplessly down at the tender nape he had coveted for so long. "He's been hiding in the courtyard each night. Listening . . ." A fresh shudder rocked her shoulders. Her voice was so soft, 'twas nearly inaudible. "He believed I was naught but a wanton harlot who would welcome his attentions . . . because I welcomed yours."

Remorse staggered Austyn. Had he been standing, he would have fallen to his knees. 'Twas not his father who had reduced this proud, beautiful girl to cringing shame, he realized, but himself.

He tipped her delicate chin up, forcing her to meet his gaze. "You're right. You shouldn't have hit him. You should have hit me."

Holly's face was no less lustrous than the candlelight, but as Austyn gazed down at her parted lips, the tears trembling on her dark lashes, he realized her physical beauty had never been the true threat to him. The passing seasons might mist her hair with silver and etch seams in the satin of her skin, but 'twas the beauty of her spirit that would never fade. The beauty of her spirit that had shone through her ridiculous disguise to blind him with its radiance.

'Twas that beauty he had sought to deny by seeking the supple grace of her body only in darkness. That beauty he had feared as he had propped pillows beneath her stomach and guided her face away from him, as if he could pretend she was another woman. Any woman at all. But the shimmering melody of her pleasure, the arch of her slender spine, the milky nape where he had longed to press his kisses, had always belonged to Holly.

His Holly. Generous and stubborn and fiercely protective of those she loved. And brave. Braver than any warrior he had faced on the battlefield. Brave enough to bash a rapacious madman upside the head with a lute. Brave enough to defy her papa when he sought to force her to a fate not of her making. Brave enough to offer her body as a sacrifice to his own selfish lust.

His remorse was but a pale shadow of another emotion, an emotion he had believed buried forever when he had laid his mother to rest in the rich Welsh earth. An emotion both tender and tremulous, yet possessed of the power to topple kingdoms and tempt a man to risk his soul for just one night to savor its priceless wonders.

A blade of irony twisted in Austyn's gut. As long as he'd stubbornly clung to the notion that he could never love Holly, he'd been free to keep her for his wife.

Holly stiffened as her husband's arms slipped away from her. She hugged herself in a vain attempt to duplicate his warmth. "You're going now, aren't you? I made it too bright and you're going away."

But instead of seeking the door, he moved to the table to pour a stream of wine into a silver goblet with leisurely grace. He eyed the glowing tapers with satisfaction, then frowned. "Where are all the flowers? Aren't there supposed to be flowers in here?"

Holly winced with belated guilt. "They were making me sneeze," she lied, "so I had Winifred take them away."

Her bewilderment grew as he returned to the bed, slipping to his knees so that they faced each other on the turbulent sea of sable.

He lifted the goblet. "A toast to my bride."

His solemn expression touched a wistful chord in Holly's heart. Before she could give voice to her yearning, he was pressing the rim of the goblet to her lips. She drank deeply, savoring his honeyed homage as if her thirst for it could never be sated.

He drank in kind, then let the goblet roll from his fingertips to the floor. Cupping her face in his hands with a fierce tenderness that both beguiled and frightened her, he gazed deep into her eyes

245

and said, "I worship thee with my body, Lady Holly of Tewksbury."

Austyn kissed her mouth.

At the first brush of his warm lips, Holly's teeth stopped chattering. Dazed by delight, she thought she might have died and gone to heaven after all. 'Twas a miracle this, a mingling of spirit and flesh more intimate than all the earthy pleasures they'd shared in darkness.

A veil of tears blurred her vision as she realized what Austyn had just done. He had taken her to wife. Not some petulant stranger garbed in an outlandish disguise and a withered chaplet of bluebells, but she, Holly of Tewksbury, clothed in shredded damask, yet somehow as naked and vulnerable as Eve must have been when God first delivered her to Adam.

The ceremonial reverence of his kiss made her feel as fresh and pure as Eve before the fall. 'Twas as if his chivalrous gesture had restored both her lost innocence and her hope for the future. She wouldn't have been surprised had she glanced in a mirror to discover the ugly marks left by his father's fingers had faded away, washed clean by her husband's regard.

Her cry of joy was muffled by his mouth as she threw her arms around his neck, binding him to her heart as she had longed to do for so long.

Austyn would have been content to remain thus forever — rocking Holly in his arms, sipping tenderly at her lips, pausing only long enough to murmur hoarse regrets and broken endearments into the rumpled silk of her curls.

'Twas she who drew her mouth from his and began to nuzzle the sensitive skin at the base of his throat, she who slipped her hands beneath his tunic to sift her fingers through his chest hair.

'Twas Austyn's turn to gasp when those entrancing hands fluttered over his abdomen to seek the points of his hose.

He caught one of her wrists, bringing it to his lips to soften the impact of its brief bondage. "You don't have to do this," he murmured, unable to resist sampling the spot where the fragile tracing of veins pulsed beneath her skin. " 'Tis not what I want."

The gentle press of her belly against his loins proved him a flagrant liar. "Perhaps 'tis time you thought about what *I* want," she said. "I should warn you that my papa always claimed me a very spoiled girl."

Sensing that she needed to prove her own power after being rendered so powerless by his father's attack, Austyn favored her with a crooked grin. "Then far be it for me to deny you."

He sealed his pledge by guiding her hand back down to his hose and pressing her palm to the throbbing measure of his desire for her. A desire that had stubbornly refused to abate since the first moment he had laid eyes on her in the garden at Tewksbury. As she folded her lithe fingers around him, he threw back his head, gritting his teeth against a groan of ecstasy.

Austyn discovered with that single touch that he could deny her nothing. Not even when she fanned her hands over his shoulders, pushed him to his back, and began to undress him like a child. When he lay naked with only the plush sable to tickle his skin, he reached for her.

She drew away from him, her eyes sparkling like polished gemstones. "You may look, my lord, which is more than you allowed me, but you may not touch."

He cocked his head to the side, entranced by her boldness. "You wouldn't?"

A provocative smile spread across her face. "Watch me."

The extravagant candlelight made watching her an unparalleled pleasure. Sitting up on her knees, she drew both cotte and chemise over her head. As she shook out her tousled curls, Austyn found himself giving fervent thanks that her hair hadn't yet grown enough to shield those magnificent breasts from his gaze. His hands were already aching to caress her, to cherish each succulent swell and hollow of her flesh as he should have on their wedding night. He was only too eager to repay the debt he had incurred when he had robbed her of her virginity with such callousness.

But Holly had in mind a more diabolical reparation.

This time when he reached for her, she cast the velvet loops on the bedposts a glower of mock threat. "Restrain yourself, sir, or I shall be forced to restrain you."

He fell back among the pillows, his empty hands knotting into fists. "Dare I beg you for mercy, my lady?"

She grazed his lips with her own in a tantalizing caress just short of a kiss. "Don't waste your breath."

Austyn had never dreamed revenge could be so sweet. Especially when that revenge was exacted with such exquisite care from his own willing body. Holly nuzzled his fevered flesh, only to return to his mouth after each thrilling foray, as if to gorge herself on a feast she had been denied for too long. When her ripe lips strayed to the taut planes of his abdomen, his hands caught in the coverlet, bunching great wads of it between his fingers.

She glided up his body, the softness of her breasts teasing his chest, and brushed his mouth with a kiss as artless and bewitching as a virgin's. Austyn groaned his delight. But it seemed that reprieve was only a prelude to a more delicious torture. For those same innocent lips drifted back down his quivering body and parted like the petals of a flower to enfold him.

Austyn did not seize the velvet bonds. He seized the bedposts themselves, squeezing until he was sure they would crack off in his hands.

"Sweet God in heaven, have mercy, woman!" he choked out, arching off the bed in an instinctive thrust that doubled both his torment and his pleasure. He survived her generous assault without shattering only by plotting in scrupulous detail his own sensual retaliation.

When Holly once again laid those delectable lips against his own, he kissed her with savage abandon, thrusting deep and hard with his tongue.

248

He had taught her only too well. She tugged at his lower lip with her teeth before murmuring, "Would you deny me, husband? Shall I beg your pardon and take my leave?"

A lance of pain speared Austyn's heart. At the sudden somberness of his expression, the teasing light fled her face. She made no protest when he enveloped her in his arms and rolled her beneath him, molding her to his body as if God had fashioned them to fit that way.

"Stay," he whispered hoarsely, knowing it was the last time he would ever entreat her to do so.

As Austyn bore her back against the mattress, Holly breathed a sigh of utter delight to be allowed the once forbidden luxury of wrapping her legs around her husband's waist to coax him deep inside of her.

Austyn knew he had much to atone for, but this was both the sweetest and most excruciating penance he had ever endured. He cursed his own stubbornness for denying them the blessing of candlelight through all those dark nights. 'Twas sheer bliss to draw back and watch rapture flicker and dance across Holly's exquisite face. To watch her creamy cheeks flush with rose and her cherubic lips part in half-gasps, half-moans that inflamed him beyond bearing. To flick his gaze downward and witness the primal splendor of her body arching to welcome each of his bold thrusts.

She was a beauty, aye, but for this one last night, she was *his* beauty. His bride. Enchanted by the mask of pleasure mellowing her features, he slipped a single finger into the slick valley above where their bodies were joined and applied a most delicate friction until her gasps escalated to panting whimpers and her eyes fluttered back in her head.

Those first shivery pulsations gloved him in ecstasy. He drove himself hard against the mouth of her womb, muffling his roar of sweet agony against her lips as the love of a lifetime spilled from his loins in a searing cascade.

The pearly pall of dawn hung over the chamber when Holly awoke to find the bed beside her empty. Her spirits plummeted as she believed for one desolate moment that the preceding night had been only a night like all the others, when Austyn took his pleasure, then took his leave with equal disregard.

Biting back a wistful sigh, she reached toward the hollow in the mattress where his big, virile body should have lain. A trace of warmth still lingered in the rumpled sheets. Her sigh escaped in a joyous sob of relief.

Laughing aloud, she rolled into the hollow, tumbling and writhing with childish abandon, then buried her face in the pillow to breathe deep of Austyn's masculine spice.

As she flopped to her back and gazed up at the wooden canopy, the silken threads of memory wove a shimmering tapestry before her eyes. Instead of fleeing her company after that first sweet convulsion of ecstasy, Austyn had pillowed her head on his chest and stroked her damp curls away from her face, hoarsely begging her forgiveness for all the nights he had abandoned her and vowing to make amends.

She'd lost count of the number of times he had sealed his pledge during the fleeting hours between midnight and dawn. Equally precious to her were those moments when sated exhaustion had seized them both and she had snuggled against his warm chest, savoring the delectable sensation of feeling both safe and adored. If she rolled away, he would scowl and mumble, then wrap his arms around her waist and drag her tight against him, bumping his chin on her head. She would smile a small, secret smile to learn he was possessive even in slumber.

Then would come the first sleepy stirrings of his loins against her rump, and the wondrous cycle would begin again.

Holly's stomach gave a petulant growl. She sat up, wondering if Austyn had gone to seek some cheese and sausage so they might sate an appetite of a more mundane nature. The tapers had melted to squat nubs of wax. A faint chill clung to the air. She peeked over the edge of the bed to discover Austyn's hose were missing, but his tunic still lay in a careless heap where she had cast it the night before.

On a whim, she rose and tugged the garment over her head, hugging it against her skin as if she could absorb Austyn's essence through her pores. The coarse wool made her tingle. She could not resist a giddy twirl to admire the way it belied around her calves. She stumbled against the table.

And had to grab its edge to keep from falling when she realized the tower door stood ajar, beckoning her into the misty morning.

Chapter 27

Holly crept down the stairs, keeping her back pressed to the wall without realizing it. She picked her way gingerly over the handful of castle dwellers who had chosen to sleep on benches and blankets in the great hall. The main door was cracked ajar, inviting in a sliver of pallid light.

She slipped through the narrow breach and padded into the inner bailey, pausing at its boundary to search the sky as if seeing it for the first time.

The brooding vault delivered no vain promises of sunrise. 'Twas the sort of late summer day more easily mistaken for early autumn — the whisper of a cooling breeze blowing off the river, the skittering surprise of a leaf forsaken too soon, a glimpse of ruby in the verdant emerald crown of an oak. 'Twas a subtle reminder to savor the sighs of summer while they lasted, for winter's icy breath was drawing nigh.

Holly had forgotten how immense the world was. With no walls to enclose it, it sprawled in an unbroken vista of soaring peaks, vast moors, and impenetrable forest, all bound by the pewter thread of the river flowing through drifting veils of mist toward the mighty sea.

Her breath caught in her throat. She was seized by a shiver, a primal fear that such an unbridled wilderness would surely swallow her whole. She longed for the familiar walls of her tower cell, the cozy nest of her blankets. She might have gone creeping back into her hole like some timid mouse frightened by the castle cats had she not seen the man standing at the crest of the bluff overlooking the river.

The sight of her husband standing with one foot braced against a rock, his dark hair sifted by the caress of the wind, would have given her the courage to walk through the flames of hell itself.

Her fear lessened with each step that drew her nearer to him, until finally her invisible fetters fell away, making her limbs feel lighter than air. She wanted to run and skip and frolic across the dewy grass like a newborn colt. But Austyn's curious stillness stopped her. He seemed oblivious to her approach. His eyes were glazed, as if he could see beyond the bend of the mist-shrouded river to the distant sea.

Not wanting to startle him, Holly reached out a hand and gently rested it against the curve of his lower back.

At the tentative touch, Austyn looked down to find Holly smiling up at him. Holly somehow managing to turn his graceless tunic into the robes of a queen. Holly with bare feet, tangled curls, puffy eyes, and lips still faintly swollen from the voluptuous kisses they'd bestowed and been granted during the night. She'd never looked more beautiful, which made what he was about to do both easier and far more difficult than anything he'd done before.

Holly knew the instant she saw the expression on Austyn's face that something was wrong. As her smile faded, he drew her into his arms and kissed her softly. There was something so wistful, so inexplicably sad, about that kiss, that instead of allaying her apprehension, it only worsened it.

He caressed her shoulders with wrenching gentleness. "I'm sending you home."

She took a step away from him, as if distance would provide a shield against further blows. "I *am* home."

"But you're not safe. You'll never be safe at Caer Gavenmore." Anguish flickered across his face as he cupped her throat, gently fitting his fingertips to the faint necklace of bruises gifted to her by his father's hands. "What happened last night only proved that."

253

"I'm not afraid of your father. You're strong enough to protect me from him."

Austyn's shell of calm determination shattered. "But who will protect you from me!"

Holly flattened her palms against the beguiling warmth of his chest and gazed up into his haunted face, praying her eyes reflected the tenderness and trust brimming from her heart. "I'm not afraid of you either."

"Then you're a merry fool!" A tiny crack shot through Holly's heart as he caught her wrists and pushed her hands away from him as he had done so many times before. Sinking to a sitting position on the rock, he drove his fingers through his hair. "Have I not already proved that my love is capable of bringing you naught but disaster and death? Oh, 'twould start out innocently enough. You'd get a speck of ash in your eye from sitting too near the hearth and I'd accuse you of winking at Carey. The next thing you know," he drew a finger across his throat, "you'd both be lying dead on the flagstones and I'd be left to finish my supper alone."

Holly didn't know whether to laugh or cry. Only yesterday she had planned to entreat Austyn to return her to Tewksbury this very morn if he could not love her, and now he was determined to send her away because he did.

He buried his head in his hands. "How am I to make you understand? This jealousy is like a crippling sickness that flows through my veins. It poisons everything I touch and twists love into something monstrous and hurtful." He lifted his dark-lashed eyes, letting her see for the first time the full extent of his despair. His voice lowered to a defeated whisper. "I can't even look at you without thinking about losing you."

A tremulous sob of laughter escaped her. "But you won't lose me if you grant me leave to stay here by your side. I would never willingly abandon you." She knelt beside him, resting a hand on his knee. "To dare to love is to court hazard, is it not? 'Tis a risk

I'm more than willing to take."

He cast the grave behind them a dark look. "My mother took such a risk and it cost her her life. I'll not imperil you so."

Holly was slowly coming to fear that there would be no swaying him. She had fought so hard, but it seemed her heart's blood had all been spilled for naught. The realization made her both furious and afraid. "So what you're truly trying to say is that no matter how much you claim to love me, you could never find me worthy of your trust."

Frustration sharpened his voice. " 'Tis not you I find lacking, but myself."

She curled her lips in a haughty sneer that would have done Nathanael proud. "And if this dreaded 'Curse of the Gavenmores' turns out to be naught but a lot of superstitious gibberish?"

Austyn sighed. "It matters naught if the curse is true, so long as I believe it to be."

Holly could not dispute his twisted reasoning. She swallowed her pride, bowed her head, and whispered, "You could keep me locked in the tower. If 'tis the only way . . ."

He tilted her chin up with one knuckle, his eyes smoldering with that same frosty fire that had first drawn her into his arms. "I'd wrap myself in chains and cast myself into the deepest dungeon in hell before I would cage you again."

Holly rose stiffly to her feet, savoring the fleeting sensation of towering over him. "Then I shall cage myself. If you want me removed from your household, sir, I suggest you order Carey to fetch the battering ram and catapult. For I'll not set one dainty foot outside that tower until you cease this nonsense." She whirled around and began to march toward the castle. "If this Rhiannon wants you so badly, she's going to have to fight me. The witch crosses my path and I'll pluck off her little faerie wings and give her a taste of 'mortal doom.' "

"If you won't go to save your own soul, then go to save mine."

255

Austyn's voice tolled in her ears like a death knell. Holly froze, allowing herself the brief luxury of hating him. Hating him for knowing her so well. For issuing the one challenge she did not have the armor or the weapons to resist. He could have cut her no more deeply had he slapped her across the face with his steel gauntlet.

She spun around to find him standing, his feet braced for battle. Her impotence made her want to lash out, to hurt him as he was hurting her. "If you were going to request such a noble sacrifice of me, perhaps you should not have risked getting me with child. What if you're sending me back to my father with the Gavenmore heir in my womb?"

Austyn's jaw clenched as he inclined his head. Whether at being reminded of the tender communion their bodies had shared or at the thought of bidding farewell to his unborn child, Holly could not say.

"If you should bear a male child, then keep it as far away from me as possible. I've naught to offer him but a birthright of damnation."

Holly set her chin defiantly and dashed a tear from her cheek. "I know 'tis not uncommon for a husband and wife to reside in separate households, but what if I am not content with this mock marriage you propose? What if I choose to offer my hand to another?"

She knew it to be the cruelest blow she could have dealt him. Austyn's reply when it came was soft and edged with bitter resignation. "If you choose to remarry, I shall lie before both God and king to see that you're granted an annulment. There's no reason you should spend the rest of your life paying for my folly." He lifted his eyes to her face. "But you are, and always will be, the wife of my heart."

'Twas as if his vow split her heart asunder. Holly felt her face crumple into a mask of pain. "The only folly I ever committed,

256

sir, was loving you!"

With that impassioned cry, she turned and ran blindly toward the castle, seeking the refuge of the tower for the last time.

The cracked oval of the hand mirror reflected a flawless oval face. The dark brows were lightly winged, the arch of the cheekbones high and pure enough to survive for decades without betraying a trace of wear. Only the violet eyes betrayed the hollow soul of the mirror's owner.

Holly rouged her pursed lips to an inviting pink, then ran her tongue over them, thinking absently that rouge tasted much more pleasant than ashes. She adjusted the ruby at her throat and slipped a gold fillet over her curls. Let her husband accuse her of thievery if he dared! The woman who had once owned these gems and trinkets bore more kinship to her than to him. If he protested, she would simply claim them as payment for pleasures rendered.

Ruthlessly stamping down an urge to steal a last wistful glance at the rumpled bed, she drew a thin line of kohl beneath each eye to enhance their feverish glitter. *You mustn't cry anymore,* she chided herself sternly, *lest it smear and streak down your cheeks like a mummer's face paint.*

'Twas just as well Austyn was sending her away, she thought, touching the tip of her pinkie to the fragile depressions beneath her eyes. Another sennight in his contentious company would have doubtlessly worn irreversible creases into her skin. No woman could be expected to endure such dizzying flights of joy and despair without displaying the scars of it. And she hadn't spent all of those years avoiding the sun and anointing her skin with sheep fat just to end up as wizened as Elspeth.

As if the unkind thought had invoked her, a quavery voice behind Holly said, "My lady, Master Carey has prepared the horses."

Holly laid aside the mirror and swept her ermine-trimmed mantle in a graceful bell as she rose from the stool.

257

Elspeth could not contain a gasp. She had been present at Holly's birth and witnessed the cream-and-pink miracle that had slipped effortlessly from her mother's body with a perfectly rounded head and tiny, dark eyelashes as fine as feathers. She had gripped Holly's chubby little hand on her third birthday when a visiting Arabian prince had demanded the honor of her hand in marriage. The twelve-year-old lad had wept and stormed when her papa had refused, but Holly had simply tossed her silky, black curls in disdain and toddled off to dig for worms in the garden.

Elspeth had studied Holly's beauty in all of its guises, but she'd never seen her mistress look quite so breathtaking. Or so brittle.

'Twas as if she were a princess sculpted from ice. The notion made Elspeth afraid for her. Ice might be hard, but 'twas also fragile — vulnerable to heat and apt to shatter under pressure.

"Would you please bear my train, Elspeth?" Holly asked, drawing on a pair of miniver-lined gloves. "I should so hate for it to get dusty in this tomb."

As Elspeth dutifully fell into step behind her, Holly set her shoulders to a haughty angle. She refused to crawl away from Gavenmore with her train between her legs. Her heart might be shattered, but she was determined to leave with her pride intact. Let her beauty be a slap in the face to Austyn and all of his faithless kinfolk, dead or alive!

Both the great hall and inner bailey were crowded with onlookers. A gasp went up at her appearance. Some, like Winifred, were openly weeping. Others did not bother to hide their relief. Perhaps now their precious master would be safe from the destructive wiles of comely women, Holly thought bitterly. She held her head high, long accustomed to the impolite stares of those less lovely than she.

Carey waited with the restless horse — a piebald gelding, a small bay, and a dainty gray palfrey perfectly suited to Holly's height. Carey's face was somber. 'Twas impossible to miss the reproachful

258

look he cast the hill.

From the corner of her eye, Holly saw Austyn — a shadow garbed in black standing beside his mother's grave. His very presence there was a silent testament to the righteousness of what he was doing.

Without so much as a disdainful glance in his direction, Holly accepted Carey's hand and mounted the palfrey sidesaddle, spreading her skirts in a pretty fan over the beast's flanks.

As Elspeth settled herself on the bay, Carey looked as if he would have desperately liked to say something, but Holly flared her nostrils with such aristocratic scorn that he did not dare.

She folded her gloved hands over the reins and announced with the aplomb of a young queen, "We may proceed."

Proceed they did, past the gawking spectators, past the crooked gatehouse, past the rubble of the abandoned curtain wall. Past the point on the road where one could look back and entertain the childish illusion that Caer Gavenmore was a celestial palace perched on a bed of clouds.

Holly no longer believed in castles in the clouds, nor in the princes who inhabited them. Under the guise of smoothing a rebellious curl, she lifted the back of her hand to her eye, leaving a single smear of kohl on the pristine silk of her glove.

Chapter 28

Holly huddled deeper into her mantle, wondering how it was possible that the world had succumbed to winter in August, forsaking both the indolent pleasures of summer and the crisp delights of autumn. A pall of gloom hung over the forest. The brisk wind took spiteful glee in rattling the leaves and hurling gusts of cold drizzle into her face.

They'd already wasted a day and a half of their journey crouched beneath a shelter of pine boughs, watching the rain unfurl in a dense gray curtain. They might have spent another interminable day doing the same had Carey not feared they would run low on provisions. So they had emerged from their sodden nest and plodded on toward Tewksbury, their spirits as glum as the weather.

Even Elspeth seemed to have lost her gift for chatter. After catching her rubbing her gnarled knuckles as if the dampness pained them, Holly had ignored the nurse's croaked protests and insisted she don the fur-lined gloves that had belonged to Austyn's grandmother.

Holly could no longer feel her own fingers on the reins. She only wished the hollow ache in her chest would subside to numbness. After years of fearing she was naught but a pretty shell, she had finally discovered she possessed a heart as vital and vulnerable as any other woman's only to have it ripped out by the roots.

'Twas just as well, she supposed. She would have no further need of it. It seemed she was destined to spend her life being worshiped from afar, never again to know the loving intimacy of her husband's touch.

You are, and always will be, the wife of my heart.

Austyn's pledge echoed through her mind in a bittersweet refrain. He had probably believed the words when he spoke them, but she was certain a few months of solitude would tarnish his noble intentions. Under the benevolent guise of setting her free, he would seek that annulment they'd discussed and woo some mild-tempered maiden with calf-brown eyes and a face like a horse to his marriage bed. Holly would bump into them at a tournament or Mayday celebration, smile graciously to hide her pain, and compliment the herd of coltish children frisking about their heels.

One of her hands fluttered to her abdomen, giving silent testament to a hope she'd barely dared to acknowledge. Austyn had made it painfully clear that he had little interest in any child she might bear him, but she could not help but wonder if his resolve might not soften if she presented him with a squirming son. A precious little man-child with dark locks and the hint of a mischievous dimple in one chubby cheek. The dull ache in her chest sharpened to yearning anguish.

"Stop torturing yourself," she muttered beneath her breath, earning an uneasy look from both Elspeth and Carey.

The rain had nearly ceased. A canopy of branches spanned the narrow path, muting the feeble daylight to premature dusk. Holly's nape prickled. She glanced over her shoulder, hard pressed to shake off the sensation of malevolent eyes peering at them from the tangled bracken.

She swallowed hard to calm her nerves, remembering what a fool she'd made of herself when she'd succumbed to similar fancies on the journey to Gavenmore. This time there would be no Austyn to draw her into his lap and dry her tears. No Austyn to hoist her up on his mount and offer the comforting expanse of his back as a pillow.

She was not the only one affected by the sinister atmosphere of the forest. Carey's hand strayed to his shoulder to check the readiness of his bow. Elspeth lowered the hood of her cloak, her gaze darting from tree to tree. They all breathed a sigh of relief when the tunnel of foliage opened into a mist-shrouded glade.

Holly's sigh surged to a cry of astonishment as she saw a cowled figure standing at the edge of the clearing. Ignoring Carey's shout of warning, she threw herself off the palfrey and ran to meet him.

" 'Tis only Nate!" she called to Carey, smoothing away the priest's hood to reveal his familiar features.

Carey settled back on his mount, his face darkening with a scowl that would have done his master proud.

"Thank God you're well!" Nathanael exclaimed, enveloping her in a less than brotherly embrace.

Holly drew away from him, rather discomfited by the intimacy. "Of course, I'm well. But what are you doing out here in the middle of nowhere? Why aren't you at Tewksbury?"

Hectic patches of color brightened Nathanael's cheeks. "I was coming to rescue you from that tyrant." He shuddered. "You can't begin to imagine the dreadful fates I've envisioned you suffering at his hands."

Holly might have defended her husband, but she feared her own fair coloring would betray the variety of delicious torments she had suffered at Austyn's accomplished hands. She knew Nathanael would never believe her anyway. His pious fervor had been stirred into a frenzy by the prospect of a quest. In his estimation, a princess locked in a tower by a wicked ogre held no less allure than the search for the Holy Grail.

"How have you come so far? Is my father with you?" She searched the woods behind him, not realizing until that moment how much she longed to cast herself on her papa's neck and weep out her grief.

"We thought it best not to alarm your father unduly. Once we'd laid siege to Gavenmore and liberated you from the clutches of that villain, we were planning to —"

"We?" Holly interrupted, his smug expression sending a skitter of dread down her spine.

They slithered from the rustling undergrowth like a nest of vipers. Before Carey could slot arrow to bow, the tip of a rusty sword was pressed to his Adam's apple. Elspeth's cry of alarm was cut off mid-croak by the filthy hand clamped over her mouth. Between one breath and the next, Holly and her party were surrounded by a dozen men.

Holly had heard tales of these men before. They'd been spotted skulking at the borders of her father's land more than once. They were infamous for terrorizing their master's own villeins — robbing them of their pathetic earnings, beating old men and dragging their virgin daughters into the forest for a bit of brutal sport. They were slovenly and vicious, their eyes narrowed by an inbred appetite for depravity that made them seem more beast than human.

But somehow the man who stepped out from behind their ranks — his ebony surcoat and hose immaculate, every hair slicked back into flawless alignment, a genial smile pasted on his handsome features — made them look no more menacing than a band of bumbling pages.

"If 'tis not the damsel in distress herself! How very courteous of you to spare us the bother of rescuing you. I do find sieges to be most tiresome."

Holly had been clutching Nathanael's sleeve without realizing it. She pried her fingers loose, reluctant to exhibit any sign of weakness before this man. "Nathanael, what is *he* doing here?"

Nate's patronizing smile faltered. "Why, he saved my life. I lost my way in the wilderness. Were it not for the baron's kindness and hospitality, I might have perished."

Eugene de Legget snorted with contempt. "We found him wandering in circles, half-dazed with hunger and thirst, mumbling a rather tedious string of mea culpas beneath his breath. He was only a few feet from your father's border at the time."

263

"You never told me that," Nathanael said indignantly. "I thought I was still in Wales."

"Of course I told you. You were simply too delirious to remember." Eugene turned his oily charm on Holly. She was surprised he didn't ooze right out of his surcoat. "Once the good brother informed us of your grave predicament, we were only too willing to offer our assistance. I must confess you don't seem much the worse for wear." He reached out to finger a curl. "I like it. 'Tis rather . . . boyish."

His lips caressed the word, shedding an entirely new light on his penchant for maidens who'd yet to celebrate their thirteenth birthdays. Suppressing a shudder, Holly ducked out from beneath his hand. He shook his head at her rudeness.

She grabbed the front of Nathanael's robes. "Do these ruffians look capable of conducting a siege to you? I see no crossbows or battering rams. And where are the scaling ladders? The catapults? The archers?"

Nathanael blinked like a man reluctant to wake up from a pleasant dream for fear of discovering it had been a nightmare all along. "I — I do not know. I just assumed the baron knew what he was about. He promised we would save you."

"Aye, most likely by slipping into Gavenmore by night and slitting the throats of its helpless inhabitants. How could you be so impossibly naive?"

Eugene *tsked* beneath his breath. "Don't be so hard on him, Holly. I found his innocence to be rather touching."

She faced de Legget, lowering herself to address him directly for the first time. "Then make good on your vow, my lord. Escort me to my father at once."

" 'Twould be my most humble pleasure, my lady."

The tension seeped from Holly's shoulders. Perhaps she had overestimated de Legget's villainy after all.

His lips puckered in an apologetic moue. "But I'm afraid 'twill be quite impossible." He reached to his braided belt and unsheathed a small silver dagger.

Holly took an instinctive step away from Nathanael, then another. As de Legget stalked her, two of his rogues seized the priest by the arms.

He squirmed in protest. "I say, sirs, unhand me this minute!"

Holly's back came up against a tree. Eugene twirled the knife in his deft fingers.

"If you harm a hair on her head . . ." Carey snarled.

Elspeth whimpered, her eyes bulging with terror.

Only Holly was silent, determined to stare Eugene down with all the scorn at her disposal. She forced herself not to recoil, not even when he pressed his hot mouth against her ear and whispered, "You won't be quite so haughty when I'm through with you, my lady, for I have every intention of bringing you to your knees. One way or another."

The dagger's blade grazed her cheek. From the corner of her eye, she saw Carey start to struggle. Saw the sword at his throat notch away a sliver of flesh, sending a rivulet of blood trickling into the neck of his tunic.

"You might bring me to my knees," she hissed. "But I won't be reduced to slithering on my belly as you do."

She bit back a cry of pain as he seized her hair, hacking away a single curl with icy detachment. Drawing a folded parchment from the velvet purse dangling from his belt, he sealed the curl inside.

"This should do to ensure the effectiveness of my demands. Were I not so chivalrous, I would throw in your tongue as well. I'm sure your husband has endured enough of its nagging to recognize it."

Holly swallowed her retort, for once in her life choosing discretion over valor. She almost wished she hadn't when one of his henchman seized her around the waist, crushing the breath from her with a burly forearm. She knew she really ought to be grateful she couldn't

265

breathe. The toothless fellow smelled nearly as bad as he looked.

"Bring the horses," de Legget commanded. Two of his cohorts slunk off through the trees.

"I believed in you, sir," Nathanael said softly, looking as bewildered as a child by his rapid change of fortune.

Eugene slanted him a glance, as if just remembering his existence. Holly cared nothing for the look. A knot of foreboding tightened in her chest. As de Legget approached the priest, the dagger shimmering like quicksilver in his fluid hand, she bucked and clawed in a futile attempt to escape the giant.

The baron's heartfelt sigh would have melted winter frost. " 'Tis the most tragic failing of we mortals, don't you think, brother? That we so consistently disappoint each other. But you still have faith in your God, do you not?"

Nathanael nodded, his dark eyes somber. "Aye."

Eugene's tender smile spread. "Then give Him my regards." Grunting in satisfaction, he rammed the dagger into Nathanael's breast.

A scream of anguish ripped from Holly's throat. Carey went down beneath a sea of flailing arms and legs. The hand clamped over Elspeth's mouth could no longer muffle her squeals of horror.

As Nathanael collapsed, Holly managed to shake off her captor and stumble forward.

Even as a damning stain blossomed on the front of his robe, he stretched out a hand toward her. "Forgive me," he whispered, his eyes going so hazy and unfocused she could not have said if he entreated her or God. "Please forgive me."

Holly's fingertips grazed his; Eugene's henchman caught her around the waist, jerking her out of his reach. She wailed her frustration as Nathanael's eyes drifted shut and he rolled to his back.

Eugene reached down, coolly withdrew the dagger, and wiped the blade on the parchment still in his hand. "May God rest his pathetic soul."

266

Ignoring Holly's murderous glare, Eugene strolled over to where Carey lay pinned to the ground by four hulking men, his lower lip puffed to twice its normal size and one of his eyes already swollen shut.

"Do try not to kill him or break his legs." Eugene tucked the parchment into the waistband of Carey's hose. "Either eventuality would necessitate finding a new messenger and I really haven't the patience."

As Eugene grabbed Holly's elbow and jerked her toward the waiting horses, she winced at the sickening thud of fists on flesh and the sound of Carey's helpless grunts.

"You bastard," she spat, blinded by a hot torrent of tears as she stumbled past Nathanael's still form.

His fingers dug into her tender flesh. "Remind me to teach you to address me with more courtesy when I'm your husband."

"I already have a husband!"

His cold smile sent a shaft of pure terror through her soul. "Not for long, my lady. Not for long."

Holly soon learned that there were more grueling ways to travel than perched sidesaddle on a palfrey in the rain. Such as being trussed hands and feet and heaved like a sack of grain over the back of a monstrous destrier. Each thunderclap of a hoofbeat jarred her spine and set her teeth to rattling like dice. Cold gobbets of mud spattered her face. She shivered to imagine the effects of such torture on Elspeth's frail bones.

As the hours passed, her thoughts churned in rhythm to the horse's strides, stirring up a maddening maelstrom of grief and regret. If only her love had been strong enough to win Austyn's trust. If only she hadn't baited Eugene. If only she'd never enlisted Nathanael's help in her mad scheme. He might be safe at Tewksbury this very moment, nagging the servants about their lack of piety and chiding her papa for hawking when he should have been attending Mass.

A rush of warm tears blurred the flailing hooves.

She sought to dry her eyes by offering up a prayer for Nathanael's poor unshriven soul. But each time she closed them, 'twas not Nathanael's pallid face she saw, but Austyn's — Austyn sprawled in a puddle of his own blood, his dark lashes feathered against his cheeks. Austyn the hapless victim of another man's obsession. Was Eugene's treachery to be the fulfillment of the dreaded Gavenmore curse? Was her beauty truly to be her husband's doom?

Holly had no more time to ponder before her horse was snapped to a halt and she was dragged off its back by the clumsy paws of Eugene's personal giant. As he heaved her over his beefy shoulder, she caught a chilling glimpse of their destination.

She should have known Eugene would be too cunning to risk taking her to his own castle, where word of her captivity might spread to her papa's ears. He had chosen for his den a crumbling ruin of a watchtower so shrouded with ivy that from a distance 'twould be nearly indistinguishable from the surrounding trees. Here in this isolated glade, there would be no curious villeins, no prying servants, no chattering pages or squires to spread gossip or intervene in whatever diabolical revenge he had planned. Here she and Austyn would be completely at the mercy of de Legget and his henchmen.

Holly shuddered.

She knew Nathanael would have frowned upon appealing to the capricious mercies of a pagan faerie, but as she bounced along over the colossal shoulder, she pressed her eyes shut and whispered fiercely, "Please, Rhiannon, you may be a faerie, but if you've a woman's heart, keep him far, far away from this place."

Chapter 29

Sir Austyn of Gavenmore was a haunted man. He stood on the battlements of his ancestral home, blinking rain from his eyes to gaze toward the eastern horizon. His crimson surcoat was plastered to his skin. The frivolous border of ivy embroidered along its back weighted his shoulders like fetters of iron.

Rhiannon's revenge was naught but a mild scolding compared with his wife's retribution. The faerie queen's shade could only bedevil one place at a time. Holly's ghost was everywhere.

It waddled along the riverbank, strewing marigolds in his path. It patted anemones into place around his mother's grave, glancing up at him to reveal sparkling violet eyes and an impish nose smudged with dirt. He passed it on the stairs, lugging a tub of scarlet poppies up to the battlements.

Austyn reached out and brushed a raindrop from the withered petals of one of those poppies.

The first manifestation had occurred only hours after Carey had escorted Holly from the castle. Austyn had been in the solar with Winifred and Emrys, packing away his plans for completing the castle and calculating how much of Holly's dowry had already been spent on ordering slate and sandstone. He intended to return every penny to the earl as soon as he could recover it.

'Twould be only a matter of weeks, Austyn supposed, rolling a scroll into a neat tube with methodical hands, before the king's tax collectors would be pounding at the door, threatening to seize the castle and its meager lands if they could not pay. The prospect no longer distressed him as it once had. Without Holly, the keep was naught but an empty shell. A tomb for his dreams.

Ignoring Winifred's worried glance, he rested his aching brow in his hands. A discordant jangling drifted to his ears. He lifted his head, a crazy hope sputtering to life in his heart.

"Did you hear that?" he inquired of Emrys.

"Hear what, sir?"

Shoving his way past his puzzled steward, Austyn flew from the solar. He skidded to a halt in the south corridor, fully expecting to find the iron candelabrum bobbing up and down on its tarnished chains.

The candelabrum hung silent and still, its rusty music playing only in his head.

Austyn slid down the wall to a sitting position. 'Twas of little import that Holly's ghost had made itself invisible. He could still hear the echo of her merry laughter.

He crouched in that darkened corridor until nightfall, finally rising only to have his dazed steps carry him to the door of the north tower. When he realized where he was, he turned and resolutely sought the barren confines of his own bed. After tossing and thrashing for hours, he shot bolt upright from a fitful nightmare to the angelic strains of his wife's singing.

He bounded from the bed and pelted up the winding stairs. But when he threw open the door of the tower, hollow silence greeted him. Surrendering any pretense of sleep, Austyn spent the remainder of the night in the window seat, gazing at the bed and remembering how Holly had so generously shared both it and her warm, loving body with him. When Winnie discovered him there the following morning, he refused to allow her to tidy the chamber, fearing her efforts might banish the scent of myrrh that still clung to the rumpled sheets.

He understood why his grandfather had forbidden anyone to disturb the tower after his grandmother died. 'Twas as if the man never relinquished his hope that the woman who had once inhabited it might someday return.

Austyn's final glimpse of Holly had assured him that his hopes were no less vain than his grandfather's. He would never forget the proud set of her shoulders, the haughty cast of her features, the wounded look in her beautiful eyes. He had sent her away to protect her, yet she seemed to believe he had broken faith with her in some irredeemable manner.

After his fourth night in the window seat, Austyn decided 'twould be best to have Emrys brick up the tower door to ensure that never again would any Gavenmore man be tempted to punish a woman for his own sins. 'Twas only then that he remembered there would be no more Gavenmore men after him. The curse had not only robbed him of his wife, but of his children as well.

Austyn's hands clenched on the rain-slicked parapet as he imagined what magnificent sons Holly would have given him.

He had yet to give the order to seal the tower, for he knew that he would be walling up his heart as well, this time forever. Then there would be nothing left for him to do but spend the remainder of his days wandering the castle in search of his wife's ghost and rattling his own invisible chains.

Shaking the rain from his hair, Austyn turned away from the parapet, driven by loneliness to seek the one man who shared his exile.

Austyn slid his knight across the chessboard, then watched his father's pawn pick it off feeling nary a sting of regret. Rhys had been almost placid since his attack on Holly. 'Twas as if the ugly spell of violence had exorcised some dark demon from his soul. Compassion had tempered Austyn's first urge to cast him into the dungeon. Instead, he had committed him to Emrys's reliable care, determined that his father would never again harm another woman.

Emrys poked at the fire he had built to ward off the damp while Winifred plucked and cleaned a chicken with efficient hands, striving

271

to conceal her fretful glances at the door of the great hall, but failing miserably. Austyn's own concern was mounting. Carey should have returned more than two days ago. Perhaps he had chosen to linger at Tewksbury until the rain cleared, Austyn told himself. He refused to humor his own impulse to glance at the door between every move, not wanting to reveal his pathetic eagerness to hear news of Holly.

His father's muteness suited his own brooding temper so well that he flinched with surprise when Rhys snapped, "Check."

Stealing a glance at the door from beneath his lashes, Austyn slid his king out of the path of his father's bishop, carelessly leaving his queen unguarded.

Rhys captured her, cornering Austyn's king to cement his victory. "Checkmate."

"It seems the best man won," Austyn said, forcing a half-hearted smile as he began to rearrange the pieces for another game.

"I think we both know that's not true, son."

Austyn jerked his head up. His father's blue eyes were as clear as Austyn had seen them in years. The sight pained him. Reminded him of a time when his father had been his only hero. A time when they'd all been happy.

"I was in the courtyard," Rhys said softly.

Austyn lined up his pawns in a precise row, struggling to keep the anger from his tone. "Holly told me. 'Twas rather boorish of you, don't you think? Eavesdropping on your own son and his" — he clenched his teeth against a pang of anguish — "bride."

Rhys shook his head. "Not then. The night my mother jumped."

Austyn's hands stilled. This time when he met his father's gaze, he found he could not look away.

"I hadn't seen her since I was a small boy," Rhys said, "so I slipped up to the tower to visit her. I was the one who told her that Father was with his doxy. She started to cry. She hugged me very tightly and told me I was a good lad and she loved me with

272

all of her heart. Then she sent me away." He stared at the chesspiece in his hand. "Perhaps if I had stayed . . . if I hadn't told her about Father's woman . . ."

Austyn was surprised to learn his barren heart still had any forgiveness to offer. He held up one of the smallest chessmen. " 'Twas never your fault. You were naught but a pawn in your father's game of jealousy and revenge."

"She loved me, you know. She was a loyal and devoted wife."

Austyn fought to keep his own bitterness at bay. " 'Tis fortunate you can remember your mother with such charity."

Rhys blinked at him. "Not my mother. *Your* mother. Gwyneth."

Austyn was baffled. 'Twas the first time he had heard his father speak well of his mother since her death. Perhaps Rhys had retreated to the past, to the golden days of summer before that fateful autumn had shattered their lives.

Rhys caressed the carved queen with his thumb, his hand oddly steady. "She begged me not to send her."

Austyn frowned. "Send her where?"

His father gently placed the white queen on the square next to the black king. "Edward did not come to Gavenmore to bestow his blessing on the new castle. He came to inform me that he was withdrawing his support. That he'd decided the Welsh were a savage and ungrateful lot and their petty rebellions had convinced him his castle strongholds were naught but beautiful follies. Oh, he clucked his regret and praised me for my loyalty, but he refused to relent. Not even when I begged . . ."

Austyn became aware that Emrys had ceased stirring the fire. Winifred was gaping at his father, a bloody chicken bone clutched in one hand.

"I believed that I might yet sway him. Appeal to his sense of honor. When I saw how he fancied Gwyneth —"

Austyn came to his feet, overturning the chessboard. He heard the pieces scatter across the flagstones through the dull roaring in

273

his ears. "You sent her? You sent your own wife to lay with another man?"

Tears began to trickle down Rhys's papery cheeks, but his voice was still the voice of a man, not the whine of a petulant child. "She cried so prettily and pleaded with me not to ask such a thing of her. I told her that if she truly loved me, she'd be eager to make such a small sacrifice for our common good. Then the next morning when Edward bade me a regretful farewell and I realized it had all been for naught . . ."

The roaring in Austyn's ears reached his lips. He snatched his father up by the shoulders, shaking him like a rag doll. "You murdered her for doing your bidding? You strangled her for sacrificing her virtue to further your own greedy ambitions?"

Through a crimson haze of rage, Austyn heard Winifred's shrill pleas, felt Emrys tugging frantically at his arm, but his eyes were locked with his father's in a mortal battle of wills. What Austyn saw in those pale blue orbs was not fear, but grim satisfaction. Rhys wanted his own son to kill him. He wanted his wife's death avenged, but lacked the courage to do it himself. A ponderous burden rolled off of Austyn's shoulders as he realized the sins of the father were no longer his own to bear.

His hands slowly unclenched. Rhys crumpled into the chair.

Austyn gazed down at his bowed head with genuine pity. "Sorry, old man. I'll not send you to hell. 'Tis a far greater punishment that you should live with what you've done."

Shaking off Emrys's hand, Austyn squared his shoulders and started for the stairs, eager to escape the hall and all of its haunts.

"And can you live with what you've done?"

His father's voice rang with an authority that froze Austyn in his tracks. Time swept backward. He was nine years old again, bracing himself to receive a scolding for carving his name into the wet mortar of the moat. He spun around, half expecting to find his father straddling the chair, his face flushed with the vigor of youth.

The old man had cocked his head to the side and was watching him like a bright-eyed bird. "You were only too eager to believe the worst of your mother."

"I was a child! I thought that she'd abandoned us!" Holly's ghost tapped him on the shoulder. *Abandoned you? I think not, sir, for 'tis you who have abandoned her.*

Austyn whirled on Winifred, eliciting a gasp of alarm and a drifting blizzard of chicken feathers. "Did you hear that?"

"N-n-nay, sir. I heard nothing."

"Nor did I." Emrys exchanged a nervous glance with his wife.

His father laughed, a dry rasp that grated on Austyn's raw nerves. He was beginning to wish he'd killed the old rogue when he'd had the chance.

"Don't mock me," Austyn snapped. " 'Twas naught but that infernal witch Rhiannon. Her sole delight is in plaguing me witless."

His father nodded knowingly. "She used to badger me as well until I realized her taunts were only the echo of my conscience."

"I never knew you had one."

Austyn's sarcasm failed to ruffle Rhys. "Aye, 'twas my conscience that tortured me because I knew in my heart that your mother didn't betray me. I betrayed her. Nor did my mother disgrace the Gavenmore name. 'Twas your grandfather who shamed us all by imprisoning an innocent woman and depriving her of her only son while he committed adultery with a castle whore. Old Caradawg's young bride was probably equally blameless, burned at the stake because of her husband's wretched lack of faith in her fealty."

Holly's ghost twirled a curl around a graceful finger with saucy defiance. *If a man refuses to trust a woman he claims to love, then tell me, husband, who between them is the faithless one?*

"Cease your prattling, woman!" Austyn thundered, raking a hand through his hair.

Winifred sidled toward the kitchen, as if his sudden spell of madness might be infectious.

His father was right about one thing, he thought wildly. He ought to be steeped in shame for all the dreadful things he'd believed about his mother. But at the edge of his remorse danced a frantic hope.

"The curse . . ." he whispered.

"Rubbish, lad!" his father barked. " 'Twas never a curse, but a prophecy destined to fulfill itself by those superstitious enough to believe in it. Beauty never brought ruin to the Gavenmore men. The Gavenmore men brought ruin upon themselves and the women fool enough to love them."

I would never willingly abandon you, Holly whispered, her breath warm and sweet in his ear.

Austyn braced his hands on the table, feeling curiously light-headed. 'Twas of little import if the others heard her, for the truth rang in his heart like the tolling of a cathedral bell. 'Twas not Holly who had betrayed him, but he who had betrayed her by having more faith in an ancient curse than in the power of their love. If she sought solace in the arms of another man, 'twould be only because he had driven her to do so by his lack of trust.

Holly's ghost threw back its head and sang — a trilling hymn of joy and hope for the morrow.

With her song still chiming in his ears, Austyn snatched up a cloak and started across the hall.

Before he could reach the door, it flew open. He flinched as a gust of wind and rain struck him full in the face. A man staggered into the hall, but had it not been for Winifred's agonized cry, Austyn might not have recognized him.

Carey's eyes were feverish slits in puffs of bruised flesh. His right cheekbone was split, his left arm hanging at an impossibly awkward angle. His other arm clutched his ribs through the tattered strips of soaked wool that had once been his tunic.

Austyn caught him before he could fall. "My God, man, what happened?"

He struggled to speak through his swollen lips, but the words were garbled. Grunting his frustration, he fumbled at the waistband of his hose with his intact arm, withdrawing a folded scrap of paper. Austyn mastered his panic long enough to entrust Carey to his parents' waiting arms, then tore open the battered parchment.

'Twas not the message or map outlined in the effeminate scrawl that made him want to howl with fear, nor even the ominous copper smudge staining the paper. 'Twas the solitary sable curl that coiled around Austyn's finger in velvety reproach.

Chapter 30

Holly paced her tower cell in crisp, restless strides.

Instead of a sumptuous four-poster with hangings of pleated silk, a moth-eaten blanket lay crumpled beneath the narrow window. In lieu of a cloth-lined tub, a basin of brackish water, intended for bathing *and* drinking, sat on the barren timber floor. On the crumbling hearth, a scrawny mouse nibbled at the chunk of stale brown bread that had served as Holly's breakfast and lunch and was to have been her supper as well. Her captor had denied her even the solace of Elspeth's company, whisking away the whimpering nurse immediately upon their arrival at his lair.

As a pale moon rose in the drab sky, her desperate gaze kept straying to the pair of rusty manacles affixed by iron plates to the wall opposite the window. She was thankful Eugene had not restrained her, but the expectant emptiness of those fetters drenched her in dread. She would have almost preferred they contain the skeletal remains of de Legget's last unfortunate prisoner.

Weary of pacing, she knelt and scraped at a patch of loose mortar she'd discovered behind the right manacle, paying no heed to the damage she was doing to fingernails that had yet to recover from her original assault against them.

"I do so hope you're enjoying your accommodations, my lady."

Holly snapped to her feet at the elegant drawl. Eugene was leaning against the doorframe, an amiable smile softening his perpetual sneer.

"From the priest's blithering," he said, "I determined that your chamber at Gavenmore was similarly appointed."

She dropped him a mocking curtsy. "Oh, no, sir. We only had moldy bread crusts twice a week and the rats were much larger there."

He stepped into the chamber, closing the door behind him. "A pity. I'll have to comb the dungeons and see what I can arrange."

Holly forced herself not to recoil from his approach. 'Twas the first visit he'd deigned to pay her since taking her hostage three days ago and she doubted his presence boded well for her future, bleak prospect though it was.

'Twas doubly hard not to flinch when he cupped the vulnerable column of her throat in his hands, caressing the faint smudges that still marred her skin. "I must say your husband has exquisite taste in jewelry. But had you consented to be my bride, I'd have draped you in diamonds and pearls rather than bruises."

Holly bit back her impassioned defense of Austyn, fearful such a show of devotion would only kindle Eugene's hatred toward him. She chose instead to divert it toward herself. "I would never consent to be your bride. Not even if you murdered my husband and every other man on earth."

He flexed his hands; 'twas all Holly could do to keep from clawing at them. She didn't think she could endure being strangled twice in one week.

They slowly eased their pressure, dropping to hang limp at his sides. "I hate to disappoint you, my dear, but my offer for your hand has been withdrawn. Surely you knew your charms would pale once you'd shared them so generously with that barbarian. You're no longer fit to be my bride."

"My, my, aren't we the fickle one? Upon our first meeting, when I was only twelve, was it not you who dropped to your knees, kissed the hilt of your sword, and swore your undying devotion?"

He blinked. "I was striving to look up your gown."

"An indulgence that still eludes you."

The nasty edge of his smile sharpened even as his voice softened.

"Only for a very brief time."

Holly's confidence faltered. "But you just said I was no longer worthy of your attentions."

"I said I'd lost interest in wedding you. Bedding you is another matter entirely."

She took an involuntary step backward.

"There's no need to cringe, my dear. I can understand how that oaf's clumsy fumblings might have made you dread the act, but I can promise you I possess skills that will soon have you begging for my touch."

Holly resisted the urge to mock his arrogance as a misty image flashed in her mind: Austyn lowering his magnificent body to hers, making her his own with tender grace and irresistible mastery.

She drew herself up to her full height. "The only boon I shall entreat from you, sir, is my freedom."

Eugene's smile vanished. "On the contrary, my lady. If you persist in defying me, you'll be begging not for liberty, but for mercy."

As the door slammed and locked behind him, Holly's bravado dissipated. Betrayed by her wobbly knees, she sank to a sitting position and dragged the musty blanket around her shoulders. As the shadows of night came creeping over the unfamiliar window ledge, there were no lit tapers to hold them at bay and no Austyn to cradle her in his arms until her trembling ceased.

The knight drove his destrier through the ancient forest much as his ancestor had done over eight centuries before.

A treacherous net woven from moonlight and shadows dappled the mossy turf, but he nudged the horse's lathered flanks with his golden spurs, refusing to slow his perilous pace. The loyal beast snorted, its nostrils flaring with exertion, then strained its massive chest forward to seek another inch of speed. Once the lord who bore the title of Gavenmore would have had a powerful army of knights beneath his command, but Austyn had only his haste and his honor. He prayed they would stand him in good stead against an opponent as crafty and lacking in integrity as Eugene de Legget, the baron of Montfort.

Not once since he'd been handed Montfort's missive had he been tormented by visions of the woman he loved in another man's arms. Instead he was consumed with fears for her welfare — Was she hurt? Was she cold? Was she hungry? Was she afraid? 'Twas Holly's courage that frightened him the most. He knew only too well how her reckless defiance could incite a man to rage.

The destrier surged through a deep brook. The spray of frigid water failed to dampen Austyn's resolve, for unlike his hapless Gavenmore forebear, he was forging ahead to seek not his doom, but the woman who was both his destiny and his salvation.

As Holly sought to detach her stiff limbs from the chilly timber planks, she halfway wished she'd never succumbed to the temptation of sleep. Rubbing the cobwebs of slumber from her eyes, she rose and trundled to the window. For one wistful moment, she dared to believe she might see the sinuous thread of the river Wye unraveling between black mountain peaks.

Instead, a lush emerald carpet of treetops stretched toward every horizon. Summer had returned to England with a perverse vengeance and the brilliance of the morning sun stung Holly's eyes to near blindness. She was further tortured by the knowledge that just beyond the eastern ridge lay Tewksbury and her father.

Shaking off her lethargy, she leaned over the window ledge and gave one of the thick garlands of ivy that clung to the tower wall an experimental tug. It snapped off in her hand. Sighing with disappointment, she tossed it to the cobblestones below, earning a nasty look from one of Eugene's henchmen. Five of the brutes patrolled the boundaries of the isolated glade, clutching sharpened iron pikes in their beef fists.

The creak of the door swinging open warned her she had company.

The gleeful bounce in Eugene's step as he joined her made her more wary than before. "Languishing at the window, my dear? Pining away with hands clasped in supplication while you wait for your noble knight to come charging to your rescue?"

Holly burst into merry peals of laughter.

A flicker of unease marred her captor's smile. Holly felt a surge of triumph at having disarmed him, however briefly.

She favored him with a pitying look. "Forgive my mirth, sir, but after having spent a summer wed to that boorish clod of a Welshman, I find your romantic notions to be hopelessly naive. I can assure you that Gavenmore is as delighted to be rid of me as I am of him. He'll not waste a penny of his precious dowry to ransom me from your clutches."

"Ah, but I did not demand a penny of ransom. I simply requested an . . . audience." De Legget's sensual lips shaped the innocent word into an abomination.

"Then I fear you'll be equally disappointed," Holly forced herself to say lightly. "My husband is as stingy with his time as he is with his coin — especially where I'm concerned. Surely Nathanael told you of the impasse we reached when Gavenmore discovered my charade."

Eugene rested one hip against the sill and pursed his lips thoughtfully. "I seem to remember something about a minor confrontation. Lots of shouting and threats of violence. The peasants demanding you be burned at the stake. Gavenmore dragging you through the streets half-naked. What an enchanting spectacle! I am sorry I missed it."

Holly bowed her head, feigning a sulky pout. "He pronounced me a shrewish, deceitful witch and said I was unfit to bear his children." The barb of truth in those words still had the power to wound.

"Why those are the very qualities every mother should aspire to! You can't expect me to believe you couldn't flutter your lashes

282

and charm your way back into his good graces." He cradled her chin between two fingers with chilling tenderness and turned her face to the light. "According to your doting priest, the Gavenmore men are known to possess a potentially mortal weakness for beautiful women."

Holly kept her lashes lowered, horrified to learn that Nathanael may have unwittingly laid in Eugene's fiendish hands the one weapon that could destroy both she and Austyn. The knowledge stripped her of all defenses save the truth. Or something near enough to it to mislead a mind as shrewd as Eugene's.

Shaking off his mocking caress, she paced across the tower, then whirled to face him, giving her bitterness free rein for the first time since Austyn had bid her farewell. "Aye, the Gavenmore men have a weakness for beauty. They consume it as other men consume bread or ale. Their appetites are insatiable. I'm sure Nathanael also told you that I was forced to trade my virtue for his freedom. My husband was only too eager to partake of my *beauty* night after night so long as it pleased him to do so."

"Lucky fellow," Eugene murmured, his insinuating glance lingering at her breasts.

"Yet now that he's grown bored of me, what does he do? He publicly repudiates me. He humiliates me by sending me to live in my father's household. Why he's probably seducing some comely serving wench even as we speak!" Holly felt a tear tremble from her lashes and chart a burning course down her cheek. "I swear to you the man cares naught for me!"

Her performance was so wrenching that even Holly might have come to believe it were it not for the jarring thunder of hoofbeats, shouts of alarm, and the bellow of pure rage that drifted up through the tower window.

"Monfort! What the hell have you done with my woman?"

Chapter 31

Holly swallowed a despairing groan as Eugene snaked an arm around her waist and dragged her back to the window. The sight below was both better and far worse than any she might have imagined. Two of de Legget's henchmen lay crumpled on the cobblestones. The giant hunched over to the side in the grass, rubbing his lolling head.

Austyn sat his prancing destrier between the two remaining guards with nary a visible scratch. Nor did he look the least bit concerned that one of the ruffians had seized his reins and sword while the other held an iron pike poised at his back.

Holly's throat tightened with a helpless surge of love. 'Twas so like Austyn to charge into peril for her sake without counting the consequences. She remembered how he had swaggered into Tewksbury with naught but a single man-at-arms and his irreproachable honor and walked away with the most extravagant prize of his jousting career — a bride.

His expression was stormy, from jealousy or concern she could not say. Perhaps he believed she had provoked Eugene's attack in a vindictive attempt to punish him, she thought wildly. Perhaps he would see this as yet another damning proof of the faithlessness of women.

"I've come for my wife."

I've come for the woman.

Before Holly could recognize the echo from the past, Eugene had seized the back of her gown and heaved her up on the window ledge. The window was much narrower than the one at Gavenmore, but there was ample room for her slight form. Her head swam as blue sky and green earth threatened to reverse.

"Would you care to come up," Eugene called out, "or shall I send her down?"

Austyn hesitated for an insulting moment. "I'll come up."

"Excellent. I'll have my men escort you."

The devilish note in Eugene's voice alerted Holly, but she did not dare betray herself. All she could do was bite back her scream of warning and wince in sympathy as the pike came down on the back of Austyn's head, sending him crashing off his mount to the cobblestones.

Austyn's lips curled in a dreamy smile. He was reclining in a meadow of purple heartsease, his head pillowed against the plush warmth of Holly's bosom. Her fragrant curls tickled his nose as she leaned over and began to plant tender kisses along his brow, crooning praise for his valor in those dulcet tones of hers.

"Wake up, you bumbling oaf!" A torrent of cold water struck him full in the face.

His eyes flew open to discover Holly looming over him, her charming little face puckered not in a kiss, but in a scowl. He also discovered she was holding an empty basin, he was sitting in a puddle of spreading water garbed only in his hose, his wrists were manacled to the wall behind him, and by the slant of the sun's rays pounding their way without mercy into his throbbing head, 'twas no longer morning, but early afternoon.

A dark crescent of a moon intercepted the sunbeams as Eugene de Legget bent over to peer into his face with solicitous concern. "I offered to rouse you myself, sir, but your wife begged to do the honors."

Austyn's gaze flicked from Eugene to Holly. Her glittering eyes flared in unspoken warning.

Austyn shook his head like a great shaggy mastiff, sending droplets

285

of water flying everywhere. Holly recoiled, dropping the basin and screeching in outrage.

" 'Tis the only way that shrew could rouse any man," he pronounced, curling his upper lip in a smirk.

Holly planted her hands on her hips, smiling a smile of acid sweetness. "Oh, I doubt that most men are as difficult to rouse as you, sir. Nor so easily expended."

"Why should a man rouse himself to satisfy a woman who'll do naught but lay beneath him like a cold herring?"

Eugene patted water from his brow with a kerchief gazing from one to the other of them with unabashed fascination. "Would that be a live herring, sir, or a dead one?"

"Oh, dead, most certainly. At least a live one would have flopped a bit now and then."

Holly snorted with scorn and tossed her curls, her haughty beauty at its peak. "Not live or dead, but frozen with distaste at your clumsy fumblings."

"Frozen indeed. I feared you were going to give Master Longstaff a fatal case of frostnip."

"Master Longstaff! Ha! Don't flatter yourself."

Austyn summoned up a feral snarl with little effort, his narrowed gaze promising revenge for that snippet of sauciness.

Eugene stepped between them, plainly fearing they were on the verge of flying at each other's throats and depriving him of his own diabolical pleasures. "If you loathe your wife as much as you claim, Gavenmore, why have you come rushing so gallantly to her aid?"

Austyn did not have to fake his icy sneer as he turned his attention to Montfort. "For the same reason I came rushing so gallantly to wed her. Gold. How long do you think her father will let me keep that dowry if she gets her witless self killed? And I've earned it, by God, for being forced to endure the lash of her barbed tongue all these weeks."

286

Holly leaned around Eugene and stuck out that luscious, pink tongue at him. Austyn shifted in the puddle of water, wishing he hadn't chosen such an inopportune moment to recall the delicious torments it was capable of inflicting.

To hide his consternation, he gave the manacles a violent tug, as if he'd like nothing more than to wrap them around his wife's elegant neck. The right manacle rewarded him with a tantalizing inch of give.

He ceased his struggles as Eugene drew a small silver dagger from his belt. "Allow me to put your mind at ease, sir. You'll be heartened to know that I've no intention of murdering your beloved bride."

The blood rushed from Austyn's pounding head, leaving him dizzy with relief.

Eugene tested the blade against his thumb, then smiled tenderly. " 'Tis you who disgraced my good name before the crowd at the tournament and 'tis you I'm going to kill."

Holly's horrified gasp nearly betrayed them, but she recovered quickly, clapping her hands with childish glee. "Oh, joy! And I had feared I'd be stuck with the lummox for all eternity."

Even Eugene eyed her askance at that bit of bloodthirstiness. "Remind me to sleep with the candles lit when I take you to my bed, dear."

Austyn began working the right manacle back and forth with excruciating slowness, but increasing desperation. If he could just coax a few more inches of slack into the chain before Eugene came to finish him off . . . "If you're fool enough to bed that witch," he said, "you'll soon be begging someone to gut you in your sleep. I'd almost prefer death to a lifetime of hell spent listening to her nag."

Holly lunged for him, her fingers curved into claws. "Give me the dagger and let me at the wretch! I'll put him out of his misery."

Eugene grabbed her around the waist. "Not so fast, love. Wouldn't

287

you rather make him suffer?"

"What did you have in mind?" Austyn growled. "Forcing me to swive her again."

"Only in your dreams!" Holly retorted.

She fought back a shiver of revulsion as Eugene's grip mellowed to a mocking embrace. "On the contrary," he said, rubbing his cheek against her temple. "I thought you might like to watch while I did the honors." His eyes never left Austyn's as he slid a hand upward from her waist to cup the underside of one of her ripe breasts.

Holly's gaze was also riveted on her husband's face. She dared not even breathe. She knew a single visible flinch, one whispery thread of the whimper caught in her throat, would be the ruination of them both.

Austyn's face, so quick to mold itself to a scowl of anger or to dimple in delight, did not betray even a flicker of emotion. 'Twas so still its unholy beauty might have been set in mortar.

He raked her with a contemptuous glance, coldly dismissing the sight of Eugene's hand kneading the softness of her breast. Straining against the manacles, he flexed his arms and yawned like a big, sleepy bear. "Suit yourself, Montfort. Just don't forget to wake us both when you're done."

Stiffening with rage, Eugene gave Holly a shove. She stumbled to one knee, but was too awash in triumph to feel a drop of pain.

"The two of you deserve each other," Eugene snarled. "A shrill harpy and a merry cuckold. You'd be enough to milk the joy out of dipping a virgin in boiling oil."

Holly grinned, savoring his petulant rage. But her smile faded as he marched resolutely toward Austyn, brandishing the dagger. "If you only knew how much I loathe wasting a quick, clean death on the likes of you . . ."

Austyn began to struggle against his chains in earnest, his forearms bulging with the effort. He shot Holly an imploring look. She knew

288

him well enough to recognize 'twas not a plea for assistance, but a desperate decree for her to stay her hand.

Holly had no time to seek a weapon. No time to scream or mumble a frantic prayer. Eugene whipped the dagger back, aiming its blade at her husband's heart. Ducking beneath the baron's elbow, she threw herself across Austyn, wrapping her arms around his waist and burying her face against the consoling warmth of his chest as she awaited the plunge of the knife between her shoulder blades.

Except for the thundering of Austyn's heart beneath her ear, the chamber went as silent as a tomb. Then a breathy chuckle coaxed the hairs at her nape to tingling life. Still clinging to Austyn's waist, she turned her head to find a sneer of gloating triumph fixed on Eugene's lips. She could almost feel his invisible snare tightening around her throat.

"How perplexing. You claim to care nothing for your husband, yet you've proved yourself willing to die for him." He tapped the hilt of the dagger against his chin. "Let no one say the baron of Montfort is not a romantic at heart. I shall reward your noble sacrifice by letting him live."

The tears poised on Holly's lashes spilled down her cheeks in a torrent of relief. Austyn rubbed his chin against her curls, the only show of solace allowed him.

"Live, Gavenmore," Eugene said, mesmerizing them both with the virulent softness of his voice. "Live knowing that every time you look at your wife, you'll remember her on her back with her legs spread wide for another man. Live with the fear that she secretly relished my attentions, that she writhed and moaned not in pain, but in ecstasy. Live with the doubt that the babe she'll bear nine months from now may not be the true Gavenmore heir, but only the sniveling bastard of a man you despise."

Through a mist of dawning horror, Holly felt every muscle in Austyn's body go as rigid as steel. As Eugene pressed the blade of the dagger to her throat and tore her away from him, he bucked against the chains, bellowing with rage and anguish.

Holly thrashed and kicked and flailed, no longer caring if she incited Eugene to murder her. She would rather die than force Austyn to endure what to a Gavenmore man would truly be a fate worse than death. The tip of the blade bit into her throat.

"Holly, look at me!" Her husband's roar of command was so irresistible that even Eugene stopped dragging her along to gape.

Austyn's gaze burned with a sweet, holy fire. "Listen to me, angel," he said fiercely. "Don't make him hurt you. Do whatever he wants." He blinked furiously to clear his eyes of tears. "Your life is of more value to me than your virtue. He'll never touch what I adore in you. You will always be pure and lovely in my sight."

"How revolting!" Eugene spat.

Holly's knees crumpled beneath a staggering siege of love. Her husband's generosity had left her with no choice but to offer him a sacrifice of her own.

She drove her elbow hard into Eugene's codpiece. As he dropped to one knee, grunting an oath, she broke from his grip and stumbled toward the window.

She scrambled up on the ledge. The wind tore at her hair and molded her gown to her legs just as it had on that summer afternoon at Gavenmore when the beauty of the day had reminded her that despite its hardships, life was too precious to forsake without a fight. She refused to look down at the cobblestones below.

Instead, she whirled to face the tower, smiling through a veil of tears at the man whose faith had given her the courage to continue the battle.

"No," Austyn whispered, riveted by his wife's tender smile. "Oh, God, please, no . . ."

"Don't be a fool, you bitch," de Legget snapped, clambering to his feet. But Austyn knew he was never going to reach her in time.

Austyn strained at the manacles with all of his weight, panic numbing him to the rivulets of blood trickling down his wrists.

Eugene lunged for her. Time lurched to a halt as Holly touched her fingertips to her beautiful lips, then backed off the narrow ledge, disappearing into thin air.

Chapter 32

Austyn roared Holly's name. Fueled by an inhuman surge of agony, he ripped the manacles from the wall in an explosion of mortar. Eugene had time to do little more than emit a strangled cry of surprise before a free length of chain whipped around his neck with a nasty crack.

Austyn lowered the baron's limp form to the floor, then charged to the window. Bracing his palms on the ledge, he sucked in shuddering gasps of air, keeping his eyes squeezed shut until he could work up the courage to look down at the cobblestones below.

"Austyn?"

At the tentative whisper, his eyes flew open in horror. The cheerful blue sky mocked his grief. Dear God in heaven, he thought savagely, was he to be allowed no interval of mourning before the ghost of his beloved wife began haunting him?

"Austyn!"

The second plea sounded both more corporeal and distinctly more annoyed. Austyn slowly lowered his gaze to discover Holly tangled in a curtain of ivy a mere arm's length below the window. One of the vines snapped off in her hand, eliciting a very mortal squeal.

Trembling with disbelief, Austyn stretched out his hand. She seized it, the desperation of her grip assuring him that she was no ghost. He shouted with jubilation as he hauled her against him in a fervent embrace. They went tumbling to the floor of the tower in a breathless tangle of arms, legs, laughter, and tears.

She nuzzled her lips against his throat, as if starved for a taste of him. "I thought you were going to leave me dangling out there all day. I had no idea if the stuff would hold, you know. If you'd have dawdled any longer, I'd have gone *splat* on the cobblestones like one of Winnie's fig puddings."

"Nag, nag, nag," he murmured, kissing her lovely brow, her precious ears, the tip of her impertinent nose.

"I just knew that if I provided you with a sufficient distraction, you could best the wretch." She splayed her palms against his chest and smiled up at him adoringly. "I had nothing but the utmost of faith in you."

Austyn sobered. "And I in you, my lady." He smoothed back her windblown curls, searching her face — a face that had become dear to him for far more than its striking beauty.

Their lips brushed and lingered in tender accord. As they drew apart, gazing deep into each other's eyes, a golden haze claimed the tower. Austyn might have taken it for nothing more than sunshine striking the motes of mortar drifting through the air were it not for the gentle ripple of laughter that echoed in their ears.

He and Holly clutched each other, their eyes widening with dawning astonishment as the shimmering outline of a woman appeared before them. The wheaten silk of her hair danced around a face so exotically beautiful it made Holly feel no more comely than a troll. She tightened her possessive grip on Austyn's arms without realizing it.

Austyn would have known her voice anywhere — rich, melodious, slightly mocking. " 'Twas all I asked, Austyn of Gavenmore. That you put your faith in the constancy of a woman's heart."

The vision wavered, but before it could fade into obscurity, Austyn found himself gazing into the forgiving eyes of his mother. His heart swelled with gratitude at the generous and unexpected gift.

The ethereal halo of light vanished, restoring the mundane gloom of crumbling stone and mortar dust. A flea-bitten mouse sat up on its hind legs, sniffing the air where Rhiannon had disappeared.

Austyn and Holly exchanged a wondering glance.

"You were truly cursed," she whispered, as if the Welsh faerie might still be eavesdropping.

"Aye." He traced the curve of her cheek with one reverent finger. "But thanks to you and your unwavering faith in me, my lady, now I am truly blessed."

Holly flung herself into his arms with a sob of joy. Austyn gathered her against him, squeezing his eyes shut against a rush of raw emotion. As their lips met, the air resounded with a flourish of trumpets.

'Twas a dazed eternity of bliss before either of them realized the trumpets' fanfare was no celestial celebration of their love, but a call to war.

The glade below rang with angry shouts and threats of impending chaos. Still hand in hand, Austyn and Holly shot to their knees and peeped over the window ledge.

Two armies poured into the clearing from opposite directions, sending de Legget's henchmen scattering like rats into the shadowy forest.

From the east rode a mammoth company of knights, their banners rippling in splashes of saffron and purple, their shiny plate armor glinting in the sun. At the head of their precise formation sat a squat figure on a magnificent gray stallion, proudly bearing the Tewksbury standard.

Holly bounced up and down with excitement. " 'Tis my papa come to rescue me!"

"He might have spared a decade from my life had he come with a bit more haste and a bit less pomp," Austyn muttered, squeezing her hand.

From the west came a motley group of men mounted on sturdy plow horses, drooping nags, and lathered donkeys. They were armed with naught but rusty hoes, tattered brooms, and smithy hammers, yet their stern Welsh visages looked no less determined than the faces of their English counterparts. Their general was none other than a fair-haired Viking who drooped over the pommel of his saddle like a withered daffodil, his ribs bandaged and his left arm supported by a makeshift sling.

"Damn his obstinate hide!" Austyn exclaimed. "Emrys promised he'd lock him up to keep him from following me."

"Would that be Emrys there just behind him? My goodness, his head is nearly as shiny as my papa's armor." Holly pointed. "And look, there's Winifred beating on a kettle with an iron spoon. What a splendid Amazon she would have made!"

The two armies met in the center of the glade, showing dangerous signs of clashing.

Austyn sighed. "We'd best get down there before they annihilate each other for the common good." Ignoring Holly's squeal of protest, he swept her into his arms. "I'll be afraid to put you down for fear someone else will carry you off."

She twined a tendril of his hair around her finger, secretly delighted. "Now that you've proved your faith in me, sir, you shall never again be plagued by jealousy."

He stepped over de Legget's body without a second glance and gave her a devilish wink. "Rhiannon never promised that."

"She's *my* daughter! I shall lead the charge into the tower!" the earl of Tewksbury was bellowing when Austyn carried Holly from the castle, a beaming Elspeth trotting at his heels.

"Like hell you will," Carey shouted back, his words still slurred by the various indignities suffered by his lips. "She's *my* lady! I'll lead the charge."

"Charge, ha! You can barely walk."

Austyn tapped the earl on the shoulder.

He turned around and thundered, "Not now, lad. Can't you see I'm busy?"

Austyn waited patiently for him to swing around the second time.

295

His beady little eyes broadened at the sight of his daughter in Austyn's arms.

"Baby!" he cried, an angelic smile wreathing his dwarfish face. "My precious little baby!"

Holly squirmed in mingled delight and embarrassment as he threw his arms around her and smothered her face with kisses. Austyn demonstrated absolutely no desire to relinquish her to her father's arms. Holly feared if either one of them loved her any more staunchly, she would have been tugged in two.

"How did you know, Papa?" she asked, settling back in Austyn's arms to pat his weathered cheek. "How did you know I needed you?"

The company of knights parted to reveal a litter borne by four grumbling foot soldiers. Its occupant struggled to a sitting position, clutching a heavily bandaged chest. " 'Twas I who told him."

"Nathanael!" Holly breathed. "Good God, I thought you were dead."

"So did I." He held up a heavy chain. "But it seems my crucifix deflected the worst of the blow." He grinned sheepishly. "I hope I didn't scare you too badly. I must have fainted from the pain." At a snicker from one of the foot soldiers, he snapped, "Well, it was quite intolerable."

Her father glowered at the priest. "We'd have been here sooner had he not led us on such a merry chase. We were halfway to Scotland before we realized we were heading the wrong way."

"Now, sir, you know I've a deplorable sense of direction." Nathanael's eyes darkened as he lifted them to the tower. "The baron?"

"He'll not trouble anyone again," Austyn said firmly.

Both the earl and Nathanael nodded their approval while Carey limped over to slap Austyn on the back.

The earl's gaze traveled from Holly's face to Austyn's. "Come, child," he said in a voice that brooked no disobedience. " 'Tis time to get you home."

Holly twined her arms around her husband's neck and rested her head on his shoulder, giving her father the reassurance he sought. "I am home, Papa."

Austyn kissed her hair. "Let's not be so hasty to spurn your father's invitation. A sound night's rest in a fluffy feather bed might be just the thing." The flash of his dimple warned her that a sound night's rest was the furthest thought from his mind.

"Sounds good to me," Carey mumbled, rubbing his ribs.

"Me, too," said Nathanael, reclining on the litter.

But as Austyn sought to pass, the priest's hand shot out to capture Holly's arm. Holly felt Austyn tense, but the wistful shadow in Nathanael's eyes was brightened by his sheepish smile. "I hope you'll allow me to bestow my heartfelt blessing . . . upon the both of you."

As Austyn carried Holly toward his destrier with both her father's and the priest's blessing, he nuzzled her ear and whispered, "Perhaps tonight will give you time to get reacquainted with a friend of mine. A certain Master Longstaff who is only too eager to seek redress for a rather unkind slur you've cast upon his honor."

"I can assure you I'm more than willing to soothe the saucy fellow's vanity," she whispered back.

At her chiming laughter, a flushed young knight slid back the faceplate of his helm, hefted his lance in salute and shouted, "To Lady Holly, who possesses the fairest face in all of England!"

The rousing cheer that went up was stifled mid-note by the sweeping look Austyn leveled on the crowd. Holly's breath caught as his gaze lowered to caress her face with irresistible tenderness.

"To Lady Holly," he proclaimed, his rich voice tolling like a bell in the crystalline silence, "who possesses the fairest heart in all of England."

That heart overflowed with love as Holly welcomed her husband's kiss.

This time there was no quelling the exultant roar that resounded through the forest as Welsh and English voices united in tribute. As Austyn swept Holly in front of him on the destrier, a joyous fanfare rippled through the air, leaving the heralds staring dumbfounded at the shiny horns hanging limp from their hands.

Epilogue

"Holly Felicia Bernadette de Chastel!"

Holly hid her smile behind the tiny coif she was embroidering as her husband came stalking across the meadow. His handsome face was set in a fierce scowl, but he might have looked even more intimidating were it not for the three-year-old who had secured her perch on her papa's massive shoulders by tugging at his ears.

He stopped at the edge of the blanket to avoid trampling his infant daughter, who slept in a basket with her thumb nestled between her cherubic lips, and dangled a sheaf of parchment in front of Holly's eyes. "Do you know what this is?"

Laying her embroidery aside, Holly absently twirled an ebony curl belonging to the six-year-old napping in her lap. "A letter from the Baron of Gloucester," she speculated. "Ruminations on the weather. A snippet of gossip about the king's mistress. Complaints about the size of his goiter . . ."

Austyn snapped open the missive, but had to pry his daughter's hands away from his eyes before he could read it. " 'Don't think me impertinent, Gavenmore,' " he read, " 'but it has come to my attention on more than one occasion that your eldest would make a suitable bride for a lonely widower such as myself.' A lonely widower indeed! A desperate old lech, he means!" Austyn wadded the letter into a ball, growling beneath his breath.

His daughter batted gleefully at his hair. "Papa's a big ole growly bear!"

"Papa's not a growly bear, Gwynnie. Since the king restored his title, he's a growly earl." He gently disengaged her from his shoulders and sent her off to toddle in the grass with a pat on the rump before sinking down beside Holly on the blanket. His expression was bleak. "It's starting already, isn't it? I thought we'd have a few more years of peace."

299

Holly leaned her head against his shoulder. " 'Twas inevitable, you know. Why Felicia and Bernadette are nearly eight."

Austyn frowned. "Where are the twins today?"

"They're off with their uncle Carey, learning how to shoot a bow."

Austyn shuddered. "I hope he wore his padded hauberk."

"I'm sure he did. I think he learned his lesson when they dropped the tub of poppies on his head. I've not seen him without his helm since. And then there was that little incident when they burned down the north tower while roasting chestnuts on the hearth."

Austyn shook his head. "I never have figured out how that sheet got stuffed up the chimney . . ."

Holly bit off a piece of thread and murmured something non-committal. She much preferred the spacious solar Austyn had built in place of the tower. A solar whose door was never locked unless they wished to steal a few precious hours of privacy away from the inquisitive eyes of their offspring.

Austyn ruffled his sleeping daughter's hair, then ran a finger along the baby's downy cheek. "They're all so beautiful."

Where once there would have been despair in his voice, now there was only pride and a perpetual sense of wonder that their love had brought such grace into the world. Even Austyn's father had shared a brief taste of it. After tenderly cradling his first granddaughter in his arms, Rhys of Gavenmore had died quietly in his sleep. He now rested beneath a blanket of anemones at his wife's side, at peace at last.

Holly reached up to caress the tendrils of silver at her husband's temples, thinking as she always did how very striking they were. "I fear that in the next few years you're going to come to learn that there are more vexing trials than possessing a comely wife. Such as fending off the suitors of six lovely daughters. I hope you don't fancy yourself still cursed."

Austyn drew her into the warm circle of his arms. "You and the

300

girls will always be my dearest blessing." He brushed her lips with his, igniting the passion that still flared so quick and bright between them.

The thunder of hoofbeats disturbed their tender reverie.

"Oh, Austyn, you didn't!" Holly exclaimed as the fully armored rider approached, the celestial turrets and graceful arches of the newly completed castle providing the perfect backdrop for the dainty warrior.

He shrugged, bestowing upon her one of those crooked smiles she never could resist. "Your father donated the armor, but it had occurred to me that one of our daughters should be able to fend off her own suitors."

The lithe rider brought the horse to a prancing halt, then reached up and dragged off her helm, sending a torrent of raven curls cascading down her back.

An impish giggle bubbled from her lips. "I saw you kissing Papa, Mama. How disgusting!" She tilted her pert nose in the air, sniffing with disdain. "I shall never bestow my kisses on any unworthy man."

Austyn grinned. "That's my girl."

Holly pinched him.

The rider wheeled the horse around and urged it into a canter. Wrapped in each other's loving embrace, Austyn and Holly shook their heads in wry wonderment as they watched her gallop fearlessly around the outskirts of the curtain wall encompassing their home.

She had inherited her mother's grace and sense of mischief along with her father's jousting skills and stubborn courage. Several min-strels and a handful of poets had already pronounced the dark-haired, blue-eyed sprite the fairest lady in all of England. Holly was only too eager to relinquish the title to her beloved eldest daughter, who had been conceived twelve years ago in one of the softest, fluffiest feather beds at Tewksbury . . .

Lady Ivy of Gavenmore!